SWEETGRASS

SWEETGRASS

Growing Up in Montana

VIOLET SUTA MORAN

Copyright © 2025 Violet Suta Moran

Printed in the United States of America.

ISBN: 978-1-968148-19-5

All rights reserved.

This is a work of nonfiction. Names, characters, businesses, places, events, and incidents are either the products of the author's memory or used to recall a certain time or place. Any resemblance to actual persons, living or dead, or actual events is purely coincidental.

*This book is dedicated to my three sons,
who love the Suta Rock Farm and their mother who grew
up there and wanted to know more about both.*

Standing: Buzz; Seated (l to r): Jeff, Violet, and Morgan

CONTENTS

Author's Note ix

Introduction	1
Pop	9
Mom	17
Big Sky	31
Night Sky in Montana	37
Suta Farm Land	43
Machines	47
Mustard	51
Wind, Wind, Wind	55
Rock Picking	63
Green Cake	70
Ode to Hildegard	72
Charlie	78
Weather	81
Chinooks	89
Gumbo	93
Hanging with My Brothers	98
Rimrocks	102
The Pete and Hannah Suta House	111
An Outstanding Outhouse	119
How Did We Live Without Electricity?	123
Outbuildings on the Farm	130
Camping with Alice	133
Living Without Running Water	137
Laundry	140
Laundry Soap	146
Ironing Clothes	149
Telephones	154
World War II Conservation	159
Hannah Lozing Suta	161
Wild Flowers	165
Scents	171
Sounds on the Farm	174

Animals on Our Farm	176
Branding Day	183
Haying	189
Ford Fairlane	193
Cooking with Mom	197
Three Meals and More	205
Coal Stove	209
Feeding the Men in the Fields	213
Garden	216
A Woodpecker Visited My Parents	220
Raising Chickens	224
Making Butter	230
Mortimer Snerd	234
County Fair	240
Boarding The Plane	243
One-Room Country School	247
Beth Volbrecht	254
School Bus	257
Transition from Country to City School	263
My Hillbilly Relatives	270
Sunburst, Montana	275
Band from Sunburst	281
Sweetgrass: My Hometown	285
Country Gatherings	292
Needlework	299
Fun On the Farm	304
Easter When I Was a Child	313
Christmas When I Was a Child	318
Sermon at the Funeral of G. Peter Suta	324
Jerry Auctioneer	328
Selling the Pete and Hannah Suta Farm	332
Acknowledgments	336

Violet Suta, age 1.

Pop's father, Alexander Suta, built this one-and-a-half room homestead in 1921. Mom and Pop lived there with four children.

Author's Note

Mom, what was it like to grow up on the farm? How did you live without a phone or electricity? Did your house always look the way it does now? Why did you pick rocks? What did you do for fun on the prairie? Where did you go to school?

My sons were asking these questions as adults even though they had vacationed on the Montana farm every year of their lives. Their questions made me realize that they couldn't see what was different eighty years ago.

Both of my parents were children of immigrants who homesteaded near Cut Bank, Montana. Pete Suta and Hannah Lozing met at a country dance held in a one-room schoolhouse, were married 22 December 1931, and raised six children on a nearby isolated treeless dry-land farm. I was their fourth child born in a one-room shack.

This book is a compilation of stories written to answer the questions of my sons. It gives a glimpse of my life from about 1937 to 1950. I helped my mother carry buckets of water from a well, wash all clothing by hand, and cook using a coal stove. When I wasn't in the one-room school, I joined my family in picking rocks so that we could plow the prairie into wheat fields.

—VSM

Back (l to r): Margaret Suta (Rudy's wife), Hannah Suta, Peter Suta, Willie Suta, Alexander and Teresia Boyza Suta (Peter's parents); Front (l to r): Louis George (Margaret's son), Ben Suta, Henry Suta, and Violet Suta

Back (l to r): Teddy, Henry, and Benny; Middle (l to r): Hannah, Pete, and Violet; Front (l to r): Dian and Rudy

Introduction

The focus of this book is on Violet's experiences of growing up on the Pete and Hannah Suta farm. You can locate the farm on a map of Montana by going north from Great Falls on I-15 until you hit the Canadian Border. Eight miles south of there you will find Sunburst, and twelve miles west is the Suta Farm. The road from Sunburst used to be narrow, crooked, and graveled or muddy, with another 1 ½ miles of an unpaved trail from the "Suta corner" to our house. The road was greatly improved in the 1980s.

This area is treeless, semi-arid, hilly and rocky. The Rocky Mountains are not far to the west, the Sweetgrass Hills to the east, and Canada just eight miles to the north. The winters are long and cold, and the west wind blows constantly. The climate and the sparse population tend to make Montana natives independent and self-reliant.

Peter and Hannah lived in the one-room homestead built by Peter's father and helped his father farm his land. Hannah told us that Peter was not being paid by his father because it was Hungarian tradition for the oldest son to take over all the work. In fact, Mom paid the $2.00 license fee for their marriage. She said that Peter's mom sometimes gave her meat with mold on it as payment for Pop's work. When their fourth child was born in 1937, Hannah insisted that she and Peter purchase land of their own and build a house that would not be so drafty and cold.

Peter and Hannah Suta raised six children spaced in two groups of age, as follows:

> **Theodore Peter** b. 16 Oct 1932 in Sweetgrass, MT
>
> **Henry Alexander** b. 14 Jul 1934 in Sweetgrass, MT
>
> **Benjamin Emil** b. 1 Dec 1935 in our homestead, Sweetgrass, MT
>
> **Violet Hannah** b. 4 Nov 1937 in our homestead, Sweetgrass, MT

Ben and Violet were actually born in Grandpa Suta's homestead because of blizzard weather. We had a wooden closet that Violet could fit behind, and she made everyone laugh by saying that Daddy found her there.

A nine-year period of no babies was broken when the fifth child, Dian, arrived on Violet's birthday.

> **Dian Theresa** b. 4 Nov 1946 in Shelby, MT (on the author's ninth birthday)
>
> **Keith Rudolph** b. 9 Mar 1949 in Shelby, MT

Peter and Hannah were able to buy a nearby 325.64 acre plot of land that had been abandoned by a disillusioned homesteader for $174.22 back taxes plus a $75.00 legal fee. Peter's father was angry that he was leaving and refused to help him buy the property. John Farbo, a friend of Peter's, backed his purchase in return for mineral rights on the land. The price of the land was a bargain, and there never were any minerals produced to give to Farbo.

Topography and History of this Land

The landscape was shaped by the most recent ice age about 15,000 years ago. As the ice moved slowly south, it mowed down hills and mountain ranges, mixing pulverized rocks with soil, resulting in rolling tree-less prairie hills punctuated by occasional gumbo flats that were the lake beds of the melting ice mass. So strong was the ice mass that it changed the course of the Missouri River from flowing into the Hudson Bay to becoming a tributary of the Mississippi river. The resulting land is rocky, especially where mountain ranges had existed in its wake.

The land became prime buffalo grazing range. The Blackfeet Indians arrived in this area in the early 1700's and pushed the Salish (Flathead) and Kootenai Indians west into the Rocky Mountains. Smallpox epidemics in 1837 and 1869 greatly reduced the Blackfeet population. In addition, white hunters made the buffalo almost extinct by 1884 leaving the Indians without what had been their main food source. During the severe winter of 1883–1884 around 600 Blackfeet Indians starved because game had become scarce and the U.S. government did not deliver the supplies that had been promised in the treaty that required the Indians to give up their land.

And then the Enlarged Homestead Act of 1909 was passed to give land away to permanent settlers so that the Indians would be dissuaded from trying to return. Both sets of my grandparents, Henry Lozing and Alexander Suta, claimed free land and homesteaded north of Cut Bank, Montana, just a few miles from the Canadian border and about seventy miles east of the Rocky Mountains. The land was all dry prairie, but homesteaders were required to "improve" their land by beginning to farm or get permission to graze domestic animals.

The state of Montana is large, and the topography varies from mountains in the west to flatland in the east. Our farm was located in north-central Montana, very close to the Canadian border, where there were rolling hills.

Violet Suta Moran

Dry-land Farming on the Prairie

Dry-land farming is exactly as it sounds. There is very little rainfall and no water available to irrigate. There is no source of water, no lake, river, or stream. You look around and see nothing but grass and more grass. The prairie goes on forever in every direction. And it looks the same in every direction. You have to look closely and appreciate small things to notice the beauty of the prairie. I remember once reading that it "takes soul" to love the prairie.

There were rolling hills on the farm where I grew up. Looking across the land it looks flatter than it really is because with the elevation and clear atmosphere you are able to look across obstructions. Because of the lack of moisture, the yield of grain is low making it necessary to have large acreage. The 320-acre plot of homesteaded land was not adequate to grow enough grain to support a family. We added more acres as time went on, but our farm would be considered small by Montana standards.

It Isn't All Flat Prairie

I get irritated when people tell me that they drove through Montana, and there was nothing to see except the Rocky Mountains, which are in the western part of the state. Montana is a large state, and there are other small mountain ranges scattered around. In the Southeast are the Badlands, where Teddy Roosevelt spent a lot of time. In many areas there are rimrocks, almost like cliffs, which dammed the water from melting glaciers millions of years age.

There are 600 named buttes in Montana, and others that didn't get a name.

Buttes are dramatic geological formations looming like massive islands above the surrounding sea of prairie. They are typically landmarks standing alone above the prairie, while mountains tend to run in chains. The term butte is native in particular to Montana, derived from a French term applied to isolated, detached hills that arise abruptly and are too high to be called hills and not high enough to be called mountains. Buttes were formed by erosion. A butte can stand alone because the top is usually a hard cap rock that is resistant to erosion and protects the softer layers beneath. There are often pillars and spires nearby that are slender isolated columns of rock. The tops of buttes are generally flat, and the sides are steep, either straight or slanted.

A Mesa differs by having a larger rop surface area than a Butte but is not as large as a Plateau.

When there are more than 600 of these buttes scattered around the state, it's hard to avoid seeing one. When you have seen one butte, you have not seen them all. Every butte differs from others, and they look different from every direction because of their formation and the shadows they cast. It takes a person who expects only a city landscape to say that this land is flat and boring.

Charlie Russell, famous western artist and sculptor, painted many scenes that include his favorite butte near the city of Great Falls. His paintings of Square Butte differ but all include Indigenous people wearing their buffalo-skin clothing and riding horses. On top of that butte and other buttes, people were able to see 100 miles in the distance.

Although there was not a butte located specifically on our land the Sweetgrass Hills were so visible that they seemed to be part of our farm. The Sweetgrass Hills are actually buttes and West Butte, the highest point at 6,983 feet, is higher than the highest spot in most states, and higher than many mountains.

My place at the kitchen table faced east and at every meal I had a magnificent view of the landmark Sweetgrass Hills about fifty miles to the east.

History on Our Farmland

Our farmland held visible evidence of historical events.

Some of our land had never been disturbed by farming. We easily found circular rings of rocks which were placed by the Blackfeet Indians to hold down the edges of their tepees made of buffalo skin. Inside the larger circle was a smaller circle which would have been the fireplace for cooking and warmth.

Besides seeing historical evidence of Indigenous people having lived and traveled on the land, there was also evidence of trails going across the land for different purposes.

We could identify a "Cattle Trail" that was used to herd cattle from one state, such as Texas or Oklahoma, to another state, such as Montana. This was done to move cattle to a place where the grass was more plentiful and nourishing. It was expensive to trail a large herd of cattle but that was offset by the increased value of the fattened cattle. The Sweetgrass Hills was a destination for that purpose and got that name because the cowboys identified that grass as being plentiful, particularly sweet, and good for the cattle.

The "Whoop-Up Trail" led from Fort Benton where the trade boats had to dock because the Great Falls of the Missouri River stopped them. Whiskey and other supplies had to then be transported by horses and wagons to Fort Whoop-up near Lethbridge and other settlements We found a trail that was probably used for this purpose.

The deep tracks of the "Rum Runner Trail" were in 2020 still visible on the edge of some of our fields where they had not been plowed over. This trail was used for smuggling whiskey and other liquor from Canada to the United States during 1920–1934 when there was prohibition in America. There must have been a lot of smuggling runs during those years because the tracks made by their vehicles left very deep ruts.

This area is also known as the Hi-Line since it is the northernmost track of the Great Northern Railroad.

Captain Meriwether Lewis was in this country during his return trip of surveying the western lands in late July of 1806. He camped at Camp Disappointment, which is between Cut Bank and Browning, about forty miles west of our farm. On the morning of July 27, in a camp farther south, he and his men had a fight with some Blackfeet who were attempting to steal guns and horses. Two Indians were killed. This was the only armed fight with Indians on Lewis and Clark's entire journey. It made the Blackfeet hateful of Americans for over a century.

Between 1888 and 1910, this area was used as open range for large cattle herds. The Conrad Cattle Company dominated the Marias River country, including land much farther north into Canada. Homesteads in size from forty to 320 acres covered this land by 1916. Four out of ten homesteaders gave up and left while those who stayed broke-up small fields for farming using horses and a one-pronged plow, and usually had a large garden, poultry and some livestock. The droughts of the 1920s and the depression of the 1930s caused more of these homesteaders to pack up and leave. My ancestors bore the hardships and stayed.

One of the 600 buttes in the southeast was named Pompey's Pillar by Lewis & Clark, honoring Sacajawea's son.

Peter Suta, known by the community as Pete and by family as Pop.

Pop

Pop was the most appropriate name for our male parent. He was an informal person who wore farm clothes and was clearly the boss, not a quiet, thoughtful business man who would discuss relationships and religious topics. Pop was opinionated and would tell you what he thought without mincing words. A little colorful language helped to convey his message, such as, "Why the hell did you do that you dumb knot-head?" We children enjoy calling ourselves or each other a dumb knot-head when we do something stupid.

Pop was the oldest in a family of four boys. His parents had immigrated from Hungary; met, married and started a family in Vine, West Virginia. They claimed homestead land the U.S. government was giving free to people who would settle in the northwest. Hungarians were known to be excellent farmers and many roamed Europe looking for land of their own. It is not surprising to find quite a few of them in the farmland of North-Central Montana and southern Alberta, Canada.

As a child Pop rode horseback or walked to a one-room country school on the Fitzpatrick ranch about six miles away. I've been told there was a Hungarian tradition that the oldest son was expected to relieve his father of working as soon as possible. Pop was taken out of school at the 3rd grade to assist his father who was known to never like working. Pop was always a hard worker and I'm sure he was doing most of the work when he was a very young man.

When Pop was eighteen years old he apprenticed as a blacksmith with Moses Bello, a friend of his father. This skill was useful in his entire life because he could make or repair many parts of machinery on his farm. He built a special fire pit (blacksmith's forge) in a corner of the shop that could tolerate the extremely high heat required to make iron malleable. Pop had a lot of strength to be able to hold a heavy piece of very hot metal clamped in one hand while pounding on it with a heavy hammer in his other hand. He also became an expert welder.

Pop worked for his father and had no money. Mom paid the $2.00 fee for a marriage license out of the small portion of her earnings that her father allowed her to keep when she worked as a Mother's Helper.

After they were married they lived in Grandpa Suta's 1 ½ room homestead house until their fourth child (Violet) was born. Mom insisted that they needed to buy some land and get their own house that would have insulation on the walls and no spaces letting in the wind and snow.

Mom worked hard and tried to be a partner in their farm, working outdoors as well as indoors, and arguing about things, such as when it was time to seed. Pop was contrary and tended to reject suggestions from other people. We children joke that it is a trait of our family that you can get one of us to do what you want if you suggest doing the opposite.

Mom and Pop experienced stress and rough times in their marriage during early years. They had no money but had a mortgage on their farmland, needed to build a house and had to buy or borrow machinery while supporting four children under the age of six.

One of Pop's extra jobs was with the WPA branch of the Public Works Administration to help improve the road west of Sweetgrass which was not much better than a trail on

Sweetgrass

the prairie. Another way Pop tried to make money was to drill water wells with Cyril Fitzpatrick. They found water at many places but never on Pop's land. Mom had to continue carrying buckets of water from a well. Pop and Cyril at the end of their work day would drink heavily in Sweetgrass bars. Pop never drank by himself at home but once he got into a bar with a friend it would be hard to get him out.

I can understand the stress Pop had of starting a farm with little or no money. But he placed tremendous burdens on Mom who experienced those same stressors plus many more in having to clothe and care for their children and prepare family meals. Mom planted a garden, raised chickens, and got a milk cow as soon as she could. Pop didn't give much consideration to Mom, but he never failed to thank her at the end of every meal.

We spent family time picking rocks so that we could farm the land. Even though I was one-year old when we moved onto the farm, I joined my older brothers in doing what we could to help Mom while Pop was on the tractor. When Ted was nine years old he was able to help Pop by driving a tractor that had a stick shift.

On the rare times when the whole family went to town Pop would stop at a bar, drinking and visiting with a friend while the family waited. Mom kept blankets in the car because we couldn't keep the engine running all the time. If Mom tried to talk Pop into leaving, he would get angry and stay longer. She would send one of us kids in to try to get him to take us home. I was often sent in because I was his "little girl," but I hated being hugged and slobbered on by him and his friends who were drunk. Fortunately we didn't go to town very often.

Later we all saw his painful experience of gout as appropriate payback for his drinking episodes. The extreme pain of gout prevented him from taking even a single drink for the rest of his life.

Pop thought education was important and yelled at his children that they should learn and not have the same problems he had with reading and writing. He hated having to ask Mom how to spell a word. He supported all six of his children going beyond high school, but he would often holler at us, "Get your damn nose out of that book and do something worthwhile." He berated us for not learning anything "useful" in school; like how to calculate the amount of seed needed for a given field, how to stack bales of hay, or how to make a fence gate. Pop could figure out everything like that by himself.

When Pop was in the hospital having a quadruple bypass, staff were treating him as a little old man who just came from a nursing home, and he started acting feeble. I phoned neighbors of his and asked them to take Polaroid pictures of some of his large machinery, farmland, and the forty-two feral cats he cared for. I posted those in his room and told a couple of nurses to come and see the pictures. All the staff started coming in and asking questions about his farm and the work he was still doing. He really perked up and worked harder at rehabilitation. Sometimes kindly treatment can be demeaning.

Pop seldom let Mom know how much he appreciated her. When he and I were alone in the hospital room he said, "I don't know why I get so mad at Hannah sometimes. I couldn't replace her with even two or three hired men." Of course he wouldn't say that to her, so I did, and she was very pleased.

Here are some examples of actions and statements that illustrate Pop's least desirable behaviors:

Mom kept a packed suitcase under her bed because she never knew when Pop might announce they were going somewhere and would be staying overnight. When he thought of something, he wanted to do it right away.

Sweetgrass

Mom kept a wooden apple crate in the basement packed with things we would need for a picnic if we went to Glacier Park.

He would come into the house and tell Mom he was going to town, and she could come along if she wanted. Immediately he would pull the car up to the house and honk the horn. My sons think it is ridiculously funny if they drive up to the house and honk the horn.

Mom and Pop could fly United without setting a date because their son Henry was a pilot. Most of us lived out of state and we didn't know when they were coming to visit until we got a call from the airport in our town. Pop couldn't understand that our work schedules were not as flexible as that of a farmer.

Pop moved quickly and didn't like to wait for anything. But he would have other things to do if we said it was time to leave for an event. On the rare times we went to a movie, we had to stay for the beginning of the next showing to piece the story together.

He was a good driver in snow and mud but otherwise he was unsafe because he drove too fast. In Canada he tried to say that the speed limit of 120 kilometers per hour meant he could go 120 miles per hour.

He thought he had to pass anyone in front of him because, "You never know what that guy is going to do."

Pop knew I had to arrive early before a band concert because everybody tuned up to me when I was first-chair clarinetist. That's when he drove slowly to inspect other farmer's crops. But he was proud of my playing, didn't complain about me practicing the "squawk box "every night and agreed with the band director to buy me a new expensive clarinet.

When backing out of angle parking, he believed that the guy coming up the street was looking forward and therefore could watch out for him. In his defense he had severe arthritis in his neck and could not turn his head.

He loved to take visitors to Glacier Park and would talk and point out the scenery with both hands. Visitors may have been too frightened to take their eyes off the mountain road.

Driving through Glacier he didn't want to stop saying, "Why would you want to take pictures when there are better ones on postcards."

He would try to stop us from buying souvenirs saying, "You don't need more Jin Junk."

If you did something he didn't like you might be called, "A God damn knot head." We kids have adopted that to call ourselves and laugh when we do something wrong.

"By God if something is worth doing, it's worth doing it right."

When I arranged a tour of a very large dairy operation in Wisconsin he objected, "Why should I go there, I already know how to milk a cow?"

He would physically wrestle another man over the restaurant bill, but Mom had to beg for spending money.

He had a friendly innocence going up to an artist in Glacier who had posted a "Do not Disturb" sign. Pop asked what he was painting, which looked pretty obvious, but it resulted in a long, friendly conversation.

In a restaurant with waitresses wearing skimpy uniforms, a male waiter approached our table. Pop looked up and growled, "What the hell did we get you for?"

A nephew who lives in a secluded part of the mountains brought his girlfriend to meet my parents. Mom and Pop agreed that she looked dirtier than any farmer. Pop told us she was a "Slop-hound," a derogatory term we children occasionally use privately.

After strokes slowed Pop down and he had to live in a nursing home, his condition gave him time to relax and show his sense of humor and gratitude for others. Staff in the nursing home called him "Sweet Pete" a name that we children would not use even though we loved him and knew that he loved us.

Mom and Pop were always together day and night for more than sixty years and weathered all storms. They were a team and both worked very hard. After sixty years, both of them said that they had a "good marriage." In fact, Pop denied that they had ever argued about anything. Pop surprised us after Mom developed Alzheimer's by learning to cook a bit, clean house, and care the best he could for Mom.

Ole and Lena

Mom died almost ten years before Pop. We knew he didn't want to be without her and thought maybe his delay in following her might resemble that of Ole and Lena in this joke:

When Lena died, St. Peter met her at the gate saying that there was a spelling test to enter Heaven but not to worry. He said, "You've been a good person Lena, and you have had a hard life, so you deserve to be able to enter Heaven easily. The test for you is to spell the word Reno." Lena spelled R-E-N-O and was welcomed into Heaven. Several years later, St. Peter asked Lena to relieve him at the gate for a couple of hours. While St. Peter was gone, who do you think arrived at the gate but Ole!!!

Lena told him about the spelling test required for entrance into Heaven. Ole said, "Well, Lena you know I didn't have much schooling, but we had a good marriage, and I know you will treat me as well as I always treated you." "Yes, Ole," said Lena. Spell, "Albuquerque."

Hannah Suta holding baby Ben, with Ted on the left and Henry on the right.

Mom

Mom's parents were both Germans who grew up until the age of sixteen in the village of Freudental near Odessa, Ukraine, Russia. The village was entirely German as allowed by Catherine the Great. One of the Czars descended from her decided to rescind her promise that the Germans would not have to serve in the Russian army. The Czar wanted to conscript them, but the Germans were strongly opposed to fighting with the Russians. As a result, over three million Germans fled Russia around 1900, many coming to settle in America or Canada. Although Mom's parents grew up in the same village, they didn't meet until living in South Dakota. Henry probably had been helping his father farm rather than attending school.

Mom's parents and other relatives claimed free homesteads given by the United States. The best farming land was taken by the time they arrived, but they were happy to have their own land.

Mom was a non-identical twin and only one-month old when her family took the train for 15 hours from South Dakota to their homestead in Montana north of Cut Bank and bordering on Canada. At that time, Mom and her twin were the fourth and fifth children. More children were born until there were seven girls and then an eighth child who was a boy. Their homestead house had only two rooms, one room being a small kitchen. At bedtime, all of the girls had to go outdoors to climb a step ladder into the attic where they each had a pallet of goose feathers (not down) and two large nails in the wall to hold their only clothes.

Mom's mother became depressed after the birth of the eighth child and was hospitalized for six months in the State Mental Institution, there being no other choices for her care. She had many physical ailments. She did well at home for almost eight years when she became depressed after the death of a thirteen-year-old daughter from ruptured appendix. Mom talked once in a while about how awful it was that Louise was in great pain, and they had nothing to relieve the pain. Mom carried anger that Grandpa Lozing didn't take Louise to the doctor until it was too late, although it was the end of February with deep snow, and they had to travel twenty-four miles to the doctor. Mom was always a caring, loving person.

Mom attended a one-room school where her family apparently were the only non-English speaking children. She had not been taught the English language. Any time she spoke a German word the teacher would hit her knuckles hard with a ruler and make her stand in a corner facing the wall. The other children laughed when this happened, and Mom remembered her hurt long after she became an adult. But there were no classes and no radio or television to help her learn English. Mom's sisters dropped out of school early.

But Mom was smart, learned English, and completed eight grades of school. She wanted to continue going to school and become a teacher, but there was no high school near her.

Even if there was a school available her father might not have allowed her to attend because she had to work to support the family. Even through grade school she had been working as a "Mother's Helper" to earn money. At some places she had to do all of the Mother's work rather than just helping. At one farm the owner told her that he noticed how hard she worked, and therefore he paid her the exact same wages that he paid his male farm workers. That was astonishing at the time and amazes me even now because women never had equality. Mom proudly mentioned this once in a while throughout her life, as well she deserved to do. Mom continued to always be a very hard worker.

Our family lived in the one-and-a-half room shack built by Pop's father as his homestead house. When their fourth child (Violet) was born, Mom put her foot down and insisted that they get some land of their own and a better house.

We moved to our own place when I was one-year old. Mom was always a very hard worker, and she wasn't about to stay in the house. She took all four of us children out to pick rocks with her so that Pop would be able to break more land for farming. I don't know how she managed to care for four children under the age of five and do all of her other work; caring for chickens; cleaning chickens for cooking and canning: cooking meals, carrying buckets of water from the well, doing laundry by hand, ironing, sewing, mending, planting a garden, and hoeing among other tasks. As we kids got older we were all given chores to do and did what we could to create success with our farming. I had my own child-sized garden hoe as soon as I could walk.

Ted and Henry helped Pop as much as they could outdoors.

We had to sweep and scrub the floors, do dishes, feed chickens and gather eggs, clean vegetables, hoe the garden and other chores. Ben remembered that he and I had to dust furniture every week whether it was wood or not. We polished the stainless steel legs of our kitchen table and chairs every week with furniture polish. The floors had to be swept and scrubbed, and we had to gather eggs every day. These are just a few of the chores we did.

Caring for four children under the age of six while having every modern convenience is about all the women of today could handle, but Mom did a lot more work than that by going outdoors and trying to help Pop as much as she could.

When Pop was on one of his drinking binges, which fortunately only lasted one day at a time, we would modify our dinner. Pop always wanted his meal to include meat, potatoes, vegetable, and bread. There were a couple of meals we children liked when he was not home. One was "Graveyard Stew," which was torn pieces of toast in a bowl of hot milk with a little butter and sugar if desired. This was delicious made with the bread that Mom had baked. Other times we made a whole meal of wild mushrooms we collected from the prairie and then fried. It took all four of us kids to collect enough mushrooms to make a meal.

Mom got a Singer treadle sewing machine which she used for about forty years to make and repair clothing. She made the dresses that I wore, usually without using a pattern. The material that she used was from flour or feed sacks. Flour used to come in 100-pound bags that had a printed pattern, usually floral. Many dresses were made for women and children out of this sack material, thus the term "flour-sack dress." I would select material for my next dress from the stack of bags at the grain elevator rather than in a store. Flour manufactures designed prints for their bags to give people material they could use for clothing, home décor, or other purposes to help them get through the depression.

Mom later store-bought her material but early creations still had a resemblance to the old flour sacks. She would adorn my dresses with rick-rack trim or ruffles, not realizing that I didn't look good in ruffles. I would get to accent my wardrobe with "stylish" long brown cotton stockings held up with an uncomfortable garter belt. The stockings drooped down immediately and none of the other girls wore them.

My brothers fared little better by getting to wear hand-me-downs. Ted would get a shirt new or handed down from a relative, then it would go to Henry and then Benny. There was some visible mending and patches and not much life in the clothes by the time they were handed down to Ben.

One year close to Christmas, I came home from school to a big surprise. Mom had made dresses for all of my dolls out of a blue silky material and lined them up on the sofa. I didn't play with dolls very often, but I must have had more than twenty. Relatives didn't know what else to give a little girl, and there weren't many choices of gifts in the stores near me. I really don't know how Mom made those tiny dresses without any patterns or special equipment to be able to sew in small areas, such as inserting sleeves.

We never went to a doctor. I think our isolation on the farm kept us away from the germs of other people and we didn't get sick very often until we started school in town.

I seemed to get a sore throat more often than the boys. Pop would rub Mentholatum (not Vicks) onto my throat and upper chest while sitting behind me. Pop had very strong hands and used a lot of pressure. It hurt a lot and made my skin red and sore. Then they wrapped a warm cloth around my throat and put me to bed with a hot toddy.

Mom made a hot toddy to drink which is a little whiskey in hot water with some sugar and sometimes butter. She believed in gargles and made them out of vinegar, salt, pepper and warm water. She believed the stronger, the better. If you were miserable from the cure, then you should get better.

I remember one winter Mom lined up the four of us kids in the kitchen and went down the line giving each of us a tablespoon of Cod Liver Oil. Cod Liver Oil contains Vitamins A and D which are fatty acids that prevent blood from clotting easily. That wasn't a problem we had. There are many other claims about it, but without good evidence. I have no idea why Mom gave it to us, but my research says that it doesn't harm children, and it didn't harm us then.

Mercurochrome was the magic cure for any cuts, sores, puncture wounds or other external wounds. It stung when applied and left a red stain that made you believe it would heal anything. Mom didn't baby us and would say, "It will heal by the time you get married."

When we started going to school in Sunburst and were exposed to more people, we got every childhood disease during our first year or two and gave them to Mom and Pop because they had never had mumps, measles, German measles, and chicken pox. As adults they usually became sicker than we kids were. But Mom always had to take care of all of us.

My Mother was a true partner in the success of the Pete and Hannah Suta farm. I have never seen another woman in our community work as physically hard as she did both indoors and outside in the farm fields.

I worked alongside her in everything she did indoors and much of what she did outdoors.

I did a lot of the cooking.

Mom washed the kitchen walls and painted every year, and I was right there doing the same thing to help. Mom liked color and would usually paint one wall of a room a different color than the other three, no matter what my opinion was.

Mom didn't drive the tractor but while Pop was in the house drinking coffee and eating the food she had made for his between-meal lunch, Mom went out and greased all the sprockets in his machinery.

Mom always cleaned the seeder which had to have every little kernel of grain cleaned out of all the nooks and crannies before a different grain could be planted. It is important to not mix different grains because that would lower the price paid to the farmer. I heard Pop telling another farmer that nobody ever got the seeder as clean as Mom.

Pop hollered at us kids, but it wasn't as hurtful as when he hollered at Mom. We had learned to let it go—we had each other for support and could laugh about it with each other. Neither Mom nor Pop ever spanked or hit us. They raised their voices to tell us what to do or what they didn't like but they didn't belittle us as some parents do. They didn't act as though they loved any one of us differently from the others. They didn't use any disciplinary methods other than telling us to do what they wanted, sometimes with a raised voice.

During harvest, Mom would watch out the kitchen window for Ben to drive from the field with a truckload of grain to empty into the granary. She would run down the hill to go inside the granary to shovel grain away from the auger. She didn't want Ben to go into the granary as we all had heard stories of children and adults dying of suffocation because the grain shifts, and it is like standing on quicksand. Mom knew from experience that this could happen easily and quickly. Shoveling that grain away from the auger was very hard work. In addition, it was difficult to breathe inside the closed granary with no fresh air and chaff flying around. I know she did this mainly to save the life of her son, but I think she actually liked hard physical labor. It made her feel she was doing something more worthwhile than housework. When she ran down the hill to help Ben, I was left in the house to cook supper. I could fry chicken for dinner by myself when I was seven.

Mom always kept the inside of her house clean. She found time to bake bread twice a week and she was always cooking something good for a large number of people.

Mom had a green thumb and really loved her pots of Christmas cactus that normally blossom once a year but for her blossomed abundantly at least twice a year. She could start a new plant by just pinching off a leaf and putting it in water to sprout. I tried that and instead of the leaf sprouting it rotted from being in water for so long. She said her secret was that she talked to her plants every day, but she must have used special words because that didn't work for me.

Mom knew the tone and volume of voice to use when she wanted us kids to stop what we were doing or to do something she wanted done. She might raise her voice and use a stern tone. We listened and did what she said but we weren't obeying out of fear of punishment because we weren't punished. She never spanked any of us for discipline.

During the first years on our farm Mom planted her garden near the house and just to the east of the kitchen. That ground was on a hillside and couldn't have been the best choice because water would run off the plants and down the hill. But I think the garden being nearby made it easy for her, or her children, to gather vegetables to be cooked. My brothers and I would play in the garden, eating some of the vegetables. We might have thought we were getting away with something, but Mom wasn't upset at all about us eating vegetables. She could also keep an eye on whether we were hoeing the garden as instructed or were just playing around.

Years later we had a larger garden on a flat piece of a field where there was enough space that Pop could use a machine to weed the large space between rows. Then we only had to hoe the soil close to the plants. Pop also could drive the water truck over to water the garden.

Mom loved the beauty of flowers. She planted rows of flowers in the garden but didn't often cut and bring them inside. She just liked to see the flowers in her garden.

She had a raised flower bed built along the east side of the house where she could water and visit some of her flowers. The dog, not Fido, decided that it was a good place to take naps. She put chicken wire around the bed to keep off the dog and cats. Despite the chicken wire, some chickens discovered this nice loose soil that was easy to scratch and roll around in when they wanted dirt to clean their feathers. It was a losing battle for Mom, but she wouldn't give up. One year when I went to visit she immediately and proudly showed me that there was a rose blossoming in that raised bed. One lone red rose on a small bush. But to her it was wonderful,

Another of her plant battles was definitely a losing one. For several years she tried to plant a small tree on the north side of the house where she could see it from the kitchen window over the sink. If it wasn't the animals destroying that poor baby tree, it was Pop "'accidentally" running over it with the snowmobile or cutting it down when swathing weeds around the house. I'm not sure if he didn't see the tree or was being ornery, which was a possibility with him.

Mom finally got a lilac bush to grow just below the north-facing kitchen windows where you stood when doing dishes. It grew large enough that it reached above the window sill, and you could see the flowers and smell that wonderful scent when it blossomed. That lilac bush grew very large and blossomed profusely on the day we held the farm auction, despite the weather being cold and snowy.

Mom loved little children, and they all related well to her. Even crying babies would stop crying when she took them from their mother. She kept small toys for children inside the bottom drawer of her electric stove where most people keep lids or cookware. She didn't mind children being underfoot. She wanted them to be in the kitchen where everybody was talking, and the children weren't left out. There never was a child injured from being near the stove. Adults fondly remember being able to play with those little toys in the stove drawer.

At Mom's funeral more than one child came to me quietly crying with tears on their face and told me, "Hannah really loved me." I assured each that, "She certainly did love you a lot and she would want you to always remember that you are worthy of love."

When Dian got married I noticed that all the siblings of her husband lived near their mother and one son even lived next door. In the car with Dian and Mom I told Mom, "You might be thinking that Philomena is a better mother than you because her children live so close to her while your children all moved away." I continued, "You did a better job than her; you raised us all to be independent and able to live our own lives. You didn't hold on too tightly; we were allowed to make our own decisions and mistakes, and you didn't give us lectures about how to live our lives, but you taught by example." I went on to say that "Unlike Phil, you raised your children to be mature adults."

Mom told me, "I feel like I didn't raise you because you were so young when you left home. I had no choice but to let you leave." I replied, "You are totally wrong. I learned everything from your example."

Mom loved to go ice fishing. She and Pop each had their own private ice fishing shacks and would haul them onto the nearby Fitzpatrick Lake. Mom would clean all the fish they caught and freeze them so that in the summer when her children and families visited she would have enough fresh trout to fry for everyone.

That lake was close, just behind Baldwin's place, but even before the Hutterites blocked the lake, Pop had started refusing to take Mom fishing when she would ask. We believe the problem was that she caught more fish than Pop and he was jealous. Mom simply used a marshmallow for bait while Pop used fancy lures. But she always cleaned all the fish and didn't brag that she had caught more fish than Pop.

She also liked to have huckleberries to make pie for us when we visited. She had to buy huckleberries instead of pick huckleberries after Uncle Bill Newmiller saw a bear on the other side of a bush from Mom and refused to take her berry picking again.

When Mom made a birthday cake she always hid in the cake a ring, a dime and a nickel after cleaning each with boiling water. When the cake was cut your future was predicted by one of these in your slice of cake. The ring meant you were going to get married, the dime that you were going to be wealthy, and the nickel meant that you were going to be poor. I have no idea where Mom got the idea to do this as a tradition, but it was fun.

A Women's Home Demonstration Club was formed in the area where Mom lives. I noticed as Mom talked about the women in the Club that she preferred the women who were much younger than her. Also, when we visited with a woman about Mom's age, she would say to me, "She's so old." When I pointed out that the woman was about her own age Mom would say, "Yes, but she's so old." And indeed most women Mom's age did look and act much older than her. I am like Mom in that way because I too stay active, like to be around women younger than me, and look at other women my age as being older than me. In fact, younger women tell me just as they told Mom, "You are my inspiration. I want to be like you when I grow up."

When Mom bought clothes for us, she always bought them two sizes too large. Then she would say, "Don't worry, you'll grow into it." Well, I never grew very much, and she gave me a nice terrycloth robe that was huge. But she was right, and I grew into it when I was pregnant. Also, when reading to Morgan and Jeff on the sofa I could cover up the feet of both of them with that robe.

When Mom worked as a Mother's Helper, her father let her keep a little of the money she earned. She saved for six months to buy a picture she saw in a catalog. It is a picture of flowers, of course, about 16x20 inches. The frame is narrow but is carved in a lovely pattern. When she became older, she embroidered a picture of flowers and inserted that into the frame. She gave it to me as a Christmas gift and I treasure it.

Mom could teach us all about recycling. I never received a letter from her that wasn't written all over an envelope that had held a bill. She wrote on every smidgen of that paper.

Mom liked to recycle jokes too, but she never could remember the punch line. That caused all of us to laugh harder than we would have laughed at the joke.

One Christmas when Mom was visiting Dian in California she said that she would like to go fishing in the ocean. It was Christmas time and there weren't any tourist boats. Dian booked a fishing venture on a professional fishing boat that didn't usually take tourists. The ocean was very rough that day and every fisherman on board, including the captain, became very seasick. Everyone was seasick and vomiting over the rail except Mom, and she even caught a large fish. The men were all impressed and Mom really enjoyed that day.

Mom was a true partner in the success of the Pete and Hannah Suta Farm.

Addendum: Mom had a few common sayings:

1. When we got hurt, Mom would say, "It'll be better by the time you're married."

2. When she got mad at something, she would say that "It isn't worth a hill of beans."

3. She taught us the following speech, "Ladies and gentlemen, horses and mules, I've come to tell you that you're all damn fools."

4. When something small but positive happened, she would say, "Like the little old lady said when she took a pee in the ocean, every little bit helps."
5. She liked the Carnation milk poem. "No teats to squeeze, No shit to pitch, Just punch a hole in the son-of-a-bitch."
6. She often said, "you can't make a silk purse out of a sow's ear." Although the analogy is gross, I decided that it helped trainers and supervisors to realize that not everyone can be taught to be successful in a position.

Violet sitting at her special place on the prairie.

Top (l to r): St. Mary's Lake; Weeping Wall, ca. 1965
Bottom (l to r): Jackson Glacier, ca. 1963; Avalanche, 1965

Big Sky

Montana is known as the big sky state, and it deserves that name.

You can actually see beyond the horizon because the elevation differential allows you to see over obstacles. At 4,000–6,000 feet above sea level you are closer to the sky than you had been before. Or closer to heaven as some would say. You are looking through less atmosphere and it is clear, not cloudy or hazy from pollution or humidity.

Every year after I moved to Wisconsin I returned to Montana for what I consider my spiritual renewal. There are two places in Montana I need to visit to draw my comfort and restore my identity. One is the Rocky Mountains of Glacier National Park and the other is a specific spot on the prairie where I grew up.

Glacier National Park

I need to annually visit Glacier Park for regeneration. I have traveled to many other countries in the world where I have seen more spectacular mountains and fantastic views, but they don't give me the same inner feeling of being filled up and expanded by the Holy Spirit as I feel in Glacier National Park.

The Rocky Mountain range in Glacier National Park is definitely rocky, craggy, and rough. There are lovely mountains elsewhere that are covered in trees, but many mountains in Glacier are exposed rock with sharp edges and no trees. You can see different colors in the layers of earth that make up a given mountain. The white of the glaciers highlight the stark formation of the mountains. Unfortunately, global warming is causing the glaciers to melt.

When Glacier Park was established in 1910 there were 150 distinct glaciers and as of 2022 there were only twenty-five active glaciers remaining. These remaining glaciers have clearly diminished in size. The decrease of glaciers in size and numbers is extreme enough that it is visible to my naked eye compared to what I remember from my childhood. Some glaciers are completely gone. There is a portion of the Going-to-the-Sun Road named the Weeping Wall because the snow and glacier melt coming down the straight rock wall made it feel like you were driving under a waterfall. The water pounded on the roof of the car, and you had to close the windows to prevent a lot of water from coming inside the car. There now is only a trickle of water instead of a waterfall. If the mountains could weep they would surely be weeping now but without tears because climate warming has caused a loss of the glaciers.

It is hard for me to select a favorite spot in the park since I love the entire place. But I do have a special feeling for the Many Glacier area because the views are often reflected in the lake.

I suppose I love Glacier Park because it is about as familiar as home. I grew up only about seventy miles east of Glacier Park and we could easily drive there and back in one day. I went there many times in my childhood. It is the only place that my father didn't mind visiting frequently with the family.

Special Place on the Prairie

My special place on the prairie was on the land west of my house. I feel like the first person on earth when I visit this land that had never been farmed. I was able to sit on that piece of land, surrounded by rolling hills, and not be able to see even one single building or evidence of current society. It is rare to find a spot where you can be totally out of sight from civilization. This section of land was leased from the State of Montana and was designated for grazing animals. It had never been plowed.

    Sitting on that spot I had a clear and unobstructed view of the beautiful Sweetgrass Hills about fifty miles to the east. There they stood jutting out of the prairie all by themselves. The Sweetgrass Hills look like a short range of mountains, but they are actually several buttes in a group formation next to the Canadian border. This grouping is unusual because buttes usually stand alone surrounded by prairie. The tallest of the group is actually higher than many mountains in other states. Turning around and looking toward the west I could see an outline of the Rocky Mountains. It is quiet there because the noise of farm machinery is usually far enough away to not be heard and there is rarely an airplane crossing the sky above me. My mind could roam in any direction while I sat there. You might say that I was meditating but it was not to any method and not even my intent. I never felt as though I was wasting time or ought to be accomplishing something while I was there. I never even took my needlework to do, or paper and pen to write down thoughts, or a book to read. I was simply quiet there and did nothing. I miss that special place.

    The prairie is so vast that you feel your smallness in the overall world. Astronauts looking down while circling the earth would not even see me as a speck of dust. Yet at the same time there is a feeling of being huge because I am alone in standing on this land, in this specific location, as though I own the world. In this place you are very small and very large all at once.

The vastness can create a loss of dimension, a loss of depth. If a tourist is driving from the east for a vacation in Glacier Park, they may see the Rocky Mountains ahead and think that they will be at their destination in about an hour. But they will be surprised when they have to drive and drive the rest of the day before getting there. The effect of space is disconcerting. With no trees or large buildings to frame the view, people cannot judge depth or distance. There is no perspective.

It is difficult to take landscape pictures that show what you see with your naked eye unless you are a professional photographer. If you get far enough away from your subject to give it meaning in relation to things around it you will not see the specific thing you were hoping to show. If you get close to the subject it loses meaning and you will wonder later why you took that picture. For example, I was taking a picture of a one-room country schoolhouse that was old and starting to fall down. When I framed the entire building surrounded by a little of the landscape, the decrepit condition was not so apparent. If I focused on the front door falling off the hinges and with paint peeling off you then wouldn't know that it had been a schoolhouse and where it was standing. The picture lost meaning.

As an adult living in the beautiful city of Madison, Wisconsin I have complained a lot about the hazy, light blue sky compared to Montana where the sky is usually a clear bright blue color with white clouds and the sun shining. The sky looks that way in the winter as well as in the summer. My son Jeff told me that he couldn't understand why I complained about Wisconsin being hazy until he moved to Boston and noticed that the sky was definitely cloudier than Madison.

Sunshine

The main reason the sky looks bright in Montana is because the sun shines an average of 189 days a year in the north-central area where I grew up and a whopping average of 300 days in Bozeman where I went to college. Compare those days of sunshine to the average of eighty-nine days in Wisconsin and you can understand why I complain about the lack of sunshine in Madison. In Montana, the sun usually is shining even when it is very cold outside. It was unusual but I can honestly say that I have experienced the sun shining while I was being rained or snowed upon.

    When sitting on the prairie I was always conscious of the past when native Americans and buffalo freely roamed that land. I imagined the Blackfeet Indians camping at that location. There were two or three large circles of heavy stones obviously placed to hold down the bottom of a tepee from blowing away by the ever-present wind. In the center there was a ring of rocks arranged for a fire. On the land nearby were short stacks of flat rocks here and there which I assumed were trail markers made by the Indians—they certainly were not stacked by any of my family. On the surrounding prairie were a couple of places where stones were piled in a rectangle about the size of a person. I believe these were shallow burial sites covered with stones to protect the body from being ravaged by wild animals. The Indians preferred to place their dead person on a hammock in trees out of reach of predators, but our land did not have any trees.

Photo of moon in bright blue sky seen at 10:30 pm.

Rain can be visible.

Night Sky in Montana

I could not talk about the Big Sky of Montana without mentioning some of the amazing views of the night sky. The stars and moon are bright and clear on any given night while on my farm because there are no city lights to interfere.

The Milky Way

The Milky Way was often visible because of the sky being clear with little or no light and low humidity. It is a huge collection of stars, dust and gas. It's called a spiral galaxy because if you could view it from the top or bottom it would look like a spinning pinwheel. The Sun is located on one of the spiral arms, about 25,000 light years away from the center of the galaxy. The Milky Way looks like a congregation or a party of many stars.

When I was a very young child and someone referred to the Milky Way I thought they were talking about the small town of Milk River across the border in Alberta, Canada. We could clearly see the lights of Milk River about fifty miles away because the elevation of that town was higher than my home. Being able to see that far away is a phenomenon of the big sky. I no longer confuse the small town of Milk River with the magnificent Milky Way.

Violet Suta Moran

Aurora Borealis

The Aurora Borealis or Northern Lights is one of nature's most spectacular visual phenomena. It appears in a clear night sky as swirling rivers of light. On the Suta Farm I remember the lights filling the sky as being mainly a greenish-blue color of various shades. The lights move and dance unpredictably, sometimes barely perceptible, then suddenly growing vivid and moving wildly. The Northern Lights are an amazing colorful display of light commonly seen in the night sky in the northern hemisphere. They occur all the time but are most active and visible in the northerly sky between September and April.

    The Northern Lights occur when solar winds with electrically charged particles enter the Earth's magnetic field. The particles collide with atmospheric gases to create blue, green, red and violet curtains of light in the sky. They were frequently visible from the Suta farm. I didn't know that what we called The Northern Lights were the same as the Aurora Borealis. I saw the Northern Lights so often while living on the farm that I guess I took this incredible sight for granted. Later when I heard adults around me saying that seeing the Aurora Borealis was on their "bucket list" I thought it must be a rare sight. It was a long time before I learned that the Aurora Borealis and Northern Lights were the same thing. I knew the Northern Lights that I had frequently seen from the Suta farm were phenomenal but thought I was missing out on something even more spectacular. Now I realize how fortunate I was to frequently see this incredible sight every year that I lived on the Suta Farm.

    But I have to admit that what we saw from the farm in Montana was not as stunning as when I saw the Aurora Borealis farther north in Iceland. In Iceland there were more colors of vivid hues, the display across the sky was larger, and the continuous dancing movements of the lights were magnificent.

Sweetgrass

Sunsets

Sunsets in Montana were always remarkable. We did not always appreciate the beauty of the sunset because our farm was directly west of Sunburst, and we were usually driving home with the sun shining brilliantly in our eyes. It was hard to avoid this discomforting event because it took longer for the sun to set when we could see so far to the horizon. The brilliant gold and red colors were not in the same configuration every night. Sometimes the sunset is so bright that it seems to be completely in shades of red rather than gold. I think all sunsets are beautiful but those seen from our farm were always spectacular. All I can do is to suggest that you picture in your mind the most beautiful sunset you have ever seen and then think about what a personal fortune it would be to see that almost every night.

There are similarities in sunsets with each starting from vivid shades of gold radiating out from the center of the sun to gradually spreading out farther from the sun and turning a lighter shade of gold. There usually are shades of blue and pink reflected on clouds throughout the sky. The entire sky becomes a breathtaking modern painting of pinks and blues. And streaks of orange. My niece Carol calls the Montana sunsets "strawberry jam and grape juice smeared together," but that sounds like a mess to me. I do not possess the poetic words to eloquently describe sunsets; and there are differences in the sunsets every night.

Sunrise

Sunrise seen from the Suta Farm is also a spectacular sight as the sun suddenly "bursts" over the Sweetgrass Hills. That is how the town of Sunburst got its name. It seems that sunsets are gradual and create a big show of colors and shapes while sunrise occurs quickly, popping up as the intact sun with rays shining from the center. The sun hides behind the Hills until it is ready to be seen.

The difference is in the higher elevation of the Sweetgrass Hills. When we were driving east from the farm the Sweetgrass Hills would elevate the sunrise, and we would not be blinded to the extent we were blinded by sunsets. I'm a night-owl, and it always seemed that sunrise came too early. I could describe sunrise better if I had more often gotten out of bed that early in the morning.

Lightning

Lightning strikes are visible from a long distance across the Big Sky. Jagged sharp strikes are stunning as they hit the ground and then thunder roars, louder and more immediately if the lightning strike was nearby.

Sometimes the lightning is circular and encompasses the entire horizon. You don't know where to look while that is happening. It is a surreal feeling to be in the center of this activity.

I like to see and hear a big lightning storm. Sometimes I lie on my back under the sunroof in my living room to watch or sometimes look out a window, even though I know you aren't supposed to be close to a window at that time. Lightning puts on a dramatic show. Lightning felt significant because it created hope that rain would fall on our dry land. Farmers might go to town if the roads were good. They might be thinking that the crop will be good now and we can spend some money. Dry land farmers were almost always happy when rain was falling. There was joy in rain.

Dry Storm

Sometimes Mother Nature would fool us by making us think rain is coming but it doesn't. There might be thunder and lightning across the sky and a dark cloud over your head which does not release any rain at all. We tried to track dark clouds across the sky to see how fast they were moving and when they might drop their load of moisture on our land. Because we could see so far we could estimate where the rain cloud was going and how quickly. If we received only lightning, thunder, and darkness it was called a "dry storm."

Rain is visible in Montana

I'm not talking about being able to see raindrops on your windshield or splashes as raindrops hit a puddle of water or seeing wet drops forming on your sidewalk. Looking at the clear Montana sky, you can see denseness or a dark gray section streaking from a cloud onto the earth. This is a delineated dark gray section of the sky, not just general cloudiness.

From the darkness you can tell whether the rain is coming straight down or at an angle from the sky. The rain is cruel to come down at an angle while the poor farmer below the dark cloud was expecting the rain to fall directly on his land. The denseness of that dark portion of the sky also reveals how heavy the rainfall is at that location. This is absolutely amazing. There may be some other place where you can see rain like this, but I do not know of another "Big Sky" location.

I know that I have seen these streaks of rain in the sky from at least 60 miles away. We could make a rough estimate as to which of our neighbors was getting rain. This was possible because we were accustomed to the loss of dimension in the Big Sky atmosphere and were sometimes able to judge distance. We knew most of the farmers who lived in the entire county and approximately where they lived. With that knowledge and because we could see clearly for a long distance we could make this judgment of who might be receiving rain.

I never thought this was strange or astonishing because I had seen it all my life. Visitors who see this or have just been told about it find it hard to believe. But it is true that rain is visible in Montana.

Violet Suta Moran

Aerial view of the home and farm buildings.

Farmland is divided into strips and seeded every other year. This postcard photo is not our land because the strips show up better. This is Square Butte, which artist Charlie Russell used often.

Suta Farm Land

On 3 April 1932 Peter leased 320 acres of land from Peter and Clara Itherbide for three years. This land was directly north of his father's place. Peter agreed to seed 100 acres, summer fallow 100 acres, and break an additional eighty acres during the lease. Peter's father agreed to provide the machinery except Itherbide agreed to provide the combine and two men during harvest. Peter got two-thirds of the crop. We believe that Peter farmed this land until he moved onto his own place in 1938.

Pop bought the 325.5-acre John Schutze homestead in 1937. Pop wrote the absentee owners who answered that they would sell him this land for $1190. Pop discovered they had not paid any property taxes since 1929. Instead of paying their asking price, Pop was able to buy the place for $174.22 in back taxes plus a $75 legal fee. John Farbo loaned him the money for one-half of the mineral rights in lieu of interest. In addition, Pop leased 480 acres from Martin and Ingeborg Jacobean for one-quarter of the crop and hay.

Over the years Pop purchased and leased more land. He bought the land that he had been leasing from the Jacobeans in 1941 for $4100, including the Walden Kaisser homestead and three smaller homesteads. Near this time he also purchased eighty acres of state land. In 1949 he bought some land from Paul Jesse for $3600, which he traded to Ted

Violet Suta Moran

Simmes for part of the Everett Kron homestead. Following his father's death in 1952, he traded his brother Rudy the land that he inherited plus some money in return for the James Hudson homestead. He later bought the Philip Schnett homestead and leased some state land for grazing. During the late 1940s and early 1950s, he and Mom's brother, Gilbert Lozing, leased 5000 acres for grazing on the Blackfoot Indian reservation.

We cared for a total of about 5000 acres as the Suta farm of which about 2000 acres was under cultivation. The remaining land was used for hay and grazing the cattle. We called our land a farm, but it was also a ranch. We had a fairly small farm by Montana standards for dry-land farming. Most of the land that Pop purchased was prairie which had a lot of rocks to be picked before the land could be broken for farming.

Breaking up new ground and rock picking was a constant summer effort from 1939 to the early 1950s. Our soil was seemingly composed of an infinite number of many kinds of rocks. Even after the initial picking, rocks would work their way to the surface from cultivation and frost. These required annual removal from the summer-fallowed farm land. Our land was hilly and very rocky, thus breaking it for farming required a considerable amount of hard rock picking. Mom would say, "No rocks, no crop," as if rocks added to the land's fertility.

Our soil wasn't rich enough and we didn't get enough moisture to yield a good crop every year. As dry-land farmers we began to practice strip farming when I was very young. Instead of plowing or planting a large field, the land is divided into strips that are seeded every other year while the unseeded strips were summer fallowed. Summer fallowing gives the soil a year to replenish nutrients, conserve moisture, and retain the top soil from being blown away by the constant winds.

Sweetgrass

The summer fallow is periodically disced to kill weeds. In earlier years of my life, Pop worked the summer fallow two or three times in a summer and was proud that his fields always looked clean and void of weeds. That practice was later learned to expose the soil to erosion and loss of moisture. Later best practices were to leave some type of cover over the soil. New types of equipment and methods of farming are used to benefit the land and research continues.

Grains that we planted were mostly wheat and barley. We grew a lot of mustard until Canadians were given higher prices.

We raised oats as hay and grain for the animals.

We grew flax a couple of years.

One year we grew rye for cattle food, but when tied into bundles and shocked, the slippery bunches would slide to the ground.

Later Pop bought a Minneapolis Moline pull-type combine.

Grain was unloaded into a truck and then shoveled into the granary. It was not practical to haul the grain directly to the elevator because we lived twelve miles from town, which was too far to haul the grain during harvest time. The truck had to be available when the combine hopper needed to be emptied. We had to have granaries at home to store the grain until there was a good price to sell to the elevator in town and when there was time to haul the grain into town. Pop operated the combine and as soon as Ted was old enough, about nine years old, he ran the tractor. Pop would hire a truck driver until Henry and Ben were older.

There was always a great hurry and stress to get harvest done while the grain was at its peak and the weather was good. It wasn't unusual to get a little snow or frost during harvest, but these problems usually cleared up in a day. At least one year we got early snow that didn't melt, causing us to finish harvest in the spring. By spring the grain was good only for feed. Harvest time always brought out a lot of yelling and cursing from Pop because of the stress to get everything done quickly before the weather turned ugly.

We raised some oats and had some seed for sale. One day a husband and wife came and said, "My name is Longcake, and I've come for some oats." For some reason, Mom thought that this was funny and laughed whenever it occurred to her.

Dry-land farmers continually devise farming methods to conserve moisture in the soil. Plow blades are angled to make furrows that might hold rainwater. The stalks of grain that remain after harvest used to be plowed under the soil but now are left standing until spring to prevent erosion.

Instead of discing to eliminate weeds we later used a rod weeder and a noble blade, which has a long knife blade that stays underground to kill weeds at the root when pulled by the tractor. These methods were designed to kill weeds and to keep the trash from last year's crop on top to control erosion and conserve moisture, and prevent the top soil from being blown away by the constant winds.

Our farm had rolling hills, and Sweetgrass Hills are in background.

Machines

Sometime in the mid-1930s Pop bought a 21-32 Twin Cities tractor. This tractor had iron wheels until 1941, when he bought rubber tires and rims for $310.

Pop bought an International Harvester combine in 1950. He hated this combine so much that he traded it the next year for a Massey Harris. That combine was the only piece of machinery that he kept for only one year. In spite of Pop's warnings, Uncle Rudy bought it used from the dealer and soon hated it equally.

In 1952 Pop bought a second Massey Harris with a canvas header. This combine was a pain because the header constantly plugged. He made the boys run it while he ran the other combine which had an auger header.

In about 1947 augers became available for unloading the grain from the truck into the storage bins. An auger functions like an escalator for the grain to move from the truck into the granary. Pop bought a Howrey/Berg auger that was by far the worst one ever invented. The BS&B motor was on the top, so you needed a ladder to start it, and it almost always started poorly, especially when warm. It was very dangerous to keep your balance while standing on the top of a stepladder to start this stubborn auger. That was a terribly stupid design, and I'm thankful none of my brothers fell from the top of the ladder. Pop was busy with harvest and

Self propelled combine with Pop driving.

Pop's first tractor, a Twin Cities 21-32 with iron wheels.

didn't pay any attention to complaints because he wouldn't want to go out shopping for an auger while the grain was in the fields. It didn't have a clutch so when it got plugged, which was frequently, we had to turn the auger backwards by hand. Moreover, the mouse-infested pit frequently plugged up and was difficult to unplug. We had to have granaries at home because it would take too long to haul loads twelve miles on a narrow graveled road to the Sunburst elevator. The combine had to keep moving and the grain had to be stored.

Harvest was done using an International Harvester combine pulled by a Twin Cities tractor.

When the grain bins were partly full, someone would have to go into the bin and shovel the grain back while the auger was running, a very miserable and dangerous job. Miserable because you can hardly breath with chaff filling the air and no fresh air. Dangerous because grain is like quicksand and you could sink down and suffocate. Ben almost got buried in the grain once so Mom didn't want him to go inside the granary. She watched from the kitchen window and would run down the hill to meet Ben coming in with a load of grain. Unloading took two people anyway and she would go into the grain bin herself, something you couldn't imagine any other farm wife doing.

Pop was on the combine and didn't need to unload so he didn't see a problem. He then decided to build his own grain elevator, a project that lasted several years. This elevator was partially successful, but it was disliked by anyone who had to unload a truck during harvest time, which seldom was Pop. The elevator shaft wasn't high enough to completely fill the bins, thus requiring shoveling.

The current combines are self-propelled, not needing to be pulled by a tractor. A truck can be driven close to the combine and grain can be dropped directly into the truck. When necessary the truck sometimes drives alongside the combine while the grain is being emptied. Time is of the essence during harvest time.

The growing season is short in northern Montana and everybody has to hurry. Harvest time always brought out a lot of yelling and cursing from pop, there was a lot of stress to get harvest done while the grain was at its peak and the weather was good.

We fairly often got snow for a day or part of a day during harvest. There was at least one memorable year when the snow was early and heavy and never melted at all during the winter. We had to finish harvest in the spring. By spring the grain was good only for feed. And that spring was very stressful when cutting the fields of ruined grain and trying to get seeding done at the same time.

Because of the short growing season traveling combine crews are often paid to help. These crews come with all their equipment from Kansas or Nebraska where grain ripens earlier and work their way north.

In earlier years, our family did everything ourselves. Pop operated the combine and Ted ran the tractor as soon as he was old enough. Pop would hire a truck driver until Henry and Ben were older.

In the mid-1950s Pop began buying round metal grain bins which were considerably easier to load and unload than Pop's elevator.

In April 1949, Pop bought a new Minneapolis Moline model U tractor. We used this tractor for cultivating, mowing hay, post-hole drilling and all kinds of lifting after we installed a Farm Hand. Pop put chains on the tractor and a blade on the Farm Hand which he used to push snow in the winter. He would work all day snowplowing around the house and road, then the winds would blow it back even deeper, and he would repeat the process.

Mustard

I loved the farm when we were strip farming and mustard was one of our crops. A ripening field of mustard is totally covered with brilliant gold flowers. The dark strips of plowed soil on either side functioned like picture frames. I thought these were my personal flowers, planted for my pleasure and clearly visible on the hillsides facing our house.

I was surprised my first year of college to have an English professor suggest that I write a paper about growing mustard. When I began my research in 1954 I was amazed to discover what the instructor apparently already knew from her orientation to Montana. The area where my family's farm was located, the northern part of Toole County, Montana, raised two-thirds of the world's mustard.

This changed in the early 1960s when new trade laws allowed Canadians to truck their mustard into the United States and sell it for more money than we were being paid, subsidized by our Government. I am still angry and puzzled over how mustard became a political pawn in international relations.

Now mustard is planted in Alberta, Canada, just across the border from where I lived. I can see those beautiful mustard fields when we drive the eight miles it takes to reach the border for some other purpose, such as visiting the Sweetgrass cemetery, which butts up against the U.S./

Violet Suta Moran

Mustard field in full bloom.

Canada border. While those mustard fields are strikingly beautiful, they are not my flowers.

Mustard is a sturdy plant that grows wild in almost any location and is universally hated as an obnoxious weed. It invades any field and grows in scattered areas on the dry prairie. Even when not in bloom, the mustard plant can be identified because it branches out instead of growing straight up on a stalk like wheat and other grains.

Mustard seeds are very tiny, and when we raised mustard the machines for seeding and combining had to be cleaned thoroughly and adapted to the small size of this grain.

Mom assumed the job of cleaning out the seeder between grains while Pop had his cup of cold coffee in the kitchen. The seeder had to be cleaned very carefully because the price we would be given when we sold the grain could be reduced if mixed with another grain.

Sweetgrass

If a farmer wants to sell his grain as "registered," meaning it is pure and will receive a higher price, someone has to walk through that field and pull out every wild mustard plant. My brother Ben and I have done that. Dairy farmers really hate to have mustard growing on their land because when eaten by a cow it will make her milk taste bad. There are other plants that will make a cow's milk unacceptable, including wild onions or garlic and milkweed. If her tainted milk is inadvertently mixed with other milk the entire supply will have to be discarded costing the dairy farmer a lot of money.

A pair of brothers who grew up on a dairy farm in Wisconsin were rewarded by their father with a penny for every mustard plant they pulled out of the ground. They pulled so many mustard plants that they have created a chain of furniture stores named "Penny Mustard Furnishings."

When someone asks what we grew on our farm and I name mustard as one of the crops, they usually are surprised. People never think about the mustard they put on hot dogs as coming from tiny mustard seeds grown on a farm. There is a "Mustard Museum" in Middleton, Wisconsin that displays, gives tastes, and sells a huge variety of mustard condiments.

Mustard seeds apparently have been growing around the world for thousands of years. The tiny mustard seed is the basis of several parables in the King James bible. The shortest is found in the Gospel of Luke 13 and reads: *"It is like a grain of mustard seed, which a man took and put in his own garden. It grew and became a large tree, and the birds of the sky lodged in its branches."* Parables usually have three parts: 1) the picture part of this simile is the tiny seed growing into a large plant, 2) the reality part interprets the birds of the sky as gentiles seeking refuge and 3) the point of comparison, which must be in a parable, is the growth of the Kingdom of God which also started from small beginnings and spread everywhere.

On my family farm we planted crops other than mustard, primarily wheat, and some barley and oats. We also raised a

Violet Suta Moran

grain named "rapeseed" which yields oil that is processed to become canola oil. A couple of years we planted flax seeds, and the fields were lovely when ripening with light blue flowers. A large field of these blue flowers is beautiful, although definitely not as striking as a field of mustard in bloom.

When driving near mustard fields that are blossoming, in Canada, I ask to stop so I can enjoy a long look at those flowers and take pictures.

Even now, more than half a century after we stopped raising mustard, my heart still yearns to look out my window and see those fields of spectacular mustard flowers that were planted just for me.

As a young child Violet loved the mustard flowers that she thought made the farm look beautiful.

Wind, Wind, Wind

Wind, wind, wind, always wind. There was always at least a strong breeze in Montana. There may almost always be wind in the entire state of Montana but the area where I lived is known as the place most likely to have strong winds. And I can vouch that it did and still does. I've been told that the wind is directed specifically at our region as it comes from the west through the Marias Pass.

Travelers on the north/south route of I-15 between Shelby, Montana and the Canadian border are surprised to see a large official highway sign warning them of "DUST STORMS, LIMITED VISIBILITY, NEXT 1 MILE." Drivers who are not familiar with this area have ignored this warning at their peril. There have been vehicles of all types, trailer-homes and even large commercial trucks that have been blown off the road and onto their side or into the ditch.

You might have seen similar signs elsewhere when you are crossing a high bridge warning you to "Beware of ice on bridge" or "Beware of wind on bridge." But you look around here on this Montana highway and see that there is no bridge and the land is flat and dry, so you ask yourself, "How can there be a danger?" But this isn't an empty warning.

On normal windy days there will be a strong wind with periodic "gusts" of wind suddenly blowing harder for a short period of time. You can be driving down the road coping well with the strong wind and then an unexpected and extra-strong gust of wind can rock your car and cause it to swerve. You have to be alert while steering. You also have to be careful when walking on a windy day because strong gusts of wind can cause you to stumble or lose your balance. When walking into the wind you might take two steps forward and one back. People who are walking have to lean at an angle in order to stay upright.

The wind leaves you with grit in your eyes and face, grinding between your teeth, and filling up your hair. You will get dirt inside your ears. Your clothing becomes impregnated with dust. I become irritated and angry about the wind because I don't like dirt and gravel blowing into my face. The gravel used in rural Montana is not finely ground and the large pieces hurt when they hit your face.

Windstorms roar loudly and you can still hear the wind ringing in your ears when you go indoors, like coming out of a loud rock concert where you forgot to wear earplugs. A strong wind is tiring and can go on for days. You can hear it while indoors like a "white noise" that doesn't put you to sleep but becomes irritating as it continues. A strong wind might flatten the crops making it hard for the combine to cut the stalks because they are lying on the ground. If the grain is ripe, a hard wind will even shake out some of the seeds.

I didn't hear the term "Dust Devil" very often, perhaps because they actually were so common. People in Montana would simply say, "It sure is windy today." A Dust Devil whirls around in a circle looking like a mini-tornado. The bottom point grabs onto some dirt and gravel and then just whirls quickly in a circle while moving forward or changing directions.

During the "dirty thirties" from 1930 to 1940 plus some years earlier and later there were a lot of dust-storms in the United States. There were strong winds blowing away the top soil, making the sky dark and eliminating visibility. They were

Sweetgrass

called "black blizzards" because visibility would decrease to zero as it does in a blizzard of snow. Topsoil from the west and mid-west farming areas of the United States was blown to Chicago and New York. The farmland was a dustbowl.

These terrible dust storms were due to a combination of factors: drought, poor farming practices and bad federal land policies. There was drought that lasted for most of the entire decade, longer than drought usually lasts. Farmers had large fields and planted row crops that allow the soil between the rows to dry out and freely blow away. Government policies are always complicated but then and now the government actually seemed to encourage farmers to ignore climate change and plant in the same way they always had.

I distinctly remember one time as a young child in the 1940s when we were at Margaret and Rudy's house for dinner, about five miles from home, when a dust storm began abruptly. We ran to our car not realizing how bad the storm was until after Pop started driving. Light from the sun was suddenly eliminated and the road disappeared from view. It didn't make sense to try to turn around on the narrow country road with no visibility, so we continued toward home. My oldest brother Ted rolled down a window and put his head out into the hard blowing wind to try to see the edge of the road and prevent Pop from driving into a ditch. Ted's face and eyes were hurt from the blowing dirt and gravel which he described as " like knives hitting my face." It was fortunate that Pop was familiar with the road and could guess about when there ought to be a curve or a turn. There is a saying often used in winter but here it was literally true that "You couldn't see your hand in front of your face." These were called "Black Blizzards."

I remember only one time of being in such a terrible dust storm, having been born in 1937, but Ted remembers that there were several of these incidents. While I don't recall being in another black blizzard obliterating all vision, I do remember being in many situations that were brown dust storms with very limited visibility.

Dust storms like this were happening everywhere in the thirties, stripping the topsoil from the farms in the west and Midwest and blowing it all the way to the eastern part of the nation. The experts had to figure out ways to keep the soil in place. Farmers were forced to change some of their practices.

There are some farming methods familiar to me. Strip farming is when a narrow strip of plowed soil is protected on both sides by strips of grain so that the wind might be slowed down and reduce the loss of top soil. Planting and plowing fields is done on a rotational basis rather than growing a crop on the same field every year. Hills are plowed in a circular pattern or contour farming rather than straight up and down. When harvest has been finished, the stubble or bottom part of the grain, is left on the ground all winter to protect the soil rather than plowing the field right away. These are some examples, but farmers and farm experts are always trying to find better methods to prevent topsoil from blowing away, to retain moisture in the soil, and to replenish the health of the soil.

In the 1930s President Roosevelt created the National Resource and Conservation Service partly to initiate programs that would conserve soil. Several things helped stop the black blizzards. Rains fortunately arrived in 1939 to reduce the drought. The government planted 220 million trees as shelterbelts to slow the wind and to help keep moisture in the soil. Some farming techniques were changed to restore the soil.

Sometimes government programs intended to help farmers can have untoward effects. There is crop insurance by the government which encourages farmers to plant more if there is a problem with their yield this year or if the price of their product is lower than the previous year. One example of a bad result of this policy is that in 2024 Nebraska farmers were tearing out their shelter-belt trees to eke out a few more acres to plant row crops that receive federal subsidies. As far as I know, the government does not do much to reward practices desirable to reduce climate change.

There are different crops that could be planted that might hold the soil in place and replenish the soil. But it is hard for a farmer who is accustomed to planting wheat to make a drastic change in planting something they haven't planted in the past. A different seed might require different farming machinery, techniques and different timelines.

There have also been tornadoes which in that area of Montana are called cyclones. I remember having tornado level winds but not an actual tornado where I lived.

As the buffalo grass dries out from lack of rain and the grain crop ripens, there is a serious fire hazard. A lightning strike or a spark from an engine can set the whole prairie ablaze. The ever-present wind moves the fire along at ten miles an hour or faster. The fire becomes so wide that there isn't a possibility of putting it out. The farm neighbors will all gather and try to wet down buildings in the path of the fire to save as much as possible. Just a few years ago, maybe 2010, my nephew Mark's daughter Kimberly was driving a combine when a spark started a fire and burned the entire large field. Farmers can't cry over things like this, so they made jokes about how quickly Kimberly finished harvesting that year.

I remember one time when I was young that many of us lined up in front of a small prairie fire near Uncle Gilbert's place and kept hitting the ground with wet gunnysacks to try to extinguish the fire. My memory isn't clear, but I guess we must have been successful. I don't remember anybody getting burned from this amateur work. If you're going to try to put a fire out by yourself, you must be sure that it is a small fire. Otherwise, it is best to evacuate and call the professionals.

Wind is finally becoming useful and lucrative as farmers are being paid by energy companies to allow wind-chargers to be placed on their land. The farmers don't do anything to create energy, but they deserve compensation for the inconvenience of avoiding the wind-charger posts when working on their fields.

The wind often made a field of grain look as though waves were moving across a green ocean. This looked especially beautiful when the top of the grain was beginning to yellow and the stalks were tall and bright green. I loved seeing this on a hillside with the Sweetgrass hills in the background.

If the wind is blowing very hard when the grain has ripened and the stalks have become less flexible, the wind can cause some of the grain kernels to be knocked out.

On 1 November 2024, I called my brother who lives in Cut Bank, Montana and listened to his report of the current weather. He said, "It isn't strange that the wind is blowing hard, probably more than fifty miles per hour, but it's strange that there are winds coming from both the north and south at the same time, dueling it out I guess. But it's a beautiful day despite the wind. The sun is shining bright, the sky is a clear bright blue, and the temperature is around sixty." Winds this strong, fifty miles per hour or more, can be called a "windstorm," but people simply say, "It's damn windy today."

Strong winds are not unusual. The wind makes it hard to open and close car doors or your house door. As soon as you force a door open, the wind causes it to slam back on you. Some businesses, particularly restaurants, build small entry porches enclosing the front door so that a strong wind doesn't blow directly into the dining room every time a new customer opens the door.

Summertime brings days that are beautiful, but they were often spoiled by the ever-present wind blowing dust into our eyes and dirt into the food of a picnic. The wind made it hard to light an open barbecue grill and then it prevents the heat from cooking the food. My husband repeatedly tried to demonstrate his skill of grilling chicken, but it continued to be half-done.

That wind was always whistling at the windows and around the corners of the house. I particularly heard the wind whistling when I lay down in my bedroom. I guess it became like "white noise" putting me to sleep. I remember that whistling wind gave me a feeling of coldness in the winter, but I have now, sixty years later, become nostalgic and have memories of home when I hear the wind whistling around my condo.

Dust storm warning on the Interstate Highway.

Picnic Rock, where I thought Mom couldn't see me. She could.

Top (l to r): Ring of rocks to hold down teepee, 1964; Rocks used as tools
Bottom (l to r): Rock dam for cattle; Picking rocks with Mom, Pop, Uncle Gilbert while Ted and Henry were in summer school

Rock Picking

One summer my three sons and their families came to the mountains of Montana for a reunion with the Suta family. After a few days in the mountains, we all felt the need to go to the prairie and visit where my siblings and I had lived, the farm we playfully named "The Suta Rock Farm."

We went into the Quonset hut, a rounded metal large storage building, housing our beloved Hildegard, a 1932 International truck. I was talking about Hildegard to my granddaughters Hannah and Becca who were maybe five and three years old. I explained that this truck was used when we were picking rocks and pointed out that there were some rocks in the truck bed. I showed them the pulley Pop had installed to be able to crank up the front of the truck box so the rocks would slide off the back. I said, "We were really happy to have this pulley so that we no longer had to unload the rocks by hand." Hannah looked up at me and said, "Okay Grandma I understand that. But why would anybody want to pick rocks?"

Such a good question, but it was hilarious to the adults. We doubled over laughing. None of us ever "wanted" to pick rocks. It was necessary because rocks can cause damage to expensive farm machinery. There was no choice. We would have been happy if we never had to pick a single rock. We had to pick rocks on land that we wanted to plow.

We children thought it must be possible for rocks to grow on our land. New ones appeared every year on the same fields. We considered rocks our most prolific crop and that is why the farm is named the Suta Rock Farm. Actually, it was my son Morgan who painted that name on the hay fence the summer he spent on the farm when he was fifteen. Smart Morgan. Pop did not like that name. He had worked very hard to make a living for his family and this could be taken as an insult. But everyone else thought it was funny and appropriate. We adopted that name even for financial and legal papers.

Where did rocks come from in the first place? Believe it or not, rocks are made of stardust blasted out and made from exploding stars. In fact, our corner of space has many rocks floating around in it—from really fine dust, to pebbles, boulders and house-sized rocks that can burn up in the night sky to make meteors or "shooting stars." The moon and planets are just the largest rocks made from space dust stuck together over billions of years.

New rocks actually appear each year because they may be forced out of the ground by frost or uncovered by the plow.

Indians Use of Rocks

When we were picking rocks, we were happy to come upon a former Indian encampment where we could save time because the Indians had gathered rocks for their own use.

Sometimes we came across a mound of rocks that I surmised were covering a grave. The Indians preferred to put a dead body high onto a tree or in a hammock between a couple of trees and leave it there to dry. On our land, as vast as it was, there was not a single tree to be found. Bodies of their dead had to be buried in shallow graves and covered with rocks for protection from predators. I have read that Indians are buried with prized possessions but we never attempted to see if this was true.

At their campsites we found many heavy rocks placed in circles where they anchored the bottom of tepees to prevent them from blowing away in the characteristic strong winds. Sometimes there would be a second circle of rocks when two tepees were erected with a space of air between to provide insulation from the heat or cold. Inside the large ring of rocks would be a small circle of rocks where the people obviously had built a fire for cooking and heat.

We found rocks as heavy as five pounds that had been used by the Indians as work tools. To become a tool, the rock would have a groove worn all around it to securely hold leather hide attaching it to a wooden handle. Making that groove would have required rubbing one stone against another for a very, very long time. A strip of leather was wound tightly around that groove and the handle and then soaked in water. When dried, the leather would shrink and tightly hold the rock and handle together so it could be used as a tool.

Rocks were not always found in the perfect shape for a desired tool. The Indians would have to patiently chip off pieces of the rock and work to make it the desired shape. The rocks we found probably each had a specialized use just as do utensils in my kitchen.

- There were large rocks with a flat head that could be used for pounding things or killing animals.
- A smaller rock with a flat head that was the size to hold in your hand would be used to grind dried corn or to grind grains into flour.
- A large rock with one side chipped off into a sharp edge could be used like an axe to cut branches and wood.
- Progressively sharper rocks would be needed to repeatedly scrape across the inside of a buffalo skin until it was clean and soft.
- A rock with a very sharp edge would be needed as a knife to slice meat into strips that could be dried for jerky.

- Rocks with very sharp edges would be used as one-sided scissors or knives to cut leather for bowls or items of clothing.
- A pointed awl was necessary to make holes for threading narrow strips of leather to hold two or more pieces of leather together to make clothing or other items.
- Some bones were already shaped as natural kitchen utensils that could be used as spoons or ladles to stir and serve foods.
- Indians knew how to use rocks to pound the hooves of animals into a powder which could be mixed with water to make a paste.
- The Indians made very sharp arrowheads to shoot and kill animals. Arrowheads found on our land were not made of the best rock for that purpose.

Rock Picking

We had to pick rocks before we could "break up" the hard land and plant seeds of grain. Mom took all four of us children when we were under the age of six into the fields with her to pick rocks. Personally I don't know whether it would be harder to pick rocks or to take care of four pre-school children out in the middle of a farm field. And Mom did both at the same time. This was our quality family time together.

Picking rocks is hard physical labor for an adult. You have to bend over, grasp a heavy rock with both hands, stand up, carry the rock to the truck, and lift it shoulder height or higher to stack it on the truck bed. Then you walk back to where you picked that rock in order to pick another. The ground you walk on is uneven and requires your body to constantly re-adjust your balance as you walk back and forth to the truck.

You can put several smaller rocks into a bucket to decrease the number of times you have to walk to the truck, but that increases the weight of the bucket you have to carry. And you have to lift the bucket above your shoulders to empty it.

How many times do you think you have to do this to make a truckload? This question is like asking the number of jelly beans in a gallon jar. The answer will be much higher than you thought. We never counted the number of rocks it took to make a truckload, but we should have. I can tell you that it is enough to make your body sore and your back ache.

Your day of work doesn't end when you have filled that one truckload. You have to go back and do the same thing over and over again. Bend over, grasp a heavy rock, stand up, carry the rock to the truck, lift the rock up high enough to place it on the truck bed, and walk back to where you were so you can pick another rock. Repeat, repeat and repeat.

Mom gave me a small bucket, like a beach toy, so that I could pick rocks with the family. I was about one-year old when we moved onto the farm so I can honestly say that I started picking rocks as soon as I could walk!! My little bucket filled quickly and I kept bothering Mom to empty it onto the truck. Mom was smart and convinced me that I should pick tiny rocks because nobody else was doing that. Then she didn't have to empty my bucket so often.

Rocks that were really large, boulders, that none of us were able to lift, had to be put onto the stone boat to be hauled away. The stone boat was a flat piece of heavy wood about six feet square and low to the ground with no sides. Pop used the grader attachment on the tractor to push the boulder onto the stone boat. If the boulder was embedded in the soil, then the men had to dig the soil all around it to the bottom before they could wrap chains around it and lift it with the tractor.

Our Use of Rocks on the Suta Rock Farm

When we had picked enough rocks to fill the truck bed of Hildegard, we dumped the load of rocks onto the dam that had been made between a couple of hills to form our large reservoir. The reservoir collected rain water and water from melted snow to provide a source of water for our cattle. The rocks fortified the dam so it wouldn't leak or break.

As I have traveled in other countries, I have seen fences and buildings made of rocks. I've been told that Alec Toth talked Pop into making fences with rocks when he first moved onto the farm. Pop soon learned that was a lot of work and could damage our large farm machinery. Pop had to move all of those rocks they had started to stack for fences. We had way too many rocks, our fields were too large, and it would have taken too much time to build fences with rocks.

We had enough unused land that we could just dump extra rocks into a coulee or onto another dam.

Saving "Special" Rocks

We quickly learned that rocks which glittered of gold were "fool's gold," having no value.

Even though we didn't like picking rocks, members of my family would sometimes select a rock they thought was special and pile it against our house. The rock may have been special to that person because of the color, size, shape or texture of the surface. The rock would have "spoken" to that person. It is interesting that we never questioned why they were saving that rock. No explanation was needed.

Picnic Rock

My favorite rock did not glitter and could not have been stacked up against the house. It was a huge boulder located down the steep hill from our house. The top of the rock was fairly flat and at least four feet in diameter. It was partially buried in the ground. As a child I thought I could hide behind that large rock when I didn't want Mom to see me. I named that boulder my "Picnic Rock" because I often took dolls and cookies along for a party. Sometimes I just laid down on the ground behind the rock, enjoying my privacy and watching the white clouds change shape.

Picnic Rock has become known as something special to everybody in my family. It is a huge boulder, and no attempt was ever made to dislodge it because it was special. It was special to me first when I was very young. Then Dian and Rudy, the youngest in my family also used it. They also took cookies there, but one story Dian told me was that they just used the cookies to gather ants that they could then kill. I had always thought of Picnic Rock as having a kind, caring atmosphere. Maybe that was what they needed at the time. One time when visiting the farm I wanted my picture taken with Picnic Rock and all of my siblings immediately gathered around. Apparently Picnic Rock is recognized by the entire family as an important landmark on the Suta Rock Farm and as such it has become imprinted on the psyche of every one of us.

Everybody Needs a Rock

Everybody ought to have a special rock of their own. It might be very small, and you might not feel any vibrations, but it would be special to you. Your rock will silently communicate with you as you speak to it, touch it, and think about something. There are people who carry a small smooth rock that they can rub with their thumb to help them relax.

I have a special rock that fits perfectly into the palm of my hand, and I keep it nearby to help me think when I am stressed or stumped over a problem, writing or planning something.

I think everyone would benefit from having a personal rock.

Green Cake

One summer we hired three high school boys to join my three teen-aged brothers in picking rocks on a piece of land that Pop wanted to start farming. High school boys eat a ton of food, especially when they are doing physical work, so I was doing a lot of cooking. Mom and I were filling up their six lunchboxes twice a day for their between-meal snacks. Because they were doing hard physical work we had to give them more than a "snack." Twice a day all of those lunchboxes had to be filled with sandwiches and usually something sweet like cake or cookies. I was also having to think about baking something for dessert after dinner and supper. Can you just picture all of that food to be prepared and I was only eleven years old!!!

Of course I wasn't doing it all alone, but Mom was also doing a lot of outdoor chores and killing chickens for dinner and whatnot.

I was also taking care of my sister Dian who was about two years old. I usually stood her on a chair in front of me to help mix the batter for something I was baking. One day I had an idea that Dian would think it was fun to put coloring into the cake I was making. I let her pick out the colors she wanted to use for the cake and then for the frosting. I wasn't sure what color we would get from the coloring drops she and I mixed together.

Apparently the cake became green and the frosting purple—or the other way around. The boys thought that looked horrible and have teased me about it ever since.

When they brought their lunch boxes back they were all laughing and the boxes were very heavy. They said the cake was still in their boxes. According to them it was inedible. They said, "It was so bad that we couldn't eat it so we tried to give it to Fido, and he refused to eat it so we had to bring it back in our lunchboxes." Fido was our dog who ate any table scraps and would not have cared what color his food was. The lunch boxes were filled with rocks.

Aunt Margaret came to visit later that day, and she laughed while she ate a piece of the cake saying, "I know that anything Violet makes is good no matter what the color."

It has now been about seventy years since I put that cake in the lunchboxes of my brothers, and they still often tease me about that terrible green cake I made that they couldn't eat.

Ode to Hildegard

Elderly Hildegard is a favorite of our family. It's strange that we have such warm, sentimental feelings toward her. After all, she has a lot of quirks. But I guess her constant presence at many of our most important activities made her a member of the family.

Hildegard is a 1932 Model A2 International 1 ½ ton truck. Purchased second hand, two years old, in 1937 for $305, it was the first of many vehicles Pop bought from Buddy Dolan at Hannah & Holmes Implement in Shelby, Montana. Pop could only afford to pay $150 in 1937 and the remainder in 1938.

This was an essential and cherished piece of equipment for Pete and Hannah Suta who had just that year bought a farm west of Sweetgrass. All they had were a new mortgage on a low-producing dry-land farm, four pre-school children in a two-room house, and no money at the ending of the depression. This truck, an absolute necessity, seemed like a luxury. She has been a constant presence throughout my life.

Hildegard started out hauling grain, but most of the time she was known as our "rock truck." This made her the center of attention all summer as our family surrounded her in the fields, picking up rocks that could cause damage to the farm machinery. Rock picking was our family's idea of quality time together.

Sweetgrass

At first we not only had to put the rocks into the truck box by hand one by one but also unload them by hand. Pop soon converted the wooden truck bed into a dump truck by adding a hoist, or hand-operated crank and pulley system, to raise the front of the box and slide the rocks off the rear end. Thank goodness. Once was enough to handle those innumerable rocks.

Hildegard is beautiful in her simplicity. Her slender shape is very boxy, straight up and down, perched on high, narrow wheels. Thick unpainted slabs of wood make up the shallow truck bed. The original color of the body escapes memory. It always was weathered iron-oxide rust. Wide running boards gracefully curve down from the front fenders to help you step up into the cab. You could hitch a ride on those running boards, holding onto the door through the open window, but you never went far because you would be bounced off by the rough ride.

Riding in Hildegard was an interactive experience. You felt every hole, rut, rock, or bump in the road—there were no sissy springs on this truck. And there was no soundproofing to prevent you from hearing every decibel of her loud engine. Although riding in the back of a truck is fun for kids, you quickly learned that you would get slivers if you sat down in the wooden truck bed of Hildegard.

To help the engine get started you might have to give a little push. That's why we always parked her facing downhill, right outside the front door, like a piece of sculpture visible every time you went in or out of the house. You had to put rocks under the front tires to keep her from rolling down that hill by herself. Placing and removing those rocks taught you to move fast to avoid being run over. It was tricky to handle the rocks when you were alone.

If not parked on a hill, Hildegard sometimes had to be cranked to start. My brother Henry usually got to do that honor, placing a large metal crank into a hole in the front of the truck and using all his strength to turn it clockwise. Meanwhile Teddy manipulated the choke in and out, regulating the amount of gas going to the engine, trying to give enough gas for it to start but not so much that the engine would become flooded.

We used this vehicle to transport us to and from the corner where we would catch the bus for school. Our driveway was a one-and-a-half mile trail on the prairie. Picture four teenagers, three of them my older brothers, crowded into a cab barely forty-four inches wide. This would be about half or three-quarters the size of pickup trucks in 2025. We were packed in like sardines.

Ted, the oldest, always drove. I was the smallest and sat on Henry's lap with my head bouncing up and down against the un-padded roof. Ben was younger and smaller than Henry, so he sat in the middle, also an uncomfortable place. Ben had to keep his legs moving to avoid being injured as Ted used the stick shift on the floor. The truck had a four-speed transmission plus reverse, so there was a lot of clutching and shifting to be done. Unlike the stick shifts of today, there was over a foot of movement between each gear, making second gear and reverse very hard on Ben's knees.

During the long Montana winters we had to first brush a pile of snow off the seat before entering the cab. Obviously the doors weren't airtight, and the heater was nonexistent. Ted usually drove with his left hand out the open window, scraping ice and snow off the windshield. When we got stuck in the mud or snow, everybody piled out and pushed.

If that didn't work we would start walking the one-and-a-half miles home, usually in deep snow and freezing temperature. We also watched for Pop to come out with a tractor and pull us home on a chain.

In any kind of weather it was always a happy sight to see Hildegard at the end of a school day, standing there at the corner waiting for us, like a loyal dog welcoming you home.

Sweetgrass

Ultimately there were six kids in our family and all but Dian used Hildegard for some of their first driving experiences. Not all of the lessons learned from Hildegard were applicable to other vehicles. You needed what seemed like a mile to stop and an acre to turn around. I learned that lesson the hard way when I was eight years old and desperately wanted to drive like my older brothers. They had been taught to drive so they could work in the fields but I had to help with housework instead.

Left alone in the house one day, I decided to take Hildegard out for a quick solo spin. This was my first time behind a wheel other than steering while sitting on Pop's lap. Although I'd never driven before, I was independent enough to think I could do this without help. After driving just fine for about a mile, an attempted U-turn brought me up against a neighbor's barbed-wire fence, coasting to a stop just inches from tearing through it. My heart almost stopped before the truck did. I knew I would catch hell if I tore down a fence. Frantic attempts to get the stick shift into reverse failed and the exhilaration of driving for the first time was replaced by fear and remorse as I walked the long distance home. Although my parents were never shy about bawling us out, I don't recall getting into much trouble for this escapade. I guess Mom and Pop understood the magnetic attraction of Hildegard.

After this aborted solo trip I was then allowed to drive without any lessons. I mostly helped Mom by delivering lunches to the men out in the fields. The skill of driving wasn't difficult to master but my small size was a barrier. I had to stretch out almost horizontally to reach the clutch and then couldn't get enough leverage to push down on the stick shift as necessary to move it into reverse. Two pillows behind my back and another to sit on helped me reach the pedals and see where I was going. Having discovered my limitations I always parked to avoid the need to ever have to shift into reverse.

Exactly how Hildegard got her name is somewhat of a mystery. Pop recalls only that "the kids" named her. She probably was named after a singer we heard on the radio. "The incomparable Hildegarde" was a famous singer of pop songs and star of the 1940s NBC radio program, "The Raleigh Room." This beautiful lady who remained a star during several decades was known to have a flamboyant personality, wearing over-the-elbow white gloves and flashy long gowns in her performances, even for the radio shows. That image would match the way we viewed our own incomparable Hildegard. No other vehicle on the farm, and eventually there were many, ever had the personality to warrant a name. Hildegard alone transcended machinery.

When we first got a radio, Ted had to go outside to remove the battery out of Hildegard to power the radio. The sound wasn't loud, so we all gathered kitchen chairs together to listen to our favorite shows.

Following fifty years of active duty, Hildegard was retired and parked on a gentle slope next to the road everyone took to get to our house. Sitting there in the tall prairie grass, she was displayed as a treasured family heirloom for all to enjoy. There she functioned as a favorite playhouse for grandchildren, other child visitors, and mice. Today the seat is totally rotted but my brothers think the engine probably still worked for many years.

My brother Ben decided to claim Hildegard when we held an estate sale on the farm in 2000. None of us could stand for her to be sold outside the family. Now, in her old age, Hildegard is finally protected from the elements, stored in a Quonset Hut where she awaits loving restoration by a caring antique collector. With her personality, she probably is feeling lonely but enjoying wonderful memories of family.

Maybe we will figure out a way to keep her in the family throughout future generations.

Postscript 2024: We six children decided to sell the farm in 2018, leaving Hildegard homeless. But not for long. The youngest child in our family, Rudy, managed to haul Hildegard over 300 miles to his home in Bozeman, Montana, where he allows her to live on his land and continue to receive the affection of the Suta family. I was happy to visit her there a couple of years ago. That was an unprecedented act of love for the family and Hildegard.

Thank you, Rudy.

Hildegard, our rock truck.

Charlie

Christmas, 2018

Dearest Charlie;
I bought this little book "Everybody Needs a Rock" quite a few years ago intending to give it to someone as a gift. Every year at Christmas time I would take it out of the gift box and read it again and think about who to give it to. But I never gave it away because I loved it and I couldn't find the right person to give it to. I thought the story and illustrations were too beautiful to give to just anyone.

I have a feeling, looking at photos of you as a two-year old playing with books, that you are the right person for this book. I see that you like all books and someday when you are a little older you might also like this story. And I'm pretty sure that you will someday go on a quest for your own special rock. You might find it right away or you might have to keep looking for a long time. When you find it, you will know. It would be nice if you find one that continues forever to be special to you. But it's okay to change rocks when you find a different one because over time your needs may change.

Your first rock might be small enough to fit in your pocket as described in the book. But I have had different rocks at different times. The special rock I have now has been with me for many years, long before I became eighty years old.

Sweetgrass

It fits perfectly in the palm of my hand but is too big for a pocket. I use it as a paperweight on my desk where it is available whenever I want to hold it. You can choose any size or type of rock to carry in your pocket or purse or to sit on a shelf. It is your choice.

I probably think rocks can be special after having a lot of experience picking rocks on the "Suta Rock Farm" where your Grandpa Rudy and I grew up. Even though I hated the work of picking rocks, my mother and I, and sometimes even my brothers and sister, selected a rock that we thought was special and we made a small pile of these against our house. Each had a different reason for being special—size, color, texture, shape—even vibrations. Thinking back, I find it interesting that nobody ever questioned another person as to why they thought the rock they selected was special. It was just assumed it was a personal decision.

When I was a child there was a huge rock down the hill from our house that I thought I could hide behind when I didn't want Mom to see me. I named that my "Picnic Rock" because I often took dolls and cookies along for a party and the flat top was like a table. Sometimes I just laid down on the ground and enjoyed the privacy and quietness provided by my Picnic Rock.

Your special rock might be very little, but it will speak to you as you touch it and think about something. It can be helpful to you in your life.

With lots of love and hugs from your Great-Aunt Violet Suta Moran

Winter, 1947: Uncle Rudy buried his Chevy in a snowdrift.

18 April 1967: The South wind blew hard for five days during a snowstorm, killing four calves.

Weather

Wallace Stegner gave the best description of the weather we endured in the north-central area of Montana where I lived as a child in his wonderful book *Wolf Willow*. "....that country is notable primarily for its weather, which is violent and prolonged; its emptiness, which is almost frighteningly total; and its wind, which blows all the time in a way to stiffen your hair and rattle your eye" (3).

It has been described that this land that we were trying to farm was meant for grazing by buffalo. But the U.S. government wrote the Homestead Act to induce people to move west and "claim free land" knowing that the land was not meant for farming and the acreage being given was inadequate considering the low yield on dry land farms.

Lies by Railroad Tycoons

When the railroad was built over this prairie land, they tried to increase their ridership by lying to people, saying anything to encourage people to move to this land. They admitted the land was dry now but advertised that "rain automatically increases as the land is farmed." There were too many lies for me to list here but the least believable was that "you could grow bananas on this fertile land with this wonderful climate." The U.S. government did nothing to try to correct the false information because they also wanted the land to be settled.

The U.S. government colluded with the railroad tycoons to get that land settled to keep the railroads in business and prevent the Native Americans from moving back onto the land they had given away in treaties.

Dry-land Farming

Our family chose to farm, taking over land that had been abandoned by a homesteader. "Dry-land farming" was an appropriate description of what we had to do because it seldom rained. Our average *annual* rainfall of less than seven inches was supplemented by melting snow and we were happy when we had a lot of snow. There is a problem that snowfall has drastically decreased because of climate warming. I remember the snow being much deeper when I was a child, not only because I had shorter legs.

Winter wheat was our most popular crop because the greatest rainfall is in the spring when the seeds can begin to grow.

Irrigation Was Not Possible

It was impossible for us and our neighbors to irrigate the crops since we did not have a source of water. Our farm was not large by Montana standards, but we had thousands of acres without any lake, river or stream. We were simply dependent on the weather.

Farmers Are the Biggest Gamblers that Exist

Farmers play with stakes as high as gamblers in Las Vegas and can lose everything in an instant. A farmer can work hard to be successful but no matter how hard they work the outcome is controlled by Outside Forces such as Mother Nature.

Farmers take their chances with whatever Mother Nature will or will not provide. They have no idea when they might get rain, snow, sunshine, hail, drought or other conditions. It makes thousands of dollars difference if you seed a few days before a hailstorm or a few days after. But you have no way of predicting when the hail might come.

If Mother Nature was kind and you had a good harvest, you still have a big gamble to do. You could lose thousands of dollars if you choose the wrong day to sell your crop. The grain market can change drastically in one day without you getting any warning. As a farm family, we survived everything that Mother Nature could throw at us.

Rain—Too Little, Too Much, at the Wrong Time

With our dry land you would think that we would be delighted to receive rain anytime it came. However, not only did we get too little rain but sometimes it would rain too much and flood low-lying areas in the fields. Rain will soak into gumbo soil only if it comes down slowly and lightly; a heavy rain will not soak into the soil. The rain will slide off and gather in a low-lying area. Rain is also a problem if it falls at the wrong time, preventing the farmer from working in the fields. When a farmer is anxious to get into the fields to start seeding, it is frustrating if rain causes the fields to be too muddy. Conversely, if there is no rain after seeding, the kernels of grain won't sprout, and the shoots don't grow. During the summer it may look as though the grain is growing well, but if there is no moisture at the time the kernels are filling out, you will end up harvesting empty shells that are worthless. If it rains when you ought to be harvesting, you cannot reap that good crop if the grain is wet. There are times when grain needs sunshine rather than rain, but extremes of either can be damaging.

Hail

Hail can destroy the crop at any time, at any stage of growth. And all it takes is a few minutes. Five minutes is enough to totally hail out your crop. You can take out hail insurance but if you get hail you would be lucky to get enough money from the insurance to buy seeds for next year. Farmers may have to take out loans to live through the winter.

One year my father criticized his brother Rudy for not having even started seeding while my father was done. My father's grain had started growing when hail came along and destroyed the tender young shoots. It was early enough in the season that he could do a second seeding. His "lazy" brother happened to be lucky that he had not wasted any seed or time. Neither of them knew the "right" day to seed but had to take their chances.

Most distressing is when hail comes and destroys the grain just when the farmer is ready to harvest a bumper crop. The farmer may have paid for hail insurance but that, like car insurance, returns only a small percent of what had been lost.

Hail comes in different sizes ranging from smaller than a grain of salt to larger than a grapefruit.

My sister-in-law Maxine said that she was the only person she knew who had her bedroom hailed out. The large hailstones broke windows and damaged her wooden furniture as well as soaking the mattress. The body of their car was severely damaged and windows were broken. Of course, their crops were also hailed out.

Hail can feel very personal because it hails in strips, destroying one strip of grain and not touching the adjacent summer fallow, or hitting one farmer and not the neighbor.

Short Growing Season

The time from seeding to harvest in northern Montana is short. Seeding time can be disrupted if winter stays too long or if it rains in the spring. Harvest can be disrupted in the fall when a hard frost or winter snow suddenly arrives earlier than expected. And anything in between might happen.

We experienced snow that stopped combining in the fall and never let up until spring. By then, the grain could only be used as hay.

My son told me yesterday that he and his wife were driving through Indiana farmland one autumn evening when she exclaimed, "Look at all those lights in the field. What in the world are they doing this late at night?" My son said she, like most people, had never thought that farmers had to

Sweetgrass

hurry to finish combining before rain or snow or hail came along. Who would think about farmers working overtime, without pay?

There are combining (harvesting) crews of two to six who travel with all their equipment from Kansas or Nebraska where the grain ripens early to North Dakota and Montana where the grain ripens later. They help the farmer harvest during the short window of opportunity before snow or other inclement weather can ruin the crop. It's less expensive to pay helpers than to lose your entire crop.

Weather Is Unpredictable

Weather forecasters today can get a college degree in meteorological science and use sophisticated equipment, but their forecasts might still be incorrect. When I was a child, weather forecasts were broadcast on the radio but the person giving the forecast didn't have computers and probably didn't know any more than we would by looking at the sky.

Mom kept a supply of clothes and equipment in the trunk of the car year round to be prepared for whatever weather might happen. She and Pop might be on the road home from Cut Bank when a blizzard suddenly would arise. Sliding off the road and into the ditch could happen quickly. There is not much traffic on that road, or on most country roads in Montana, and they could freeze to death before help miraculously arrived. (Remember that I am writing about how things were when I was a child, and we didn't have cellphones.)

Temperature Can Change Quickly

People living in all parts of the country joke that "If you don't like this weather, just wait an hour and it will change." That joke is an exaggeration in most locations. However, where I lived we often experienced temperatures changing that quickly. I recall one afternoon while I was walking on the street in Cut Bank and there was a forty degree drop of the temperature in half an hour. The temperature also could rise that quickly during the warm wind of a Chinook.

The most remarkable temperature change ever recorded in the U.S. occurred at Great Falls on 11 January 1980, when in seven minutes it went from thirty-two degrees below zero to fifteen degrees above. In seven minutes! The most rapid increase and decrease of temperatures in the U.S. have occurred in north central Montana. Extremes of temperature seem to be normal.

People thought I would be used to cold weather when I moved to Madison because there was a national temperature gauge in Cut Bank, Montana, and during the winter it would frequently be broadcast on radio that Cut Bank was the coldest spot in the nation. They never reported how much it warmed up during the day and they never reported the days with sixty- to sixty-five-degree temperatures during chinooks.

I learned eventually that there is a difference in how the temperature feels in a humid climate compared to a dry climate. A cold temperature feels much colder, and a hot temperature feels hotter in a humid climate than in a dry climate. The wind and sunshine also make a difference in how we perceive the temperature.

It certainly does get cold in Montana, but often the sun is shining brightly on those cold days. When it is hot in the summer you can feel cooler in the shade in a dry climate, but shade doesn't make much difference if the day is very humid as well as hot. The humidity makes the heat feel more miserable.

Humidity also makes the temperature in Madison feel hotter and more miserable than that same temperature in the dry climate of Montana. In Montana you can cool off in the shade but shade does not make you feel much cooler in a humid climate.

During most of the winter in Montana the sky is bright blue, clear, and sunny even on a cold day. If you leave your car outside on a winter day, it is likely to feel warm from the sunshine when you open the door even though the outside temperature is freezing. Winter in Madison is depressing because the sky is hazy, a cloudy blue with little sunlight.

Blizzards

A blizzard might be a white-out reducing all visibility or it might be that you can see except when gusts of wind blow the snow. Usually blizzards occur while it is snowing and there is an intensely strong wind. But a blizzard also can occur when it is not snowing but the wind is strong enough to blow the snow that is on the ground and decrease your visibility.

There could be a sudden heavy snowfall of five or six inches in one hour. When I say sudden, I mean that there was no warning. It truly becomes a blizzard with almost zero visibility if there is wind blowing—and there is always some wind blowing in Montana. In a Montana winter that amount of snowfall could melt away the next day.

Fog

I don't recall seeing fog on the Suta Farm in Montana, but it probably does occur in parts of Montana that have more moisture than the central northern area. Last week I awoke to hear an announcement on TV that people should stay home from work because of dangerous conditions caused by thick fog. I looked out my window and could not see across the street. Fog is one weather condition we didn't have to worry about on the dry-land Suta Rock Farm.

Chinooks

See the story on Chinooks which are a phenomenon that occur primarily in Montana when a warm wind melts a foot or two of snow in just one day.

Grains Can Get Diseases

The climate is not the only thing that farmers have to be concerned about. Just as people get ill, the grain might get some kind of mold or disease that spoils the grain.

Grasshoppers

Grasshoppers are not related to the weather, but a grasshopper invasion can be more horrible than a hailstorm. It is frightening when they arrive in a large swarm that darkens the sky. There is a noise of all of them flying at once, sounding like a helicopter. They all drop down suddenly and in a day or two eat every living plant on your farm and even clothes that were hanging on the clothesline. When they leave the barren fields, other insects and bugs will have freedom to invade and finish off what little remains.

Farmers gamble that none of these untoward climate events occur to destroy their crop. But the truth is that all of them could occur during one year. Farmers just take their chances.

The Stock Market

Every day, usually about noon, radio stations all over the nation report the price being paid that day at the grain elevator per bushel of various grains. There is a big difference as it rises or falls unpredictably. The farmer can lose thousands of dollars if she sells her grain just one day before the market rises. Farmers have no control over the price their product will receive, but they gamble as to when is the best day for them to sell their grain at the elevator in town.

Chinooks

Most people do not know about the phenomenon of Chinooks that only occur in the northwest, particularly in Montana.

A Chinook is a strong warm wind coming over the Rocky Mountains from Japan. The northern and west-central part of the United States are the only places these occur. A Montana Chinook can quickly raise the winter temperature to sixty or sixty-five degrees Fahrenheit, making it feel like spring. This can occur more than once a winter and often lasts for one or two weeks. Other winds on the northwestern coast might be called Chinook but that wind brings rain to the west and might then drop snow on the Rocky Mountains and is not truly a Chinook.

The rest of the nation is unaware that the winter temperature fluctuates greatly in Montana. When I was young there was a temperature tower in Cut Bank, Montana, and the radio broadcast frequently that the lowest temperature in the nation was in Cut Bank. People assumed that the temperature of the entire winter was about the same. What they didn't know is that it doesn't stay that cold all winter.

A Montana Chinook wind can dramatically melt over a foot of snow in a single day.

A Chinook wind is called a "warm wind," but it may feel cold outdoors because the wind becomes cooler as it blows over the snow. The wind may feel cold as it blows on you even though you know the temperature has risen since yesterday and you can literally see the snow melting. After the snow is melted, the wind will feel warmer.

You have to be careful if you drive somewhere early the next morning because that melted snow may have frozen overnight to make the roads icy. The temperature will probably rise again during the second day of a Chinook, and the high temperature and bright sunshine may continue for a week or more, continuing to make it feel like spring. And there can be several Chinooks during a winter.

I miss those warm Chinooks that periodically broke up the winter in Montana.

The winter sky in Madison, Wisconsin where I live now is usually hazy without many days of direct sunlight. A cloudy, hazy sky is depressing. In Montana, by contrast, the winter sky usually is a bright blue with fluffy white clouds, and another thing I miss is the sun shining brightly even though the temperature might not be that warm.

When I was young we didn't have climate warming. Glaciers had not yet melted in Glacier National Park and the scenery in the Park, while still amazing today, was more spectacular in past years. I have visited Glacier Park every year since I have moved to Wisconsin, and I can visually see by my naked eye the significant difference in the size of the glaciers every year. It is a tragedy that many of the Glaciers have melted. I believe that I was told last summer that there were only sixteen glaciers left in the Park, down from hundreds earlier in the century.

We used to get significantly more snow, deeper snow, and more frequent snowstorms during the winters. Rarely were there accurate forecasts warning us of those storms. There were no educational programs or scientific equipment to educate meteorologists. Meteorological science has advanced both in knowledge and equipment and yet forecasts can still

Sweetgrass

be inaccurate. I never heard about a meteorologist when I was young. Forecasts were given by general radio broadcasters who didn't seem to know any more than we did. There were some people on the radio who were called "weather forecasters" but they didn't have computers or special education. We simply had no way of knowing what weather we might have the next day.

It was not unusual for Montana to get five or six inches of snow in one day. That rarely occurs today, even in the mountains, because of climate warming.

I remember being caught in a snow slide on top of Going-to-the-Sun Mountain on the Fourth of July in the early 1950s. There had been no warning of this. I'm sure that someone these days keeps an eye on how quickly snow is melting, but back then no one expected a snowslide to occur. Fortunately it did not bury any cars under snow. One car was just ahead of the slide and one just behind. We were two cars behind. It took all night for the road to be cleared enough for us to get through. We couldn't run the heater while waiting during the night for fear of running out of gas. We were thankful that Mom had warm blankets and clothing in the trunk on a sunny Fourth of July holiday. Pop got a shovel from our trunk and helped the Rangers clear the road.

These days there probably is no place in the Park where there would be enough snow to create a snow slide because climate warming has reduced the amount of snow.

I think it was 1952 when we were again in a tough situation on top of Going-to-the-Sun Mountain. This event was more dangerous as we were caught in a blizzard on the 25th of July. We couldn't stay on top of the mountain because the facilities were primitive. The information building and toilets have improved but even now they have no facilities for overnight stays. But there shouldn't be a need for an overnight stay anymore. The park rangers block the road if the weather is predicted to be bad.

We were driving on our way home and therefore were on the outside lane of the highway with little or no protection from a deep and dangerous drop down the mountain. Visibility was very poor. Ted had to hang his head out the passenger side window to tell Pop how to turn the wheel to keep us on the road.

All was forgotten the next day when the sun was shining, and the sky was brilliant blue.

I miss those warm Chinooks that periodically broke up the winter in Montana. The winter sky in Madison is usually hazy with little direct sunlight.

In Montana, the winter sky usually is a bright blue with fluffy white clouds and the sun is shining, the same as during the summer. Sky and sunshine in the winter are other big reasons why I miss Montana.

Gumbo

The soil on our land was partly gumbo or completely gumbo in some places. If you are reading this but you are not a farmer or a gardener, then you probably wonder what I'm talking about. Dirt is dirt, right? Nope. There are different types of dirt and it makes a big difference when you want to grow something in it or if you are driving on it while it is wet.

I once heard that researchers found more than twenty different types of gumbo soil in Montana. As far as I know they all have similar characteristics. It is a soil that is heavy like clay. The opposite is sandy soil which is light and allows water to flow through it quickly.

You can test this if you pick up a handful of sand and notice that it will fall through your fingers. Water poured slowly on it will flow through it quickly. Pick up a handful of soil from a good field or garden and it will look moist and crumble on your hand. Water will make it muddy. Pick up a handful of clay soil or even children's clay and it will feel heavy and just stay in a clump on your hand. Water poured on it will flow off quickly and make the surface slippery without soaking into the soil.

Gumbo takes water in slowly; it swells as it absorbs the water, and it releases the moisture slowly. Heavy clay soil is an advantage in an area where there is little rainfall because

Mud at the Suta corner beginning one-and-a-half mile driveway to the house.

Note how coarse the gravel is.

it holds onto whatever moisture it can get and doesn't let it evaporate quickly. Where I lived in Montana the average *annual* rainfall was seven inches. Where I live now in Wisconsin we could get almost that much in a day. Farming techniques have to adapt.

If a rainfall was heavy and fast the moisture would slide off the gumbo soil and collect in some low-lying area. There may be a lot of rain, but it won't do the crops much good. If the rain falls slowly, like an all-day rain, the moisture will go deep into the ground and the gumbo soil will hold onto it. Plants will be able to put down long roots to sustain themselves. Sandy soils just become dry very quickly.

When gumbo becomes saturated with moisture, it gets increasingly slippery or greasy. Cars traveling on wet gumbo roads will slide uncontrollably. Driving on a wet gumbo road is worse than driving on ice. If you are walking on wet gumbo your legs can quickly slide out from under you.

If a pickup truck with four-wheel drive plowed through a graveled country gumbo road while it was wet, there would be deep tracks fishtailing from side to side. The driver on a two-lane country road has to drive down the middle of the road to avoid going into the ditch on either side. When you come along in a car, the only thing you can do is try to stay in the ruts made by the truck. Even when you are driving in the deep ruts your car will still slide .You may meet another vehicle as you both drive up a hill from opposite directions, but you just have to take your chances that one of you will be able to stop or to move over. It is unnerving.

As the gumbo soil begins to dry out a little, it becomes very sticky. It sticks to everything it contacts and even sticks to itself. This sticky soil can build up on the tires of your car to the point that there isn't room for the tire to turn around in the wheel well of the car. You may have to stop the car and scrape some of the mud off the tires every once in a while.

If a farmer plows while the gumbo soil is still too wet, the implements might get stuck. Or the mud would clog up the machinery. If the farmer plows while the gumbo soil is drying but is still moist, the mud will stick into big clumps and then when it becomes dry those clumps would become very hard, almost like cement.

All of us had rubber overshoes to wear outside when it was muddy. These were high boots with several buckles that you had to snap as tightly as possible so that your foot would not come out of the boot when it got stuck in the mud. If you walk around your yard doing chores, you may have to stop now and then to scrape off a couple inches of mud that is collecting on your boot. Your heavy muddy boots make it hard to walk. Farmhouses have a scraper mounted on the ground outside the house for people to scrape off the mud. You can't just wipe your feet on a throw rug and get this mud to come off.

When these sticky clumps of gumbo soil lose more of their moisture they will become very hard. It is difficult to plow over this hard soil. A road grader will find it almost impossible to smooth out this road with deep ruts that were made when the soil was wet.

When I went to the garden to get a couple of carrots and potatoes, I had to use a metal tool to dig them out; my fingers were not strong enough to dig in that hard soil. If I tried to pull a root vegetable out of our gumbo soil, the green top would break off because the dry gumbo soil would have a tight hold on that carrot or potato.

There are problems with gumbo soil, but a dry-land farmer is lucky to have clay soil that will hold in the moisture for plants. That farmer just has to be careful about when to seed or plow or do any work in the fields. They have to judge the stage of the gumbo. They might have one perfect day to work the field when it is not too wet or too dry.

Farmers try different methods using different machinery to conserve moisture.

Efforts have been made to improve country roads by raising the road and installing culverts to provide some drainage. It is good to have some drainage to prevent water from pooling in a low-lying area. But having the road built higher is not a great improvement because that soil will still become very slippery when wet, and it will be more dangerous if a driver slides into a very deep ditch.

Gravel ought to be put on the gumbo road when the soil is still moist. If the road is wet, the gravel will be squished into the mud and not be of much help to a driver. If gravel was put onto a dry road, the road grader invariably would come and push the gravel off the road and into the ditch.

This may be the appropriate time to point out that there is a big difference between the gravel put onto a driveway in a big city and the gravel that we had to use where I lived. Our gravel was not tumbled, or whatever is done to make it into small round stones. Our land was very rocky, and maybe we didn't have a hill made of good gravel.

Our gravel came in large pieces, more like the end of your thumb and with rough, sharp edges. You might have to adjust your balance a little when walking on this large gravel. The large stones can make your car slide, especially when you put on the brakes. New gravel like that caused Mom to lose control and slide into the ditch, frightening her from ever driving anywhere except on the dirt trails between our house and the fields.

Hanging with My Brothers

I entered my family as the fourth child within five years, following three older brothers: Teddy, Henry and Benny. On my ninth birthday, my sister Dian was born and Mom told me she didn't believe in raising an "only" child so a couple years later my brother Rudy was born. So as far as we children were concerned, we had a first family and second family. I was the youngest of the first family and wanted to play with my older brothers. That didn't work well. I will give only a couple of examples.

    I was only a few years old when I received a unique doll that cried when you turned her over. The boys persuaded me to hit my new, precious doll with a hammer so we could see what made her cry. They had everything ready in front of the house—a hammer and my doll laid out on a wooden board. I tried to get my doll back but Ted kept holding her out of my reach. They repeatedly told me that it wouldn't hurt the doll at all and they'd give her right back. To get my doll back I accepted the hammer Ted put into my hand. Ted put his hand over mine to hit her on her head. Her plastic head shattered. When I ran crying to Mom, she asked who had broken the doll. Well, she didn't give the boys any punishment because I was the one who actually hit the doll with the hammer. Mom just asked me, "When are you going to quit listening to those boys?"

Sweetgrass

I was a slow learner in that regard and still tagged along with the boys whenever I could.

One time Henry and Benny called from the bottom of the basement stairs for me to come down there because they had something to show me. I didn't know that Ted was straddling the top of the stairs waiting to drop a block of wood down on me. It was a direct hit and I got a bloody gash on my head. He says he just wanted to scare me. Mom had to tie my hair together to close the wound. Ted remembers Mom being angry with him and the other boys that time. I guess I had to spill blood before Mom would get angry with them.

One winter day when I was about three years old, my brothers decided to test the ice on a small pond by sending me onto it because I "was the lightest." I stepped onto the ice and immediately broke through. I was totally submerged in the water and under ice. I had no idea how to stand up in water or how to move. I guess the pond wasn't very deep but it was deep enough for me to drown since I didn't know how to get out. I would have drowned if Ben had not found a stick that they stuck into the hole and hollered for me to hold onto. I held on and they pulled me out through the hole like a fish. It was a miracle that Ben found a stick because there had been no construction around there and not a single tree grew nearby. It was a very cold walk home going up the steep side of the hill to our house. Henry took off his jacket and put it over my shoulders. For my entire life I have once in a while asked my brothers what they would have done if Ben hadn't found a stick. Would any one of them have walked into that icy pond to rescue me? Their response is always the same. They throw back their heads, laugh heartily, and don't give me a verbal answer. Ted told me they did get bawled out "a little bit" by Mom for this incident.

No wonder I became afraid of going into water. But years later I attended a land-grant college that required swimming because there had been so many drownings of rural kids.

Swimming was the hardest course I took in college and that "D" was my lowest grade ever. I told this story to adult friends saying that I wasn't going to swim until I was over seventy. When I became seventy my friend Miriam called my bluff and insisted I come to beginner's swimming lessons with her—so I learned to swim a little when I was seventy, even though I didn't like it.

One summer day Mom sent the four of us, me and my brothers, to walk to Grandpa Suta's place so he could give haircuts to the boys. I was very young but the walk wasn't bad because we cut across the fields. Well, Mom hadn't specified to anybody that haircuts should be given only to the three boys. When Grandpa finished with them, he put me on the chair and started cutting away. I didn't object because of course I wanted to do what the boys did.

Well, I had been born with black hair that was naturally curly. What more could be desired by a mother who had been very anxious to have a daughter? When the four of us reached the bottom of the hill closest to our house, within sight, Mom came running out to us crying loudly! What a terrible thing that her daughter now looked just like the boys! Now that I think about it, that may have been the only time I saw Mom cry like that.

I was still young when Pop tried to be nice by buying one bike for the three boys. Pop knew nothing about bicycles. First of all, nobody could ride bicycle on our country roads covered in gravel that was actually the size of large pebbles or small rocks. Nobody knew about using different tires or different bikes for that type of terrain. Only one bike for three boys was also a problem because the boys were different heights. Pop set the bike to fit Ted's long legs.

I wanted to ride that bike even though I hadn't seen the boys riding. I propped it against the garage door and kept trying to get on and pedal. Of course I kept falling over. I sprained my wrist and ankle but didn't complain to anybody for fear that I would be criticized for trying to ride their bike.

Benny had a bigger problem with that bike when he tried to ride it down the steep hill by our house. I give him credit for managing to remain upright on the bike but the big problem was that he didn't know how to stop. His legs weren't as long as Ted's so he couldn't stop by dragging his feet. He had enough velocity going down the steep hill that the bicycle continued to go up the next small hill where it ran into a barbed wire fence before it stopped. It was fortunate that the weather was cool enough for Ben to be wearing a jacket because all of his exposed skin was badly injured by the barbed wire and became infected. I don't think any of the boys ever tried to ride that bicycle again. I know for sure that I never again tried to ride a bicycle.

I was jealous and wanted to go with my brothers when they all had to have their tonsils removed at the same time. Uncle Gilbert consoled me by explaining that he had a dental appointment and I could go with him. After the dentist was done with Gilbert, they put me up on the dentist's chair. Gilbert knew this dentist was a serious alcoholic but didn't know how badly his judgment was damaged. Instead of pulling my loose baby tooth that was falling out, the dentist actually pulled a six-year molar. Gilbert thought the dentist was just <u>pretending</u> to pull that loose baby tooth. Nobody knew I had a major procedure so when I went home I just took care of "my poor brothers" by waiting on them. I did not know that I had a molar pulled until I became an adult, and one dentist finally recognized that my fourth wisdom tooth had moved down and taken the place of my six-year molar that the drunken dentist had pulled.

Alcoholism must have been a big problem among doctors in that rural area and I encountered another one. This story has nothing to do with my brothers, but the alcoholic doctor made me think of this. When I was fifteen and living in

Shelby, I chose a doctor to remove my infected tonsils. He could not get the bleeding to stop and so he sutured gauze dressings on both sides of my throat; which I know now was very inappropriate. He used sutures that dissolve to hold the dressings in place on both sides. He sent me directly home without any warning that the sutures could dissolve while I was asleep and the gauze could then choke me to death. When I was a student nurse, I assisted a doctor in the operating room who removed a lot of tonsils. He was appalled to learn about my experience.

I probably set myself up to have this experience because I still wanted to have my tonsils out like my brothers.

I don't remember us having fun with our abundant snow such as building forts and having snowball fights. I guess making me angry by putting snow down my back was enough fun for my brothers.

Ted and me.

Ted, Henry, Benny, and me.

Rimrocks

About eighty million years ago most of Montana was covered by an ocean now named the Western Interior Seaway.

The ocean was probably formed by melting ice when the ice age was ending millions of years ago. Erosion caused by moving glaciers carved out lake beds that were able to hold water because some areas around the lake were alluvial deposits. These areas around the ocean were made of sediment, residue, and remains that became generally sandstone cliffs. The sandstone cliffs or rimrocks were the dam of the ocean and are located everywhere throughout Montana. They were hard mineral rock resistant to erosion and functioned as a dam to hold water in that area. Other edges of that ocean probably were shallow because they were composed of soil, vegetation, sand and smaller rocks and were eroded by the moving ice. The area of the ocean that didn't evaporate became the steppes or prairie land adjacent to the ocean. The land above the dams of the ocean was similar prairie land.

The most dramatic rimrock remaining are those around Billings, Montana where the height of the rims range from 200 to 500 feet stretching all the way from Columbus, Montana to Miles City, Montana, a distance of forty-two miles. The rims are part of the Eagle sandstone formation and are at least seventy to eighty million years old. They are a geological

View near Cut Bank.

(l) Looking for arrowheads at a buffalo jump; (r) Little Jerusalem, two to three miles west of Sweetgrass.

Roads going up or down the rims can be difficult.

Just west of Sunburst you have to go up a rimrock to reach the elevation of the Suta place.

wonder of striking vertical cliffs overlooking Billings, the largest city in Montana. Billings and these rimrocks are located in southeastern Montana.

The rimrocks throughout Montana and down into Wyoming are similar and served the same purpose although none are as visually sensational as the rimrock around Billings. They are all part of the same geological and historical event.

They were the dams that held the water or the ocean in place.

Rimrocks are similar to small cliffs. There weren't any rimrocks on our land, but they were part of the nearby landscape. We could hardly go in any direction without driving up, down or alongside rimrocks. The rimrocks were close to us, less than six to eight miles away in most directions. They were part of the landscape of our farm and surrounding areas that contribute to the beauty of the prairie.

When the water of the ocean dried up, the land which had been under water began to look like the land above the dam or rimrock. The landscapes above and below the rim are similar but at different elevations.

This is different from buttes or mesas that are found sticking up out of the prairie as stand-alone formations. There is not a plateau of land around buttes or mesas as around the rimrocks. Buttes and mesas never functioned as dams holding in the water of a lake or ocean.

The rimrocks are beautiful sticking up out of the flat prairie. They are usually of equal height and are in a grouping like a dam that contains water, which they were millions of years ago. Groupings of rimrocks differ in length. The sides of them are angled in most places but occasionally are more vertical and steeper like cliffs.

People who live in this area sometimes specify that they live "above or below the rim." The landscape above and below the rim look similar. The prairie roads going up and down a rim are usually curvy, narrow and steep. Driving up or down the rim is dangerous if the road is not being cared for or if there is snowfall, rainfall, ice or wet gumbo soil. It can be a treacherous drive. Above the rim is land that was the edge of the ocean, and it is flat land with some hills like prairie or steppes. The land below the rim was the bottom of the ocean, left behind when the lake evaporated. Over time the land below the rim began to resemble the land above the rim.

Looking at a chain of rimrocks, there are places where the edge or rim is steeper than in other places. The Indigenous people made specific use of a steep rimrock by using that location as a "buffalo jump." The Piegan Blackfeet Indian word for these rimrocks is "Pishkun." They would stampede the buffalo to make them fall over the precipitous edge of the cliff where they would break their necks when landing. These areas are called "buffalo jumps."

The Indians would prepare for the event by placing large rocks in formation as a funnel pointed toward the edge of the cliff. While stampeding the buffalo, men would be positioned along the funnel to keep the animals moving in the direction of the edge of the cliff.

The Indians would identify the leader of the buffalo herd and would begin the stampede with that buffalo. When the lead buffalo was frightened and running as fast as possible, the rest of the herd would follow while also being chased by other Indians. In early years, dogs would help the men in chasing the buffalo over the cliff. When the Indians acquired horses, they had less need for dogs to help with buffalo jumps. They also were able to sometimes hunt buffalo while on horseback rather than staging a buffalo jump.

When a buffalo jump took place, the Indian women would be positioned below the rim where the buffalo were falling. If a buffalo didn't break its neck and die from the fall, the women would use their knives to finish killing them. A few Indian men at the bottom of the rim would use bow and arrow to help with killing buffalo that survived the fall.

This was a very efficient method of acquiring a lot of meat, skins and other desirable parts of these animals. A buffalo jump did not require as much effort as hunting a large number of buffalo. It also helped the tribe conserve precious arrowheads because they would have to shoot only a small number of the animals.

The women removed only the prized pieces of meat from the buffalo because there would be too much for them to be able to take all of the meat. They would start eating the liver while the meat was raw and still warm. The heart and tongue were always cut out because they were thought to bring great strength to the consumers. The hump of the buffalo would be roasted over a spit for the tribe to eat in celebration of the successful hunt. There would be a feast left behind for predators.

Some of the meat could be preserved all year without refrigeration by making jerky or pemmican. Jerky is made by drying thin strips of meat over a rack or on a rock in the sunlight. When they had fire they made fire pits to cook or dry the meat. Pemmican is made by chopping or pulverizing the meat finely and mixing it with fat and dried berries. The women may have stomped on this to mix the meat thoroughly with the berries. Pemmican could then be made into balls and stored for use all year.

The Indians also made shallow bowls in the earth lined with rocks which they could heat to a high temperature by fire to make primitive cooking pots or "blood kettles." They boiled the bison blood so it would coagulate and lessen its susceptibility to spoilage. Other foods could be mixed with the coagulated blood. Biscuits could be made by mixing ground grain with the coagulated blood.

A row of pishkun is beautiful sticking up out of the flat prairie. During sunrise or sunset the parade of rimrocks create undulating shadows that highlight their beauty and continually change the view as you drive alongside. They

Sweetgrass

are stunning when snow accentuates their shape. I find the view of rimrocks to be interesting and beautiful enough to sometimes take my breath away.

We didn't use the rimrocks for any purpose benefiting our farm, but they added interest and beauty to the extraordinary landscape where we lived.

The State of Montana has provided recognition of the awesome historic event of buffalo jumps by establishing "The First People's Buffalo Jump State Park" ten miles south of Great Falls on I-15 and 3.5 miles taking the Ulm exit. In the Park are descriptive posters, a picnic area and hiking trails along the "pishkun."

Entry of our house, with steps over Fido's house.

From west to east; Mom got her house with a view.

Part of our driveway from the gravelled road in tall grass.

The Pete and Hannah Suta House

My oldest son Morgan thought it was a simple question when he asked whether Grandma and Grandpa Suta's house was always the way he knew it or did they ever do some remodeling. There wasn't even a house on that location when we bought the land. The house actually had several lives from 1938–1951 with rooms and utilities added. It took my oldest brother Ted and me several hours of phone calls to try to sort out what was built when. And then it took me more than an hour to fact-check everything with brother Henry. I will start by giving you history on where we lived before we lived in that house.

After they married, my mother and father lived in the tiny one-and-a-half room shack that was originally the homestead of Alexander and Teresia Suta, Pete Suta's parents. Grandpa Alex had built that shack when he arrived in Montana to claim free land in 1915 under the Homestead Act. The first two of Alex and Teresia's four sons, Peter and Rudy, were born "out east" before they arrived; Peter in West Virginia and Rudy in Pennsylvania. There was no insulation in the house and water had to be carried from a distant well. Their Montana homestead was expanded to two small rooms after Willie and Kalmon were born.

Violet Suta Moran

When Alex and Teresia left their homestead, they built a slightly larger house directly across the road from Aunt Margaret and Uncle Rudy, in the midst of all the metal junk collected by Margaret's son Louie. That was where Grandma and Grandpa Suta (Alex and Teresia) lived when I was a child.

The original little homestead Alex and Teresia left behind is where Mom and Pop lived after they got married. The first four of us children were born while they lived there; Teddy, Henry, Benny, and Violet. Ben and I were actually born inside that house because there were snowstorms for my birth on November 4 and Ben's on December 1. I think old Mrs. Vargo may have helped Pop after the storms ended but she wasn't present for the birthing. The land that homestead was on is now a plowed field.

Pop and Uncle Rudy (late at night and after a few drinks) talked about their father liking the old Hungarian tradition where the father could retire at any age when the eldest son was barely old enough to do the farm work. Pop was officially taken out of school during the third grade to help his father with farming. Rudy and Pop admitted that they had often played hooky catching gophers and never had much schooling at all.

We had a free-standing plain wooden clothes closet that stuck out from the wall because the feet were large, and I could squeeze behind there. It made everyone laugh when they asked me where I came from and I told them, "Daddy found me behind the clothes closet."

After I was born (or "found") Mom put her foot down and demanded that they get some land of their own and a house that wasn't so cold and drafty. Mom thought they should quit working for Grandpa Alex because he mostly paid them in bad food and rarely gave Pop any money or seed. She related a "typical" incident when she was given a ham covered in half an inch of mold. Mom told me, "I felt like vomiting while I was scraping off that mold, thinking I would have to feed this to my kids."

Grandpa Alex was so angry about Peter leaving that he refused to loan him any money or even help him sign for a loan and did not speak to him for six months. Pop had no money because his father had not been paying him.

Pop obtained our first piece of land, about 325 acres, with the backing of John Farbo, a friend. It had been the homestead of a man named Schultz and he must have defaulted because it cost only $174.22 for back taxes plus a $75 legal fee. The deal was that Pop would give Farbo half of the mineral rights in exchange for the money. Instead of striking oil on our land as expected, it yielded only some natural gas. Henry jokes, "That poor guy probably got only enough money from the gas royalties on the property to buy himself cigars for a year." We used the gas later when we installed two wall heaters in the living room and obtained a gas burning kitchen stove.

Our new family house was built by Pop and Alec Toth (pronounced tote), an old family friend from Hungary. Alec Toth was a very short man and older than Pop. His favorite saying was "What for da matter for." That might be the beginning or end of a sentence or the entire sentence. With a little inflection that phrase could mean anything, favorably or unfavorably. It could mean that what was being discussed could go either way and it didn't really matter. It was an all-purpose phrase stated in response to anything.

Pop was a perfectionist, and he thought everything mattered. When Alec Toth and Pop poured cement for the foundation of the house, Alec said they didn't have to level the cement because "water runs downhill and so the cement we poured will level itself out." "What for da matter for it'll be okay." Unfortunately that did not work out.

When ready to start building, Pop discovered that the foundation was two inches higher at one end. You can imagine that a two-inch slope would have an adverse effect on building the rest of the house. By then the cement had hardened. The only tools he had to chip it off until it was level were a chisel and hammer. That was a very slow and hard manual process. Ted was six years old and vividly remembers that "Pop was cussing almost continuously while doing that work; and even added new swear words."

Built on a Hill

I was one year old when we moved into our new house.

Mom had asked that her house be built on a hill with a view and she certainly got her wish. There was a beautiful view of the Sweetgrass Hills, looking east. The sunrise "bursts" dramatically over those hills, which is how the town of Sunburst got its name. I really, really miss the view of the Sweetgrass Hills.

One disadvantage of being on a hill in Montana was that the ever-present winds lowered the winter temperature or at least made the temperature feel lower than the thermometer reading. There has been a distinct change over the years of my life with winter temperatures no longer dropping as low as in the past. I remember frequent times in my childhood when the winter temperature registered twenty below zero or lower, not including any wind-chill factor. We didn't know any measurement for wind-chill.

Another problem with locating the house on top of this hill was that the water well was located at the bottom of the steepest side of the hill. We had a winch on the well allowing us to lower a pail into the water and then turn the crank to bring up the full pail of water. We kids all carried buckets of water; Mom even gave me a small pail so that I could help. But Ted recalls that as we walked up the steep hill about half of the water sloshed out of our buckets.

I'm certain that our entire family would accept any disadvantages and choose to live on that hill with the view of the Sweetgrass Hills if we really had a choice.

The Size of the House

The house that Mom and Pop and we four children moved into consisted of a small kitchen and two very tiny bedrooms.

There were six of us sleeping in two tiny bedrooms. I slept in a crib in Mom and Pop's room until I was almost six years old. Then Henry and I slept together on a pull-out sofa in the kitchen while Ted and Ben slept in the second bedroom.

I don't remember when Henry and I were moved into different beds.

All three of my brothers, almost teenagers, slept together in a full-size bed in one room. Either Ben or Henry slept in the middle with the other two boys on either side of him.

The boys were very happy to have more room in bed when in 1946 Ted started high school and had to stay in Sunburst with Grandpa Alex because there was no school bus.

Additions Needed

Then it seems like a lot of things happened almost at the same time at our house. My sources and I had a hard time figuring out exactly what was done when. We concluded that Pop must have been working on several construction projects all at once. It's a good thing he was such a hard and capable worker.

A large addition was put onto the north side of the house. Part of the original second bedroom eventually became the bathroom. The girl's room, the boy's room and the living room, with a tiny porch, were added as part of this addition. We had two pull-out sofa beds which were useful when family visited from out-of-state.

That tiny porch gave us a second exit in case of fire but was never used by us as an entry or exit. It just functioned to confuse traveling salesmen who thought it was the front door.

The three boys still had only one bedroom, but it was larger and could hold a single bed in addition to the double bed.

Now We had a Bathroom but Couldn't Use It

Although we had a fully equipped bathroom we had no electricity and no running water. All six of us had to continue using the outhouse.

So we had a wind-charger for electricity and a cistern to hold water. "Can we use the bathroom now?" we asked.

Nope. Cannot use the bathroom until a septic tank is installed to process human waste and an area established for runoff to be safely discharged.

We were expected to go to the outhouse for bowel movements so that the septic tank would not be stressed.

And we were instructed to not flush the toilet after every use because we had to conserve water.

Finally, a Big, Useful Kitchen and a House for Fido

Finally, I think in 1950, we were able to build our last addition of a wonderful large country kitchen with an attached porch large enough to be used as an entrance for our farm workers. The kitchen was completed in 1951, thirteen years after we had moved into that small two-room house.

The former kitchen in the small house became the room known as the dining room. There was a table in the dining room, but it was always covered with Mom's plants, especially Christmas Cacti, and was never used as a dining room.

Bill Newmiller, married to Mom's sister Ella, stayed with us for a while during the winter to help build the kitchen. Uncle Bill talked a lot and had some experiences that made good stories but he never knew when to stop talking. I'm not exaggerating when I say that Uncle Bill would continue talking even after everyone had left the room. We kids enjoyed playing pinochle and canasta with Uncle Bill at the kitchen table long after Mom and Pop had gone to bed.

Our kitchen cabinets were not prefabricated. We were fortunate to have men around who were expert carpenters as well as farmers.

Sweetgrass

The large porch built onto the south side of the kitchen was used as our front entrance even though it was in the back of the house. Entrance to the porch required three steps. The concrete for those steps was poured into a hollow mold with an opening on the east side for our dog to be able to enter.

That was the doghouse for Fido, a black and white mixed mutt, who thought he was a member of our family.

When we four kids lined up for a snapshot, Fido often would quickly join us by standing in line and facing forward just like we were. He put himself at the short end of the line, appropriately by me rather than by Ted who was tallest. Fido was quite good at helping us chase cattle. We fed Fido table scraps, never store-bought dog food. When Fido was getting old and tired my parents got a new puppy. But Fido wasn't going to let that puppy have his food and water so he perked up and started eating and moving around again, playing and fighting with the puppy. Fido lived for a couple more years.

Pop built a little cabinet to be used as a washstand in the porch. It had two doors for supplies and a rod to hang towels. People could clean up a little before coming into the kitchen by filling the basin with warm water from the reservoir part of the coal stove. Farming was dusty, dirty work. The dirty water was just thrown outside onto the ground. That handmade washstand was one of the most coveted items when we held our farm auction. I don't remember the sale price, but the bidding was very active.

Pop also made a long bench that fit along one wall of the porch. That bench was used frequently for additional seating along the back of the kitchen table.

Our kitchen table was huge and made of yellow Formica with stainless steel legs. It had two or three wide leaves and could comfortably seat eight or more using the matching upholstered yellow chairs. However, those chairs were put into storage because they were too wide and we needed to be able to seat more people. Using smaller chairs and the bench behind the table, and angling two chairs at each end we could then comfortably seat fourteen or more people. And we could set up the card table in the kitchen if even more space was needed.

After we added the kitchen in 1951 we were able to replace the coal stove with one gas and one electric stove. Those drilling for oil on our land were able to only get natural gas, which we then used for heating and a kitchen stove. Gas was reliable during the frequent times in the winter when the electricity was off. And it was wonderful to have both of those stoves when cooking for a large crowd.

Other than paint and flooring, that was the end of our home improvement. There had been a lot of changes from the original, don't you think!!! After that, Mom took over and painted the rooms a different color almost every year. She often painted one wall a different color than the rest of the room, and the colors may have been a contrast rather than a blend. Mom liked to be surrounded with color since the prairie didn't have much color. I remember helping her wash the walls of the kitchen every single year before she applied a new coat of paint. We did a lot of cooking, and the walls got a little greasy and dirty.

After we older four kids moved away, there was less cooking to make the walls dirty and the walls didn't have to be washed and painted every year. However, her oldest granddaughter, Carol, often came to spend some time in the summer with Mom and recalls washing and painting the kitchen walls every year even after the older children had moved away.

That little house acquired in 1938 became a large and comfortable place for visitors and family to gather after 1951. Mom and Pop did a great job.

An Outstanding Outhouse

Everyone who ever visited the outhouse on my family farm pronounced it to be the Cadillac of all outhouses. It was built by my father and decorated by my mother.

The striking feature that immediately made a positive impression was that it had an <u>indoor</u> toilet seat, as opposed to other outhouses that had just a hole cut into a wooden bench. Pop had cut a barrel at the appropriate height for a toilet and then securely mounted an indoor toilet seat on top.

The barrel was held in place by being screwed into the cement foundation of the toilet. It was a custom at Halloween for Sunburst high school boys to make the rounds of farms and tip outhouses over, but they got the message that it was useless to try that at our place. This was a permanent building.

The room was a standard size for a one-holer at about 5x5 feet. My father took pride in this building and the quality of construction had no comparison. Pop had no training as a carpenter, but he was very smart in figuring things out. He was a perfectionist in all that he did. The structure was so secure that strong Montana winds never whistled through any cracks and neither did snow blow into the room. And those strong winds did not shake the building when you were in there. You didn't have to worry about being frightened by a mouse or other rodent because there were no cracks they could squeeze through.

The roof was made so well that there were never any leaks. The door was a smaller size than standard, so Pop had to make that by hand. The door was made of heavy wood to withstand those hurricane-force winds. It always fit perfectly and was never blown off. When we sold the farm the outhouse was more than eighty years old and it was still standing in good condition.

Mom did her part to make this an impressive place. Linoleum was laid over the cement floor and was replaced when it began to show wear or the corners curled up. She kept the floor spotlessly clean by frequently scrubbing it on her hands and knees. I remember other outhouses where spider webs hit you in the face, but Mom didn't allow spiders time to spin large webs. There were several sticky fly catchers hanging from the ceiling and a fly swatter hung on a nail for those times when a big fly would not leave you alone.

Every spring Mom painted the inside of the outhouse with new paint in a different color. The walls had not looked dirty, but Mom liked color inside the outhouse as well as in the house. It was more cheerful to sit in there with bright colors. A small window let in some light from the south.

We often did not have store-bought toilet paper but there was a box of some newspaper and good catalogs that you could use when necessary. Magazines were in a holder on the wall for your reading pleasure.

Lime had to be added periodically to break down the contents of the toilet so it didn't fill up.

Pop designed a cement septic tank on the side of the hill where sludge settled down and liquid seeped into the soil to be cleansed. I recall only one time when the septic tank had to be emptied. Pop hired someone to do the dirty job, and I never went out to observe.

This outhouse was the only toilet we had for six children and two adults until after I was starting high school and we got running water and a toilet inside the house. But we didn't stop using it when we got an indoor bathroom. The outhouse continued to be used frequently as an overflow when too many people had to go at the same time. And everybody *insisted* that Pop always use it when he went "number two."

When I was really young, Mom let me use a potty during the night. But as I grew older I had to use the outhouse like everyone else. I never felt scared on my way <u>to</u> the outhouse at night because I knew the house and people were behind me. And by using a flashlight I could see what was ahead of me. But I always felt a little scared when <u>returning</u> to the house. I was acutely aware of the <u>vast</u> darkness behind me in which there could be any kind of monster.

I often ran back to the house or at least walked very fast. We didn't have a yard light until the wind-charger was working in about 1946. It was very dark in the country with no light anywhere at all except my flashlight.

If nobody was around during the day time, you could leave the outhouse door open and enjoy a magnificent unobstructed view of the beautiful Sweetgrass Hills. They looked like a small range of mountains about fifty miles to the east. If you happened to run to the outhouse at dawn, you could see the sun bursting over the top of the hills.

Our view of the Sweetgrass Hills was so iconic that Pop had it engraved on the large marble headstone that he and Mom share in the Sweetgrass cemetery. In the cemetery the headstone is placed so that when you visit their graves you see the Sweetgrass Hills in real life just above the picture on the headstone.

Mom wanted her house to be on a hill with a view, and now she might see that same view from the grave.

The outhouse.

Wind-chargers built today are much larger than what we built.

How Did We Live Without Electricity?

People actually lived on this land before they discovered fire. I'm not old enough to know those days but I did survive my childhood without electricity. It was a huge job for the government to get electricity to us because in our rural area the houses were far apart.

But we jumped past the government timeline and got our own electricity generated by a wind-charger. The wind-charger was purchased in Shelby and erected at the southwest corner of the house with the help of the salesman, Ray Middlesworth. The purpose of our small wind-charger was to generate electricity, same as with the huge wind-chargers you now see erected all around the country to generate an alternative to burning fossil fuel.

Pop built shelves along the entire eastern wall of the basement to hold the large batteries that would be charged by the wind-charger and then provide us with electricity. Batteries had to be large because we didn't have transistors. Our first priority was to get electric lights to replace our kerosene lamps in the house and to get lights in the barn and shop to make it easier for Pop to work there.

I was surprised when I started listing all the ways I am using electricity in my condo. This long list may be incomplete. Electricity has made so many things more convenient.

USE	BEFORE ELECTRICITY
Lighting	We had a lot of kerosene lamps. There was a wick hanging in the kerosene and you could get more light by turning the wick up higher or having a larger wick. There wasn't much light for doing your homework.
	Some people made their own candles to burn.
	When we got electricity, Pop had wiring for only *one bulb on the ceiling of the kitchen*, not wanting to drain the batteries.
	We had to be sure to turn the light off when we left the room. Aliens watching would have thought we were sending signals with the lights going on and off.
Condo is heated by electricity	Our house was heated by a coal stove. Sometimes we gathered dried cow chips to burn when we ran out of money.
	After drillers discovered gas on our property instead of the desired oil, we then had gas piped to the house for heating.
	We had two gas wall heaters for the entire house—they didn't give adequate heat, and they were known to be very dangerous by starting fires in the wall. We turned them off at night and used more blankets and comforters.

Sweetgrass

In the kitchen I use an electric stove for cooking.	We used a coal stove for cooking until I was in high school. Wood was not available on our land because there were no trees. It was less expensive to have coal delivered than wood, and coal burned slower. Later Mom had an electric and a gas stove in the kitchen. Gas was reliable when the electric lines were down in the winter.
Electric refrigerator	Before electricity we cooked meat promptly and we canned a lot of different meat and fish. In the winter we cut a chunk of ice off the lake and used it to keep food. A pan underneath caught the water melting from the ice.
Electric freezer	A grocery store in Sweetgrass had a walk-in freezer, running on a generator and they had lockers to store frozen meat for the entire community. We didn't go to town very often and only took out the meat we could use promptly. Otherwise we used canned meat.
Running water from faucet	We had to go down the steep hill and drop a bucket on a rope to fill it with water. Later we had to pump a handle to get water up through a pipe.
Hot water directly from the faucet	After we carried a bucket of water up the steep hill, we had to put the bucket on the stove to heat the water.

Dishwasher washes and dries the dishes after it is loaded	When I was young our dishwasher and dryer was "Violet."
Air conditioning	Ha, ha, ha. Fan yourself with a cardboard fan. If we were too hot we opened windows to get a cross-draft.
Electric toaster can be set for darkness desired.	We made toast in the oven. When we first had an electric toaster, it toasted only one side of the bread, and you had to open it and turn the bread over. Not much better than using the oven
Microwave for heating leftovers and TV dinners	We didn't have TV dinners. Also no TV. Leftover food could be heated on stove top or in oven.
Vacuum	We didn't have wall-to-wall carpeting. Throw rugs were shaken outside. Wood or linoleum floors were swept and scrubbed; preferably on your hands and knees to get into the corners and edges.

Sweetgrass

Laundry, washer	Mom scrubbed clothes by hand against a scrubboard and wrung them out by hand.
	I was maybe six when we got a washing machine that had a gas motor. It moved the clothes around to wash so we only had to scrub dirty things. But the clothes had to be rinsed and put through the wringer again.
	See story on laundry.
Clothes dryer	We hung clothes outside in all kinds of weather.
I buy clothes that are permanent press and don't require ironing	*See story on Ironing.*
	Everything had to be ironed using heavy irons heated on the coal stove
Radio, electric or batteries	Early radios needed large batteries.
	Our whole family pulled chairs up near the radio to hear our favorite shows. Sat close together because of poor reception.
	A few shows were *Kate Smith* singing hour, *The Shadow Knows*, *Abbot and Costello*, and *Charlie McCarthy* and his dummies.
My cellphone can take photos.	We never had a phone while I lived on the farm.
	We drove to visit someone; if they weren't home we left a note.
	When a child I got a small Brownie camera that took tiny pictures.
	I have used 35-mm slide cameras and others.
	I liked the Polaroid camera that instantly developed the photo.

Television	I confess that I still don't understand how pictures can be transmitted through the air. I didn't watch TV until I went to college. When we got TV on the farm it could only pick up one station.
Games on phone	We played card games: canasta, pinocle, hand and foot, etc. We played board games, especially Monopoly. We didn't have a phone of any kind.
Movies now have reclining seats and waiters to serve food.	As a child I only went to a couple of movies—Black Beauty and Heidi. I sat on hard seats. Movies were black and white.
Electric sewing machine	Clothing could be sewn by hand (I still hand-stitch some hems). Growing up we sewed using a treadle machine, pumped by foot. It skipped stitches.
Computer with backup. Connected printer.	Paper and pencil worked pretty well. I learned to type in high school on an old Underwood using only the pressure of my fingers to make each letter stroke—had to press hard.
Sometimes when my hair was longer I used hair rollers warmed by electricity.	Women used to put a hair curling iron into the top of a kerosene lamp to heat. Sometimes the iron got too hot and started fire in a woman's hair. Some women died from these fires.

I use either a clock that runs on electricity or on batteries.	Clocks usually had to be manually wound every day. If you didn't wind the clock at the same time every day, the clock might go slow or stop.
If desired, an electric blanket can be set for desired hear.	I don't like electric blankets and prefer to just use a warmer comforter or add another blanket on the bed.
La-Z-Boy electric recliner	We had a rocking chair you moved by foot. If you wanted to recline, you could go lay down on bed.
Electric doorbells that can be set on the sound you like.	We used to knock on the door using our knuckles.

I forgot to mention that we needed to have water run from the cistern to the bathroom before electricity. In other words, we had a bathroom before running water. My brother Henry, who is fond of airplanes, made a strong point that the pump in the basement that moved that water used a 32-volt alternator that was war surplus off a B29 airplane with a 32-volt system.

Outbuildings on the Farm

Additions to the house are definitely not the only things that Pop built. I am very impressed when I think about all the things he made without ever having a class or someone to work with who could mentor him. His own father was a very poor carpenter as exhibited by the drafty homestead he built for his family.

Pop figured out all the details of carpentry without any directions. There was no internet program or TV program or course for him to take nor even a friend to call when he had a question. He just figured it out. Once I watched a couple of men trying to hang a closet door evenly and they had a lot of trouble. When it was crooked they tried to shave some off the bottom to straighten it out but that wasn't enough, and they did more. If it were an outside door we would have had to throw it away because it would not be able to keep out the cold air.

Not only did he learn by experience, but Pop was also a very hard worker. In addition to working the farm fields and caring for the machinery, he constructed the following buildings:

Our house, which has been described, along with additions.

The **outhouse**.

Chicken house with roosts and nests.

Sweetgrass

A small **Brooder house** for baby chickens to stay warm and safe from others.

A couple of **granaries**.

The **barn,** which was built with the boards from the Livery Stable in Sweetgrass. He and Alec Toth took the Stable apart board by board so that every board and nail could be re-used to make our barn. We pounded nails out from the wrong side of a board and then used a claw hammer to pull the nail out from the right side of the board. Then we had to pound the nail until it was straight and could be used again. It took time to prepare nails to be re-used but we had time, and we didn't have money to buy new nails. My brother Ted still marvels over how they hauled the boards home when the only vehicle owned at that time was Hildegard and that truck was very small. The barn was made with a hayloft because hay was kept inside those days.

A **corral** was made around the barn with swing-gates so animals could be moved between three pens.

A **ramp** was built to load cattle onto the truck so they could be driven to sale.

Pop built a **3-stall shop or garage** with sliding doors.

Pop was a blacksmith and built in a corner of the shop a **blacksmith's forge** that could withstand extreme heat.

A one-and-a-half car **garage** was built near the house.

Pop built a small **bunkhouse** where a hired man could sleep.

The **Quonset hut** which was a rounded metal building had to be erected for storage of machines in winter.

A **grain elevator,** different from a granary, was built.

Pop made **fencing** for the cattle around two or three different pastures to be able to move them to fresh grass.

In addition to wooden buildings, he designed **two major dams** between hills to create water reservoirs for the animals.

There were abandoned one-room homestead houses that could be used for other purposes. Pop used the Schulze home for a coal and wood shed and another for a granary.

Pop would buy coal and have it delivered to an old house on our property. It would be in large chunks and the boys had to break it into smaller pieces with a sledge hammer. We used old lumber from these abandoned homesteads to start a fire in our coal stove.

Pop was creative and could make things that had never been made before, such as the winch to raise the truck bed of Hildegard so that rocks would slide off instead of having to be thrown off the truck by hand.

He used his blacksmith skills and his own creativity to make all kinds of parts for machinery and buildings.

He could figure out anything. Self-reliance is a trait I think that most Montana farm people have just because you learn that you can't always call on somebody else to do what you want done. You need to use some good common sense.

Camping with Alice

"You're going camping with me this weekend," said my good friend Alice, surprising me because neither of us were campers. Discussion revealed that Alice had planned to go camping with Bob, her husband who three years ago had packed up his belongings while she was at a conference and surprised her with his announcement that he wanted a divorce. I knew that Alice would take him back if there ever was a chance. Now she thought there was a chance.

She had paid for a campsite on the sand dunes of Lake Michigan for them to spend a weekend together. And Bob at the last minute canceled out. It was a strange plan to get him back since neither of them had ever been campers. I couldn't picture them having a romantic weekend camping considering their age, excess weight and poor health. But that had been Alice's plan and she was darned if she was going to have paid for a campsite and not make use of it. I suppose this same frugality prevented her from reserving a room at a romantic hotel with a better chance of getting Bob back.

Alice was a bit of a character who could make unexpected statements, such as telling people the reason she asked to transfer back onto the road surveying health care institutions was because it was too difficult to have an affair with the Culligan Man if she had to stay at home in Madison. Alice came up with quirky ideas, such as asking friends to help with the wedding dinner she had already promised an impoverished woman in her church. Or preparing a party for the private owners of her in-laws Cemetery Association. When we arrived to help we might find that Alice had not shopped or prepped in advance. I know if I did the same thing my friends would be angry; but when it involved Alice such things just became humorous stories that only made Alice more endearing.

Alice and I were both nurses who had previously worked together at the Central Wisconsin Center for the Developmentally Disabled and remained very close friends. She became a state surveyor of hospitals and nursing homes while I started my own consulting business after resigning from University Hospital. I had recently left my husband so I was happy to sometimes join her at a nice B&B where she was staying while investigating health-care complaints. Time spent with Alice was always an enjoyable change of pace. I could do my work at the B&B while Alice was surveying a facility or investigating a physician.

Alice's appearance differed from the way I thought a high-level state surveyor ought to look. She dressed to be comfortable—in loose-fitting, well-worn slacks and top, along with heavy woolen socks showing through her Birkenstocks. Alice was overweight with a kindly round face framed by short, wavy grey hair. She was quick to smile and laugh. She dressed for personal comfort, and also because she wouldn't spend the money necessary to buy professional attire. She consciously made use of her persona. She told me, "When I go in to do a survey, everyone looks at me as the dumpy, not-too-smart, good old Grandma who lives next door." As expected, staff were not frightened of her and would approach her to reveal secrets of the facility. She delighted in the fact that administrators were usually astonished to hear at the exit report all the problems that she had uncovered. I enjoyed hearing her stories.

Sweetgrass

In preparation for our camping trip, Alice, consistently frugal, borrowed a tent from a co-worker who said she had it for many years but had never taken it out of the box. The tent was an old design that required you to insert aluminum rods, some straight and some hinged. There were no instructions anywhere and we had a horrible time setting it up. We were also in a hurry because we had stopped to visit a friend on the way and it now was starting to grow dark. After many insertions and re-insertions of aluminum rods, we started being irritable with each other. When we finally finished setting up the tent, we discovered a rain cover in the box. I'd had it with that cheap tent, and I angrily said that I wasn't spending any more time on that damn tent. I didn't know what a rain cover would do, and it didn't feel like it was going to rain anyway. Remember, this was years before we had smart phones with a weather app giving hourly weather reports.

We moved on to making a fire, having a little wine and unpacking the extravagant food we had planned for dinner and breakfast. We had made out the gourmet menu a few days ago identifying which of us was responsible to bring each item. We quickly discovered that we both brought items from the same list and were missing some important foods such as steaks, eggs and bacon. There was disbelief and some blaming over which of us had made the wrong list. But we then proceeded to make-do with what we had—eating a lot of potatoes, and finishing off another bottle of wine.

By the time we were done eating it was dark and late enough to go to bed. We unrolled our sleeping bags on the thin floor of the tent because, of course, Alice thought renting cots would have been an unnecessary expense.

As you may have expected by now, it rained heavily during the night. I became aware that there was a slight slope of the ground under our tent and I was on the downward side. Water was coming in through the floor of the tent and soaking my sleeping bag. Since there wasn't a rain cover over the tent (my bad) water also started dripping down through the ceiling. For some reason, maybe Karma, the dripping occurred only on my side of the tent.

Alice was using a CPAP machine with three long electric extension cords. We were frightened about the possiblity of getting electric shock from the lightning and rain while disconnecting the equipment and putting it into the car where it would be dry. I was wet and cold and angry, as well as sleepless.

The rain stopped as the sun began to rise, and the air was nice and warm. It was going to be a beautiful day. We cooked a make-shift breakfast with lots of potatoes and odd leftovers and laid our sleeping bags in the sun to dry. We went for a long walk under the warm sun along Lake Michigan. Walking on the sand dunes made me feel calm and happy that I was there. By the time we returned, our sleeping bags were slightly less wet, and we decided to take a nap before driving back to Madison.

You get only one guess of what happened next. Yes, it suddenly started raining heavily again. We had to take down the complicated tent and re-pack all our supplies into the car while the rain poured down.

We drove home in silence, neither of us wanting to end our friendship by discussing this traumatic weekend. Neither of us ever went camping again. And Bob did not reunite with Alice. Although I would have been so happy if he had been subjected to the same discomfort I endured on this camping trip with Alice, since it was all *his* fault in the first place.

Living Without Running Water

Water is a precious commodity when you are living where water is scarce and not readily available. In general, the area of Montana where I grew up was dry. As a farmer, we practiced "dry land farming." We never had a water well close to our house.

We tried to drill for a water well close to our house but that didn't work. Grandpa Lozing was an expert at divining the location of underground water and helped many people find water wells. We just simply didn't have any water, or oil, underground.

When we first four children were born to Hannah and Peter Suta, we lived in a tiny shack and Mom had to walk quite a ways to get a bucket of water. Of course she had to take us children with her when Pop was farming. It must have been really hard for Mom when I wasn't yet walking, and she had to carry me and a bucket of water. My oldest brother was only five years older than me so he wouldn't have been able to help very much.

When we built our permanent house on a hill, there was a water well at the base of our steep hill. It was hard work to carry adequate water up that hill. Every one of the four of us children carried a bucket of water. Mine was the size of a sandbox toy. My brothers remember that the hill was so steep that about half the water in their buckets sloshed out before they reached the top. Poor Mom carrying all the water up that hill—but she had asked for her house to be built on a hill with a view.

We had a metal bucket on the counter with an enamel ladle in it and everybody drank from that same ladle. You had to take only a small amount of water at a time because you wouldn't spit back into the bucket anything you left in the ladle. This was the same at the house of everybody we visited. Visitors and family drank out of the same bucket.

That well at the bottom of our hill wasn't plentiful nor was it good water, so it was closed when we were able to haul water into our cistern.

When we were children we all took turns having a bath with only a couple of inches of water in the square metal container used for washing clothes. We took turns taking baths with the youngest first, I think. I'm not sure of the order in which our family took baths, but I suppose Mom went last because that was her kind way of doing things.

To do laundry Mom had to scrub the clothes on a corrugated washing board and wring them dry with her hands. I can imagine it is very hard to wring the water out of men's pants. Mom was a small woman, but she always worked so hard that she had strong hands and a lot of muscle.

We didn't get running water until after we got a windmill that produced an electric current through a wall of large batteries in the basement. And we didn't get running water right away from that windmill. The initial purpose of the windmill was to produce electricity for some electric lights. It was quite a while before we made a large cistern, a cement hole in the ground, that could be filled with water and pumped upstairs by an electric machine.

The cistern was filled with water that had to be hauled from one of the Sunburst wells east of the city, about a thirty-mile round trip in an old truck that didn't even have a radio. We had a tank mounted permanently on the back of one of our pickups, known as the "water truck." One of my brothers or Pop would drive back and forth to get at least five or six loads of water to fill the cistern. They all hated having to haul water. I guess it was just too boring. I would have traded cooking for sitting in the water truck and driving it back and forth.

Next time San Francisco or anyplace else has a water shortage, they ought to put Pop in charge of water conservation. We learned how to conserve water long before it was generally talked about.

Examples that Pop enforced include never letting the water run while you are brushing your teeth—you only need enough to wet your toothbrush and rinse your mouth after brushing. You can flush the toilet after number two, but never after number one.

When washing your hands or face, you need only to get wet to apply the soap, turn the faucet off while scrubbing yourself clean, and turn the water on to rinse off the soap. The same can be said for taking a shower—just get wet, soap yourself, and then turn the faucet on to rinse your body. It's a waste to keep the water running the entire time of your shower. If you have to use water when cooking, such as for washing off vegetables or boiling potatoes, re-purpose that water by watering the garden or the animals.

While living at home, I never took a bath in more than two inches of water because Pop would start hollering for me to quit wasting water as soon as I turned the faucet on. If I didn't turn the faucet off right away, he would start banging on the door.

I think of that memory now that I am an adult with accessible water. I feel so decadent, a little guilty, and very happy when I occasionally take a bath with the tub filled to the brim.

Laundry

Stop a minute and imagine how you would do laundry if you had four children under the age of six and didn't have electric or gas power and have no source of water nearby. What a daunting task! I don't know how my mother managed to do this and other impossible tasks to raise our family on the farm.

Hannah and Peter weren't homesteaders who went to Montana to claim free land, but the parents of both were immigrants and had homesteaded. For six years after they married Peter had helped his father farm for little or no pay. During that time they lived in the homestead of Peter's parents. They now have four children while living in this one-and-a-half room shack that Peter's father built.

Water had to be hand-pumped from a well some distance away. The buckets of water had to be carried home to be heated on the coal-burning stove. Mom was often carrying a baby at the same time she was carrying a bucket or two of water.

Once she has carried water home, there is another problem—where is the soap? You need soap to get the clothes clean. But since they basically had no money, Mom had to make soap herself. I'll tell you how to do that in another story.

Farming is dirty work. The rags and greasy clothes of the men had to be boiled in a large kettle of soapy water and

Sweetgrass

stirred around with a big stick while the kettle was on the stove. The men got greasy because all machinery used grease. Boiling hot water was necessary to get grease out of the clothes. When these greasy clothes looked a little cleaner, they could be washed and rinsed like other clothing.

When Mom was starting out with married life and having babies, everything had to be washed by hand, including heavy items such as towels and blue jeans.

While washing clothes, Mom had to bend over to scrub each item in soapy water on a corrugated metal or wooden washboard propped in a square metal washtub—which doubled as our bathtub at other times. During the life of all of us babies, Mom had to wash cotton diapers by hand because there was no such thing as disposable diapers.

After clothes were scrubbed and wrung out, they were rinsed in clean water and the rinse water had to be wrung out again. Like a lot of "women's work" this required a lot of muscle. Mom always had strong hands and could open any lid stuck on a jar, even when men couldn't open the jar.

Sometimes in the summer a few of the country women would get together to do their laundry outdoors in the company of others. Laundry day would seem more enjoyable when the women could visit with each other. They were seldom able to get together because homes on the prairie were several miles apart and the women had no way to travel unless their husbands were willing to take them.

Mom told me that the Hungarian women, including my Grandma Teresia Suta, brewed "poppy tea" to put the children to sleep to keep them out of the way on laundry day. I remember the beautiful bright orange and yellow colors of the poppies growing in Grandma Suta's garden. Tea may or may not have been made from the California Poppy which is related to the opium poppy but is non-narcotic and non-addictive. Although non-narcotic, the California poppy tea could be used as a sedative or as a pain reliever. Tea could be made from the fresh flowers, or the flowers could be dried for tea.

There were no such things as playpens or child safety seats to keep young children and babies nearby, safe and controlled. Mom thought it was wrong to give poppy tea to children and proudly told me that she never gave it to her children. Our dear Mother wasn't going to take a chance on some unknown thing harming her children. She preferred to keep her eyes on her four children playing nearby.

There was always a lot of junk in Alex Suta's' yard and Mom enclosed us in pens that she made out of machinery and junk. The littlest ones, like me at that time, she tied to herself with rope.

Frankly, I don't blame the other mothers for putting the children to sleep where they could be safe from harm and not a bother.

As I grew older, Mom gave me chores to help her.

When I was still very young, two or three years old, Mom gave me a permanent assignment of emptying out the pockets of pants and shirts. Not only did my father and three older brothers have a lot of pockets but you never knew what you might find inside those pockets. My brother Ben, especially, stuffed his pant pockets as full as he could with items such as dead birds, live or dead tadpoles, sharp pieces of junk, broken glass, rocks, grasshoppers, various bugs, and garter snakes, dead or alive. Years later, Mom laughingly admitted she knew this was an awful task and that was why she assigned the job to me. She always disappeared outside while I was searching through pockets.

I still remember the thrill when I was about five years old, and we got a washing machine that had a gasoline motor. The blades inside the washing machine just bumped the clothes up and down a little so we still had to do a lot of rubbing to get out soil and stains. I was old enough to help Mom by rubbing clothes on the washboard if they had stains.

Sweetgrass

The machine had rubber wringers to squeeze excess water out of the clothes. Each item of clothing had to be fed through a double roll of rubber wringers after washing and again after rinsing. That was better than having to wring out the water by hand.

You had to be careful how you put shirts through the wringer to avoid popping off the buttons and giving yourself more work to sew on new buttons. I learned that it hurt if you weren't careful and got your fingers caught in the wringer.

Clothes were hung on outdoor clotheslines to dry, no matter what the weather was like. On a nice day we could enjoy a beautiful view of the Sweet Grass Hills, looking like a small range of mountains about fifty miles east. We did not enjoy that view very much while hanging our clothes outside during the harsh winter weather in northern Montana.

I admit that hanging the clothes outside even in the winter does make them smell better. Mom tried to wait for nice weather to do the laundry, but nice warm weather doesn't come often during the winters if you live in northern Montana.

There was a system to follow in hanging clothes on the clothesline. First you had to wash the clotheslines with a damp cloth to remove dirt and bird droppings.

Shirts and tee shirts were hung by the tail because that way the sleeves would dry quickly. Also, you wouldn't want to hang shirts by the shoulder because that would add wrinkles.

Pants were hung by the legs so the heavy waistband and pockets would dry.

Items that weren't as thick as Turkish towels were lined up so that the corners of two items could share one clothespin. We were always short of wooden clothespins because they broke.

If it was a really cold day, the laundry we first pinned on the line would be frozen by the time we were hanging clothes from the bottom of the basket. Those frozen clothes were stiff as icicles when we took them indoors to finish drying. They had to be handled carefully to not damage them when they were so stiff. After the clothing thawed a little, we hung all that we could on the lines in our dirt basement and scattered the remainder on all surfaces throughout the house.

My brother Ben insisted that it was good to hang the clothes outdoors when it was freezing cold because the freezing process helped to dry the clothes—like freeze-drying food. But I never knew when Ben could be believed. The dry climate of Montana helped the clothes to dry rapidly.

It's good that Ben thought it was beneficial to hang the clothes outdoors in freezing weather because he and I were the ones who got that job.

When I had my first baby I thought it strange that Mom started talking to me about toilet training him when he was only a few months old. I had studied child development and children usually weren't able to be toilet trained until they were almost three years old. She said mothers in her day bragged about how early they were able to toilet train their babies.

It took a lot of discussion to learn where Mom was coming from. When she had babies it was hard to get water for laundry and the diapers had to be washed by hand. It would be less work if you didn't have to wash diapers. It took a while for me to convince Mom that it was the mothers who were being trained to watch the baby's signals and then quickly hold the baby over a bucket or the toilet.

Mom admitted that babies sometimes were just tied to a potty chair and remained there as long as it took for them to "do their business." The mothers didn't want their babies to soil diapers, especially with a bowel movement because there was a scarcity of time and water for washing diapers.

Mom said that diapers wet with urine were often just hung over a chair to dry and were reused without being rinsed because of water shortage. All the babies had severe

Sweetgrass

diaper rash causing them to be cranky and cry because they were hurting. That certainly would be motivation to toilet train the baby as early as possible.

People sometimes speak longingly for "the good old days" but neither Mom or I would care to go back to those days when laundry had to be done the hard way. And it isn't done yet.

Laundry wasn't finished until ironing was done and that's the topic of another story.

For much of my adult life I had certain clothing items that had to be washed by hand because they were delicate. I had to wear nylons every work day from the time I was a student nurse until I retired after more than fifty years of nursing.

I have made the choice to wear cashmere sweaters which have to be washed by hand because they are superior in keeping me warm. But I just don't use pantyhose any longer. Knee high or thigh high nylons can substitute and are easy to put on.

We had a beautiful view from the clothesline.

Laundry Soap

When I was a child, our family was quite poor. Many homesteaders were in the same situation. Women learned to save money by making rather than buying soap to wash the family's clothing and other items.

Laundry soap was made by combining alkalis with fat, which reacts to make soap. Plants could be burned to produce some mild alkali, which is what Mom did. Or lye, which is a strong alkali could be purchased inexpensively. Fat was provided by lard rendered from the fat of an animal that we had butchered. This lye soap was very caustic to your hands, as you can imagine.

Rendering solid fat from an animal to obtain liquid fat is a process of melting the animal's lard. The lard had to have been trimmed carefully from the meat because you wouldn't want pieces of meat in the soap.

The lard had to be simmered very, very slowly to melt it into a liquid. While it was simmering, scum and fragments of meat would come to the surface and these impurities had to be frequently skimmed off. Particles of meat that remained had to be strained out of the liquid.

Mom cooked the soap in a large trash barrel over a campfire out in the graveled yard. It would be hard to render the lard on the stove because you would have had to have a very large pot to hold all of the lard from a cow or pig. It took a lot of animal lard because it cooks down as it melts. The low fire had to be kept burning most of the day. Mom had to be vigilant all day to keep her children safe from the fire. Little kids could get inquisitive about what was cooking.

When the solution of lard and lye was liquefied, it had to cool a while before it could be poured into wooden molds to completely cool and solidify.

> *Recipes for lye soap were not specific and the resulting soap was often very harsh.*
> Put wood ashes into barrel lined with hay.
> Allow rainwater to drain through a hole in the bottom.
> Boil this lye solution to desired concentration.
> Add melted animal fat and stir constantly until it begins to harden. Pour into molds and cut to size.

Laundry soap recipe.

When we became more affluent, Mom fell under the spell of radio advertising for Fels-Naphta: "Ninety-nine percent pure." Pure of what you were never told, but that was an effective ad for many years. Many homemakers used Fels-Naphta as their only laundry detergent, but others simply added a little of it to the fat and lye combination to make that solution more effective in removing soil.

When we could afford it, we used store-bought soap in the house for washing face and hands, but Mom continued for many years to make lye soap for laundry.

I was surprised when I looked for soap recipes on YouTube to find that there are many women today who are making their own soap with some modifications from the original method. They are happy to make soap because they choose to do so either for their own family or to sell. They are doing this by choice to avoid chemicals or to sell the soap as a craft product. They cannot go out and butcher an animal when more soap is needed so they have to start with a different fat or purchase lard at the grocery store. And they have learned ways to make the soap more effective, such as adding a small amount of liquid dish-washing detergent. Fragrance can be added. With modifications they have learned by trial and error, the products can be used to effectively remove old soap from material making softer and whiter, brighter clothing.

There are a lot of women today who are happy to make soap because they choose to do so.

There is a big difference between women who choose to do this for pleasure and the women like Mom who are forced to do it because of little money.

Ironing Clothes

It may sound a little stupid but after the laundry became dry, we then had to wet the material to be able to iron out the wrinkles. You cannot iron out the wrinkles if the article is totally dry unless you use steam from your iron. And we did not have steam irons until I was an adult.

Writing this story in 2025 I can happily tell you that we no longer have to sprinkle (wet) the clothes before ironing because we can get steam out of the iron to moisten the wrinkled area and be able to iron it flat. Better news yet is that many garments now are wrinkle-free and do not require any ironing at all.

Polyester material that requires little or no ironing was not invented until after my three sons were grown. I think every woman in America must have celebrated when polyester was developed as a material for clothing because it needed no ironing or less ironing than did cotton.

Polyester made a nuclear change in the lives of me and Mom by reducing the hours and days of ironing we had to do. The early polyester still required some ironing, but it was easy ironing.

When I lived at home, Mom and I ironed everything except socks and shorts. Even the material used to make jeans had to be ironed. Mom and I spent two days every week washing and ironing clothes.

We "sprinkled" water on the dry clothing so that the heat of the iron would create steam and allow the material to be ironed flat. Sprinkling is a skill that had to be learned by trial and error. Curl up your fingers on one hand and dip it into a bowl of water, holding back a little of the water which can then be tossed or "sprinkled "across the clothing. It is necessary to control the amount of water sprinkled on the clothing. You had to be careful that you didn't make one spot very wet and leave other areas dry. The goal was to have the entire garment equally moist.

You could buy or make a sprinkler by making small holes in the lid of a container filled with water. We thought the original method of sprinkling water from your hand gave you more control over the amount of moisture desired.

You could iron the garment right after you sprinkled but the moisture is not evenly spread throughout the garment. To allow the amount of moisture to become even on all areas of the garment, you had to roll the material up tightly and set it aside for a while. Judgment had to be used as to when the material is evenly moist depending on the type of material—an hour or two might be adequate.

We put sprinkled clothing into something with a cover, like the roaster pan, so the clothes wouldn't dry out before ironing. If unable to do all of the ironing on the same day, we sometimes put the rolled-up material into the refrigerator (after we got one). If left out at room temperature for several days, mold might begin to form, but that was never a problem for us.

Some items had to be starched before ironing. That required several decisions. For example, before ironing a shirt, you have to decide if the entire shirt or just parts are to be starched. The collar might be left unstarched so that it will be softer on the neck of the wearer. But some men like the sharp look of a starched collar.

You also need to make a decision regarding how strong to make the starch. Does the wearer want "light" or "heavy" starch. And do you need different strengths of starch for different items in your laundry. You might put heavy starch on tablecloths and light starch on shirts. We had to make the desired strength of starch, mixing the powder with water and boiling it until the right consistency, stirring to prevent lumps.

When we four kids started going to school in town laundry became a bigger task than when we went to the one-room school. When going to school in town, my three older brothers wore white shirts every day. The material of the shirts was cotton and the shirts would be just a sagging mess if they weren't starched and ironed. They needed to wear a clean shirt every day because teen-age boys have strong body odor. All of their white shirts had to be washed and ironed after one wearing. We country kids needed to look and smell as clean as possible even if we weren't fashionable.

When we arrived home from school we all changed into everyday clothes to save wear on our good clothes. These everyday clothes also had to be washed after one wearing because we got them dirty doing chores outdoors on the farm.

There was one year in the 1950s when the fad was to wear dresses made of paper. That wasn't very comfortable or practical. You could wear a dress only a couple of times without washing and ironing.

Ironing was done using five pound steel irons heated on top of the coal stove. Some of the irons were made with handles all in one piece. Some other irons could be connected with removable thick wooden handles. These handles had a hook on the bottom that you could open and close in order to change the handle from iron to iron. This was useful if you needed to adjust the temperature for the type of cloth you were ironing, using a hot iron on some parts of clothing and a cooler iron on others.

You had to move irons to the hottest or cooler part of the coal stove depending on the kind of material that was being ironed. There were no instructions regarding what temperature to use for ironing a specific garment. There also were no temperature gauges to show how hot an iron was, not even a 'high or low" temperature.

The temperature of the iron was 'scientifically' gauged by spitting on my fingertip and then touching the bottom of the hot iron—very quickly—and noticing how fast the water evaporated from my fingertip and how quickly my fingertip became hot. With experience I could tell whether the iron was the right temperature without burning my finger. That judgment had to be made in a split second.

There were two major decisions to make before ironing any article of clothing, and the decisions affected each other. We had to decide what temperature the material being ironed could tolerate. We wanted the iron hot enough to eliminate wrinkles but not so hot that it would scorch or ruin the material. (Different materials would scorch more easily.) And secondly we had to choose an iron that was at the correct temperature for that material. This was a pretty scientific process using only your good judgment based on a lot of experience for all decisions.

The spit method could tell me the temperature of the iron, but a process of learning was necessary to match the correct temperature to each different type of fabric. When I was five or six years old I began to practice ironing on jeans because if I happened to scorch the material, the scorch marks wouldn't be very visible. Scorching the material would happen if my iron was too hot for the material or if I wasn't moving the iron around fast enough. The material would turn brown when scorched and could even burn if left too long.

Mom and I ironed many pieces of clothing for a family of six. An electric iron would have controls for the heat rather than relying on the spit method. An electric iron would not be as heavy as a metal iron. When electric irons were developed, they could produce steam to eliminate the need for sprinkling. However, the voltage of electric irons prevented us from using them with the electricity from our windmill. We had to wait for REA wiring.

Our section of the USA was one of the last to get REA (rural electrification) because of the long distances between

Sweetgrass

our sparse rural population. REA wiring reached us sometime in 1947. *(See story on Electricity)* Before that, we produced a little electricity for ourselves by building a windmill to charge huge batteries filling half the basement. My oldest brother Ted remembers the windmill being built in 1944 or 1945 because he remembers climbing to the top. This electricity powered a few lights and a refrigerator. I thought it also powered a radio but Ted told me that he had to take the battery out of Hildegard and bring it into the kitchen to connect to the radio in the early days because the voltage was different.

When Mom could start using electric irons, she gave me all of her heavy irons saying, "you have earned these for all the ironing you have done." She labeled one as last being used in 1947, which was when REA finally reached the Suta Farm. The irons we had been using are heavy enough to be used as very good bookends.

Mending was also part of the laundry process. My brothers were always tearing or wearing out the knees of their jeans and we could sew patches on their everyday jeans. Buttons that had been lost had to be replaced. I also learned the difficult method of darning socks. I was glad that Mom and I gave that up as soon as she thought she could afford to buy new socks.

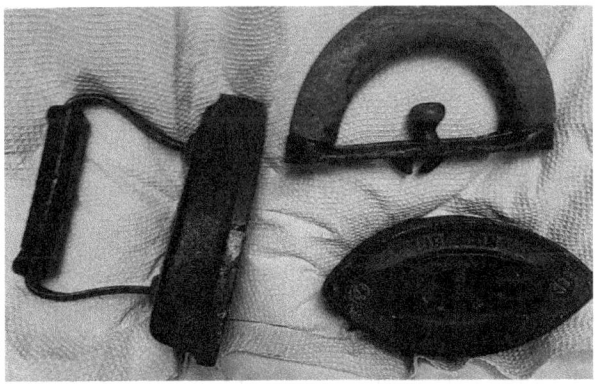

Choice of irons so you always had one at the right temperature.

Telephones

How Did We Live Without Them

It is amazing that the United States government, unlike some other countries, has not made it a national priority to insure that all citizens have access to Wi-Fi for phones and computers. Today there are still areas in the mountains or where people are spaced far apart where reception isn't good, or you can't get Wi-Fi at all.

The biggest problem without telephones is the inability to get help in emergencies. Your house could burn down before any firefighters arrive, your father might die of a heart attack before an ambulance arrives, and the police would not know that your family is being robbed or murdered until someone tries to visit you and then drives to the police station to tell them. Catastrophes occurred more often without phones, but life went on for most people.

What Did We Do Without Telephones?

Populous areas had telephones long before my family did. Many phones were the style that is made fun of in comedy shows; mounted on the wall and with a crank that had to be turned to reach an operator. My family never had that or any other type of telephone while I lived with them. I think I never even used a phone until I was out of high school. During my college life there was only one phone shared by an entire floor of classmates and that could be used only to place or receive brief verbal communication.

Farmers in my family use walkie-talkies to communicate from their farm machinery to their home.

We would drive to visit a person, and they might not be home. We simply wrote a message on a piece of paper to let them know that we had been there. We didn't have "visiting cards" as in Victorian times so we used whatever paper we could find, and paper was scarce. I remember many times writing a note on the inside of a book of paper matches.

If we needed to get information out quickly, such as about a death, we might drive to tell one or two neighbors and expect them to help pass the information on to others. Telling the local bartender, the grocery store clerk and the clerk in the post office would guarantee to get the word out because they would see many people and could pass on the information.

If you wanted to have a party, you had to plan it far enough in advance to be able to see everybody and give verbal invitations. If you had more time you could send written invitations through the mail, but then you would have to wait for their response.

Because we never knew when a visitor might drop in unexpectedly, we had to be prepared at all times with refreshments like cake or cookies and drinks to serve. Some friends and family members made it a habit to drop in unexpectedly at mealtime. People were generally happy to greet unexpected visitors. Maybe we were just more bored before television. Now that we have television you might go to visit someone in their home, and they might not even turn down the volume on the TV if they were interested in the program.

Face to face was the way we communicated, sharing information and opinions. I remember reading that 90 percent of communication is body language. Words alone, as in the text messages sent on telephones today, can be easily misinterpreted if you don't see the other person's nonverbal behavior.

Today I would not think of dropping in on a friend unexpectedly. It is common courtesy to call ahead to see if my friend is home and to ask them whether this is an okay time for me to stop in and visit or could we make a plan to get together on a future date. I think that we had a lot more visitors in the past. Maybe these days they stay home and watch television instead of visiting. And I think that people now wait to get an invitation to visit.

When my family first got a telephone, it was not a direct line for our exclusive use. I wasn't there but I think it might have been a party line with multiple people able to use the same telephone wiring. Each person connected to the line had a unique ring on their phone using a series of long and short rings. Polite people would pick up the phone only when it was their unique ring, but these "party lines" certainly gave people an opportunity for multiple people to talk at the same time, or for unethical people to listen in to another person's conversation.

Calls to a large business, such as the hospital where I worked when young, had to go through a live telephone operator who would plug in the physical connection to the person who could help you. Long distance calls likewise had to go through an operator.

I didn't have my own phone and phone number until I managed a Nurse Consulting Business starting in 1989. The phone I had was a land-line, which was not portable because it was large and had to stay plugged in to the phone line and the electric line. The phone had an answering machine which was essential. If I was out of town or teaching a workshop, I could dial a code to listen to the messages that had been left on the tape for me.

Sweetgrass

I can't remember when I got my own cellphone, but I am pretty sure that it wasn't until after I retired, when I would have been more than seventy years old.

What Did We Use Instead of Telephones?

Nothing was as convenient as cellphones, which use small computer chips and have consolidated many functions that in the past required different devices. There was no way that one person could carry all the items needed to perform the functions that can be done on one smart mobile phone.

To keep information on people we contact we used address books or Rolodex devices.

We wrote our schedules on paper calendars.

Some businesses sent out catalogs that showed pictures and description of items you could buy. Everybody my age remembers ordering their school clothes out of the large Montgomery Ward or Sears Roebuck catalog.

Many brands and styles of cameras were available to take pictures. Most of them used film which had to be developed rather than showing you the picture immediately as is done on the smart phones. I must have begged a lot to get a little Brownie camera that can develop tiny out-of-focus pictures.

Calculators, adding machines, maps, puzzles and all the games you can get on your phone were available for purchase but were not consolidated into one format.

There were radios, phonographs, tape recorders, and maps that would play music, give the news and the weather report, and show you where to go when you are driving.

When we did get phones, they were not "smart" at all. They had only one function and that was to allow a person to listen and talk to another person. The phones were not portable because they were bulky and had to be kept plugged in to both an electric line and a phone line.

After we got phones, large telephone books gave us numbers of people and businesses. We could evaluate the businesses by the ads they placed in the book. Now we have to describe to a robot on the phone what it is that we want her to look up for us.

Today There Is Misuse of Cellphones

Today people send texts by telephone so frequently it is almost like they are having a live talk, but the information can be misunderstood because they are missing most of the communication which is nonverbal.

People having a meal together can neglect eye contact. People sit together at the table, but all are staring at their phones. Teachers have a difficult time teaching because children are paying attention only to their phones.

The last couple of years my insurance agent said that instead of my rate going down because of my safe driving, my rate went up because there was an increase of accidents in my area. The main cause of accidents is because of inattentive driving, meaning that people were paying attention to their telephones when they should have been paying attention to their driving.

World War II Conservation

I didn't plan to write anything about World War II because I was very young and not fully aware of how civilians were affected. I decided this week to write a few notes from memory just because my oldest son was surprised by something I said.

My four uncles were all in the Army. All of them were in active combat, but fortunately none of my uncles were injured or killed in service. My father was not drafted because he was needed by the government as a farmer and had several children.

Even though I was less than six years old I remember a few things.

I remember saving every tiny little piece of string for the war effort.

I remember that the foil from a gum wrapper (which we rarely had) or cigarettes, as well as foil from anything else had to be saved and rolled into a ball.

I remember that many food items were rationed, and you couldn't just go to the store and buy anything you wanted as we do now. Every family was restricted to a certain number of coupons that they had to have to purchase certain items. We ate everything that was served even if it didn't taste great because a lot of substitutes had to be put into cookies and cakes instead of sugar or butter.

My mother learned to conserve paper until it became a habit and every letter I have ever received from her was written on the inside of an envelope that had been sent to her holding a bill. And even then she wrote on every smidgen of the paper, along the sides and top.

Small pieces of paper were never thrown away until both sides had been used.

Pencils were used until worn down to the eraser.

Gifts that were wrapped were opened carefully to avoid tearing the paper, and then that wrapping paper was folded to be used again and again.

Toilet paper was a luxury; any kind of paper could be used if you had an outhouse.

If you ever used food from a can, the can had to be saved for the war effort.

My uncles always wore their uniforms at home when they had a furlough. I thought they looked very handsome in their uniforms. I suppose you have to wear your uniform 24/7 because you could be called up at any time.

I wasn't old enough to know much about WWII, but I was aware that signs and ribbons displayed at houses meant that a family member had lost their life or was missing in action. Some signs just acknowledged that a person from that home was in the armed service.

I am thankful we haven't had a World War since then and I pray that it never happens.

All four of my uncles were active military.

Hannah Lozing Suta

(Homesteader, 1912-1991)
Poem by Bonnie Buckley Maldonato

Montana, Too: A Book of Montana History in Story Poems. Produced by Sweetgrass Books, a Division of Farcountry Press, Helena, Montana, 2007.

Bonnie Buckley attended the One Room Oilfield School shortly before I did. She is Dean-Emeritus of the School of Education at Western New Mexico University.

As a young child,
she and her sisters
tie shocks in the grain fields
as expected by German
immigrant parents.

Alive with ideas,
her green eyes convey
intelligence and a lovely spirit.

She observes the greater value
placed on a man's work,
and knows she can learn
his work as well as hers.

Violet Suta Moran

At age ten, her father sends her
to work as a mother's helper.
So impressed is her employer
that her pay is raised to equal
that of the hired man.

She attends the Border School
through eighth grade,
dreams of becoming a teacher,
but even high school is not
possible for this homestead girl.

She marries affable,
sometimes irascible,
Peter Suta, son
of Hungarian neighbors.

She uses money she has earned
to pay for a blue chiffon dress
and the two-dollar marriage license.

On a farm of their own,
it never occurs to her
that she is pushing
the limits of rural patriarchy.

She picks rock in the fields,
greases farm machinery,
cleans seeder sprockets,
and loses every wedding ring
she tries to wear.

The outdoor work she loves
is done in addition to keeping
her house as shiny as the green
of a new John Deere.

Sweetgrass

She paints her rooms
in happy colors, including
the spotless outhouse.

The food she cans,
cooks, and bakes
is so outstanding
that area salesmen
form the habit
of arriving for dinner.

She carries water to her flowers,
including roses, one a daring red,
in a climate too harsh for a rose.

A champion of children,
her own six are
beloved treasures.
Each, never spanked,
is taught through love
and can read
before entering school.

She knows the right words
to chastise any parent abusing
a child in her presence.

She agrees with her children
that chocolate pie for breakfast
is a good thing, but not poppy tea
used by some homestead mothers
to quiet a baby on wash day.

In later years, Alzheimer's
steals away her mind
and she burns family treasures.

Violet Suta Moran

The integrity of her life
blooms as brightly
as her snow-silvered lilac
on the day of Jerry's farm auction.

Her college-educated children
smile over a mother
who wouldn't have used
the term "feminist" or
"Renaissance woman,"
but was both.

Hannah usually wore only work clothes.

Wild Flowers

Quite a few people who have driven through Montana have told me that it looked like a desert.

As you drive through the dry prairie, you might think that there are no flowers growing on that land, but you would be mistaken. There are not a lot of tall, showy flowers on the dry prairie. It might look as though all the land is brownish dried-up grass unless you get right down to the ground and concentrate your attention on looking for life and tiny flowers in the grass. You have to take your time. The grass growing on the prairie may be the variety named buffalo grass. It is rather short and curly and is well suited to the mouth of the buffalo, animals that can graze close to the ground.

Wildflowers on the prairie.

Lie down flat on the ground on your stomach to see the variety and volume of wild flowers. There is a crowded panorama in the grass. They are not showy, and you would not be able to pick a bouquet because of their short stems. The small flowers are easy to miss because of their light yellow or white colors. There can be several varieties of those tiny flowers even if they have the same color or shades of the same color.

A book on Prairie Wildflowers states that it includes only the "showy wildflowers" of the Plains, Valleys, and Foothills in the Northern Rocky Mountain States, and then proceeds to present photographs and descriptions of 250 of those "showy wildflowers." I'm pretty sure that all 250 varieties are not present on the Suta Farm. But that gives you some idea of the large number of prairie flowers that exist on prairie land even though they may not be readily apparent to the naked eye from a distance.

I will review here only a few of the flowers easily seen on the dry land of our prairie.

Bitterroot

Bitterroot is the State Flower of Montana and grows on the dry prairies with rocky or shallow soil. The blossoms appear just above ground on very short stems. The petals could be pale pink or white to deep rose in color. The blossoms are overlapping and the flower can be from 1 ½ to 3 inches across. The journals of Lewis and Clark note that Indians dug the roots for food in the spring before they became too bitter to eat. Because of this history the botanical name is Lewisia rediviva Pursh.

Crocus

We named a large hill on the prairie west of our house "Crocus Hill" because every spring the entire north side became crowded full of blossoming wild crocus, also known as the pasque flower. That hill had always remained prairie, never plowed. The large sloping hill was very striking when totally covered with purple flowers. Apparently this pasque flower is common in South Dakota where it is designated their state flower.

Crocus flowers.

These crocus resemble the flowers from tamed crocus bulbs you buy at the store but at the same time are very different. They are pale blue to purple in color and remind me a little of tulips. The petals of the flower are more spread out and flat. Unlike the city crocus, a dense coating of fine hairs cover the stems and leaves making it look as though they are warmly wrapped in silver fur. The flower grows close to the ground.

Like the tame crocus, the wild ones push their way out of the soil early in the spring while there is still snow on the ground. They are the first flower of spring on the prairie. Pop always watched closely so that he could be the first in our family to pick a bouquet of crocus. It was a heart-warming sight to see him coming in to the kitchen with a big smile and holding a bouquet of short-stemmed, delicate flowers in his large work-worn hand.

You can buy tame bulbs which produce different colors of crocus, but our wild ones always opened into shades of lavender satin with gold centers and deeper lavender to purple outer edges.

Crocus Hill, as far as I know, was unique in the area where we lived. Crocus certainly grow in other areas, but I never knew of a place with this volume of flowers in one place. Most people near us just farmed all of their land and didn't operate part of it as a ranch so the wild crocus didn't have a chance to grow.

Crocus Hill.

The people who bought our land of The Suta Rock Farm are undoubtedly farming all the land available, including plowing under our rare and beloved Crocus Hill.

All of my family have sentimental memories of the unique beauty of Crocus Hill. My sister Dian and her daughter Nicolette one year pressed some of the flowers and gave each of us a gift of the pressed flowers in a frame under glass.

Lilac Bushes

Lilacs are not listed in this book of prairie wildflowers, but you would think they were growing wild in the city of Sunburst. They apparently are able to withstand poor soil and inadequate water and grew abundantly as shrubbery surrounding almost every yard in Sunburst.

One year our entire school gymnasium was covered in lilacs for Prom. That was a beautiful decoration but a very strong scent.

Prairie Roses

Prairie Roses could be found growing wild in unexpected places. I found many growing on the dams of our reservoirs. They grow close to the ground with a single row of petals, two or three inches across, that spread out almost flat and overlapping. They don't look like roses in the floral shop, but they have a better scent, clearly recognizable as a rose scent. They were usually a light pink, but I have seen some that are bright pink and they all seem to become white with age. Whenever I found them I would lay on the ground to smell them. Then I would pick a few petals to rub between my palms to intensify the scent and then rub the petals where I would apply a perfume on my body.

They produce a scent that is stronger and more pleasant than any rose-scented perfume or lotion you might buy. I have never found anything to compare. Most of the roses grown in a hothouse do not have much scent at all.

I have seen roses that resemble wild Prairie Roses growing on shrubs in the city, but I have never seen wild rose shrubs on the dry prairie. These shrubs are definitely not those of the common rose bushes. The flat petals and the pure rose scent are more similar to the prairie roses growing low to the ground.

Prickly Pear Cactus

The Prickly Pear Cactus is most abundant on the prairies of Montana. There are at least three species. Those growing on our land differed from the species photographed in the book of wildflowers. Our cactus grew only a foot or two tall but had beautiful purple blossoms and terrible, long stickers.

Shooting Stars

Shooting Stars are my favorite flower and I know they are loved by many people. They are delicate and striking in gorgeous shades of pink or magenta petals with yellow and black stamens. The stamens come to a point prompting the flower to also be named Bird Bills. The blossoms point downward as though they are the bill of a bird or a rocket with wings coming toward earth, being led by the striated yellow and purple point. There may be several blossoms on one stem. They tend to grow where the land is wet.

The only place wet enough on our land was around our former water well. That is where we had to pump water when I was a child. Sometimes even one of my brothers would pick a small bouquet of shooting stars.

I get excited when I see them unexpectedly sticking out from between rocks above a stream in Glacier Park. They are mainly found in western Alberta going down into California, and maybe also into the mountains of New Mexico.

It was a wonderful surprise to see a crowded 6x4 foot bed of Shooting Stars blooming in Iceland and I have a prized photograph of that.

I have thought about getting a Shooting Star tattoo, but I don't think the artist could do it justice.

Scents

The air on the prairie has a very fresh and clean smell with no pollutants as in a city.

There is what I just consider a "green" scent to the prairie, especially after a rain. It is the pure and refreshing scent of ozone. You could smell this green scent when you visit a nursery where plants are grown, there you are also smelling the moist soil. It resembles the smell of mowing your lawn. Likewise when cutting hay on the farm the scent will resemble that of mowing your lawn, but it varies depending what grain is being cut for hay. Alfalfa has a sweet, distinctive smell.

During harvest time you will notice the scent of the grain. Bruised kernels of wheat during harvest have a scent similar to bread. Harvesting mustard seeds produces a sharp, pungent scent like putting your nose over a jar of the condiment. Chaff irritates your nostrils and may also have an odor, and the fine pieces will impregnate your clothing.

Only a few of the wild flowers have a noticeable scent. Wild roses are an exception.

You can notice the smell of rain coming as well as feel changes in the air. I would describe it as a clean scent and feel of humidity.

If you are driving on graveled or dirt roads on the prairie, you can see the "dust clouds" raised by your vehicle and you can also notice the "dusty" smell. "Dusty" dirt smells different than wet dirt which may have a scent of richness. I think I have been developing an allergic response to dust which makes me sneeze a lot and makes my eyes feel scratchy. Not only do I notice this with the dusty roads in Montana, but I also notice it with old books.

Odors of the prairie change with the seasons and with your location, but you can almost always smell sage. Sage is a soft green color and is a common plant growing wild on the prairie. It is a very hardy and bushy plant and grows wild on even the driest prairie land. The scent is stronger but similar to that of the sage seasoning commonly used in turkey stuffing.

Sage is one of the plants that make a cow's milk taste bad. Other wild plants that adversely affect the taste of milk are milkweed, wild garlic ("ramps" treasured in Vermont), and wild mustard. If just one cow in a herd of dairy cattle eats these plants, the strong flavor of that cow's milk will taint the entire volume of milk collected from the dairy herd and all will have to be discarded.

Another strong offensive odor I have noticed is when a field of green peas is being harvested. The scent is stronger than that of pig manure.

There are people who buy a plot of land outside of a city and then complain about the odors of the animals who had already been living on the next plot of land. It should be expected that farms generally have some type of animal and that will result in the smell of manure, and the smell of manure is stronger from some animals than others and stronger if the animals are numerous and their housing is not kept clean. But it is impossible to completely prevent the scent of manure when raising animals.

The smell of the animals on our farm didn't bother me except when we were raising a pig or two. They were kept

Sweetgrass

in the corral by the barn west of our house and the wind often came from the west.

When my brothers were cleaning out the barn, they piled the manure behind the barn. That pile of manure sort of crusted over and did not exude the odor of manure. My brother Ben made good use of that manure by planting mushrooms. And our entire family was thankful for that.

Anybody who grew up in the fifties remembers the prevalent scent of Noxzema. Noxzema cream was supposed to make zits go away so all the teenagers washed their faces with it and then applied a layer of the cream over their zits or over their entire face. A lot of older women used it as a face cream even though they didn't have any zits. They apparently thought it would take away or prevent wrinkles and make them look as young as teenagers.

Another common scent was that of Chanel #5,which every boyfriend bought for his girlfriend. And the girls used it liberally wanting everybody to know that they had this cologne—and boyfriend.

Sounds on the Farm

There are always crickets chirping in the evening. They make a chorus with the frogs. Swallows build their nests on the buildings and are always busy feeding and talking to their babies, as are robins and other birds. We raised chickens, and they were always clucking. There is a distinctive cluck made after a hen lays an egg. In the summertime we added 350 baby chickens that were "peeping." The rooster may crow all day long, not just in the morning to wake everyone. Other fowl being raised make their own sound, e.g., the ducks and geese quacking. All the animals being raised on the farm make the sounds of their species, e.g., the cows mooing and the pigs grunting.

When the farm was active we could hear the sound of the tractor or the combine, whatever machine was being used on the fields. Sometimes the fields were too far away for us to hear the motors.

We could hear coyotes howling at night and had to be vigilant that we didn't have a sick calf or other animal susceptible to being killed by the coyotes. They became almost extinct in the 1980s because of sheepherders poisoning them to protect the sheep and lambs In the 1990s they began to come back.

If we had people picking rocks in the fields, they would come back to the coulee or the reservoir dam to empty the rocks off the full truck. Hildegard's motor makes a distinctive noise and then there is the sound of the rocks hitting each other as they roll off the truck bed. From the house we could also hear the rock pickers talking and laughing.

If it was harvest time, there would be a truck coming back to the granary with a full load of grain and you can hear the loud motor. The truck would back up to the granary and then the noise of the auger would start, grinding as it carries grain to the top of the granary.

In later years we heard the noise of a snowmobile that Pop bought to travel around the pasture inspecting the cattle. In the summer there would be a similar noise from the riding lawn mower also used to inspect the cattle and finally save wear and tear on the cars and trucks. Pop loved to give small grandchildren rides on these machines. Older grandchildren were sometimes allowed to drive the machines.

There were noises from all of the animals on our farm. You could ask a young child to make those sounds for you. Don't forget sounds made by the birds.

Needless to say there was also noise made by the people talking, laughing and hollering at one another.

Animals on Our Farm

Our farm was primarily a dry-land wheat farm, but we also raised cattle to supplement income. Most of the time we had about forty white-faced Hereford cows with one bull.

Of course there were also wild animals on our farm.

When we four children were young we milked two cows by hand, getting milk for our own use and cream that we could make into butter and sell to the grocery store in Sunburst. Some of the cats would come around hoping they might have some milk squirted in their direction and they would catch it in their mouths. I never liked milk very well, but I liked putting the thickened cream that rose to the top of the container on top of my cold cereal.

The cattle grazed on grass on the prairie and were given hay during the winter. When the reservoir froze over, Pop had to go out in the worst weather often more than once a day to chop holes through the ice to make water available.

Every year we were able to slaughter one of the steers for our own food.

Usually all of the cows had calves in the spring, around Easter when it usually was still cold. If a calf looked weak Pop would carry it into the house and lay it on gunny sacks in front of the coal stove. Usually that heat and rest were enough to revive them in a day. Mom might give the calf a little milk by a bottle. Calving time was always busy. Pop would check the cows every hour or two around the clock when one seemed ready to give birth. He didn't want a cow to have a medical emergency without prompt care. Cows and calves were worth a lot of money.

Mom and Pop with our cattle.

Pop always tamed his bulls so that he could go right up to them. He thought it was funny to stick his butt in front of the bull's face and let the bull shove him with its head without injuring him with its horns. He should have taught the bull other good behavior. One year the bull broke into the pasture where we had cows that weren't old enough to have calves until the following year. There were a lot of difficult births that year, but the worst happened when I was home from nursing school one weekend.

The cow was young, and the calf was in breach position, feet first instead of head first. They could both die. The closest vet was forty-five minutes away and this happened several years before we had a telephone. We weren't able to do a C-section. Pop was frantically trying to pull the calf out and the sweat was pouring off his face. He was upset and started cursing and hollering at me, "God dammit haven't you learned anything in that nursing school yet," and "You should have damned well learned this by now." and more in that vein. He finally chained the cow's head to a fence post, wrapped chains on the calf and pulled it out with a tractor. I definitely had not learned that in nursing school!! It was terrible but both the cow and calf survived with a little nursing care from me and Mom. I was always amazed at Pop's creativity. If you live in an isolated rural place like we did you have to figure out how to do things yourself.

We also raised one or two pigs every year for their meat. They were fed "slop" which was good leftovers from our meals or food we couldn't keep because we did not have refrigeration. These foods were tossed into a "slop bucket" in the kitchen which was emptied at least once a day and washed out to prevent odors. They were also given grain to eat. Pop liked to fatten up the pig before it was slaughtered for us to eat. We kids usually left some fat on our plate and Pop would snatch it with his fork to eat. It wasn't a surprise that he had to have heart surgery when he was older.

We had a ranch but with no horses because Pop disliked them. He had a history with horses. While courting Mom, he took a horse to visit her about eight miles away on a winter day. The horse slipped and fell on top of Pop, breaking his leg and pinning him down. One foot was caught in a stirrup and the horse was pulling him around in a circle. By the time his brother Rudy came looking for him Pop had developed pneumonia. This was before antibiotics were developed so Pop was very sick and blamed all his suffering on the horse. And he held a grudge against all horses. His brother Rudy said, "It wasn't the fault of the horse but that damn stupid fool who took a horse out riding in bad winter conditions." For the rest of his life Pop drove his pickup or car on the pasture to check on the cattle. The prairie was very hard on vehicles, especially when he drove twenty-five or thirty miles per hour over rocks and holes and ditches, but he would rather replace a car than get a horse. In later life he got a snowmobile and a lawn tractor to drive around the pasture and also to entertain grandchildren.

Sweetgrass

At night we could sometimes hear coyotes howling. That's another reason why it was important to check our cattle every day. We needed to remove and care for an animal that was disabled or ill before coyotes might kill them.

We hated weasels that grew around the dam of the reservoir. They have a pointy ugly face and a long, narrow, flexible body which allows them to sneak into a chicken house through a very small opening. We always closed the chicken coop at night, but weasels could still squeeze in if they wanted to. They are vicious and bloodthirsty murderers that will invade the chicken coop and proceed to kill every chicken just for the fun of killing but not for food. We kept a rooster with the chickens to fertilize eggs, but we also counted on him to make noise in case of danger. The weasels always invaded during the night. Mom's bedroom window was fairly close to the chicken coop, so she ought to be able to hear a ruckus. But I remember one year when the weasels killed the rooster as well as every chicken in the coop and Mom didn't hear a thing. Weasels are so sneaky and devious that we didn't bother trying to kill them. We couldn't poison them without also poisoning some of our domestic animals.

Wild animals were not obvious because they naturally have colors that blend in to their surroundings. Prairie hens and the female pheasants were dull brown like the earth. Our ring-necked pheasants were all killed off by pesticides, mainly DDT, that had been used to kill weeds in the grain fields. When we put our farm into the CRP program we stopped using any pesticides. Pop missed the animals that were no longer running around the farm. As gifts on his eightieth birthday my brothers Ben and Henry gave him pheasants to try to re-start them on the land. That made Pop very happy. But a couple of years later he didn't see a pheasant on the farm and made the assumption that they had all been killed by predators. Maybe it was residual pesticide.

The men used to shoot wild ducks that would come to our reservoir. Our dog Fido was not a very good retriever if the duck fell into the water. These wild ducks were small birds, so they were shot with shotguns. Mom and I quickly got tired of digging out buckshot and declared that we would no longer clean any wild ducks. The men could practice their shooting skills on the large gophers growing on the prairie. Shooting at the gophers was a little like a game of skeet shooting .

Pop and his brother Rudy said they played hooky when they were kids and spent a lot of time snaring gophers. Gophers were tricky because they always had more than one hole to enter and exit their home beneath the earth. You had to tie a slipknot in your string and place it above the gopher's hole. When the gopher poked its head out of the hole you had to pull the string and catch it around the neck very quickly. I don't know the success rate of snaring. One of our country school teachers, Beth Volbrecht, loved all animals but allowed the boys to snare gophers during recess as long as they promised to kill the gopher quickly with no tormenting. They never caught a gopher anyway.

Our rabbits did not look like the cute, fluffy bunny rabbits shown in Easter pictures. Ours were huge and resembled the shape and color of a greatly overgrown gopher or an ugly antelope. These jackrabbits were common on the prairie. Making fun of them are postcards on sale that picture a "Montana Jackalope." The pictures are stupid merging a rabbit and antelope, but the jackrabbits honestly were almost that large.

We rarely had a wild dog come around to our farm but feral cats came frequently. It was good to have cats around to kill mice and prevent rats. We had mice, but I never saw a rat on our farm. When we were kids we often found a bed of kittens and played with them until they became too wild and fought us.

One time cousin Louis Suta was at our place and my brothers took all of us into the hay loft to see a new litter of kittens. Louis tormented them by poking their eyes with a piece of straw. Eventually he killed all of them by wringing their necks. It seemed as though he was really enjoying himself and the four of us just watched. We didn't approve and none of us would have ever done that, but we didn't say anything because Louie was a big bully and would have fought or mercilessly made fun of the person who tried to stop him.

Pop once thought there were too many cats around our place. I don't know why it bothered him because we didn't feed them. Pop wanted us to put the kittens in a gunny sack and drown them. We refused so he was going to do it himself. Mom kept us kids in the house so we wouldn't see Pop killing the kittens. Quite a bit of time went by, and she went outside to see if he was done so she could turn us loose again. She found Pop near the barn where the kittens had been, sitting on the ground and playing with the kittens. He never did drown them.

In his later years Pop fed forty-two feral cats, some of which he partially tamed. He bought dog food for them because it was less expensive than cat food and served it in a large tractor tire cut in half.

Google identifies twenty-six varieties of birds living on the prairie, but they are not very visible. They could hide even though we didn't have trees. Probably the most common were swallows that built their nests of mud on all the buildings. There also were many robins who laid their tiny blue eggs in a nest on the ground where our dog or some other animal would eat them. Meadowlarks charmed us with their beautiful song. I wondered why so many seagulls lived on our dry prairie more than a thousand miles from an ocean. My brother Ben, who was always a joker, said that some of them had been too lazy to move when the ocean water was receding. Google says that these birds are "gulls" but not really seagulls. They like to live in Montana and North Dakota, where they follow the farmer's plow eating worms, insects, and mice as they are uncovered by the plow.

Crows and hawks were fairly common and probably ate carrion to sustain life. Mom thought all hawks were "chicken hawks" intent on capturing our chickens in their claws. When she saw hawks she would holler at Ted to grab a shotgun and get those chicken hawks. Ted says that he just waited until the hawks moved away by themselves, and they never did steal one of our chickens.

We saw bald eagles flying overhead with their majestic long wingspan, but we didn't have any place high enough for them to build a nest.

I guess I forgot to mention the undesirable skunks and very, very large mosquitoes.

After our land was no longer actively farmed and we stopped using pesticides, the grass grew lush and green. Then birds and animals started to return to the land where they had always lived. Antelope and white-tailed deer began to hang out on the land. I often saw them jumping in the field where the grass or hay that had been planted was growing high. That was a beautiful sight.

Whitetail deer.

Branding Day

Branding was not a happy time for those on the receiving end but I remember it as an exciting day when I was a child expecting visitors and lots of action on our Montana ranch. Branding animals is necessary so they can be identified and returned to the proper owner when they break out of the fence and wander away, or if stolen by a cattle rustler as still happens once in a while.

I knew that we would have visitors; definitely Grandpa Lozing, Mom's brother Gilbert; maybe Pop's brother Kalman, maybe Uncle Bill and sometimes other relatives or neighbors. In addition we often had high school boys who did summer work on our farm. Uncle Rudy and Aunt Margaret always came around noon for dinner but never helped with anything except providing entertaining conversation.

First thing to do was to herd the calves from the pasture into a corral. We didn't have a large herd of cattle because they were supplemental or a backup to our farming. We had a small herd of usually forty cows and one bull and we expected all of the cows to have calves. The forty calves had to be cut out of the herd, separating them from their mother and they weren't willing to leave her side. We all worked to do this. Pop chased the cattle in his pickup truck or car, refusing to use a horse because of a bad history with one horse. All the rest of us were on foot, running and shouting and waving our arms with a couple of dogs barking, the cattle mooing and Pop blowing his horn. This was dusty work in our dry-land country.

Most calves were the same size, about two months old in June, controlled by when Pop put the bull in the pasture with the cows. Sometimes the bull took control himself, breaking through the fence to reach the cows and he might impregnate heifers less than two years old who would end up having difficult births. As a result, there might be a few calves that were younger or older than the others and the young ones also had to be separated out from the others.

I would climb up and perch on the top of the corral to watch the action. I saw Teddy, Henry and Benny, my older brothers, pick out one calf and all run after it, trying to trap it into a corner so they could get a rope around its neck. I thought it was funny when the calf kept escaping from their grasp and they had to continue running around the corral. Pop would get impatient and yell at the boys "Get that goddamn calf over here," as if they weren't trying to do that.

My brothers were glad when Uncle Gilbert relieved them. Gilbert was Mom's brother and a real cowboy who could lasso the calves instead of chasing them around the corral. Gilbert looked like the Marlborough Man, a television ad of a cowboy riding a horse and smoking a Marlborough. The difference was that Gilbert had a real cattle ranch with horses, rolled his own cigarettes, and always had a Bull Durham tag hanging out of his shirt pocket.

Once a calf was caught, it was thrown down onto its side. It was held in place with one person leaning back on the rope around its neck and another person sitting down at the rear, using his feet to push the bottom leg forward and leaning back with the top leg in his hands. The man at the rear got kicked and shit upon. As the day went on, the straw he had to sit on became more and more soiled and I tried to throw in some fresh hay once in a while. This was one time I was glad to be different than my brothers because my job was to help in the house instead of holding down a calf.

Pop always did the branding himself, knowing the brand would be visible to anybody and wanting it to look good. The hot branding iron had to be held in place just the right amount of time to scorch the brand permanently onto the leather hide. If the iron wasn't held flat for a long enough time, then hair would grow back on the hide and obliterate the brand. Making a perfect brand wasn't easy with the calf bucking and moving despite being held.

The temperature of the branding iron was a critical factor in making a good brand. If the iron was too hot it would burn too deeply into the skin and could start a fire that might disfigure the brand, When the iron was not hot enough it had to be held in place a longer time, making the brand messy as the calf didn't lay still for this. Pop would get very upset if the branding iron wasn't the right temperature to make the brand look perfect.

Heating the irons was a special skill taken very seriously by Grandpa Lozing. He had to tend the fire carefully to have hot coals without too much flame and he had to move the irons around to get them heated just right. We had several branding irons for each letter, so they could be moved around to have one at the right temperature when Pop was ready to apply a brand.

Our brand was "lazy T H bar" placed on the upper right rib area with the capital T lying lazily on its left side, followed by a capital H and both underlined with a bar. Pop registered this brand at the State capital honoring his first two sons, Ted and Henry. As my brother Ben said, "The cattle are lucky we weren't all six children born yet."

Usually about twenty of the calves were male and had to be castrated so they would grow bigger and have tender meat. After castration, they were considered "steers" and would not behave like "bulls" around the young female heifers. Cutting out the testicles was the specialty of Uncle Kalman and he liked to fry and eat them. As he came into the house carrying a pan of freshly-removed testicles he would holler to Mom, "Hannah, here's a pan of Rocky Mountain Oysters you can fry up." Mom would holler back in her sometimes colorful language, "You can cook your own God damn balls but don't expect any help from me. And you'd better not ruin my frying pan."

None of us joined Uncle Kalman in eating this rare gourmet delicacy. I've heard this occasionally appears on the menu in high-class restaurants, especially in France, with a description vague enough to keep customers ignorant of their origin. I still wonder what they taste like.

According to Google, Rocky Mountain Oysters have a gamey quality, like breaded venison. Early ranchers started eating them because they needed inexpensive food. These could come from bulls, bison, pigs, or sheep. Most commonly referred to as oysters because of their slimy appearance when raw, some other names used are cowboy caviar, prairie oysters, swinging beef, Montana tender groins, and bollocks.

When Kalman wasn't around to do the castration Pop would do that in addition to branding and vaccination. The vaccine was given in the soft part of the bend of the leg and prevented three diseases, including brucellosis, blackleg, and something else.

The noise of the day continued until everything was done. The calves were bawling for their mothers who were bellowing back. Pop was shouting and cussing about everything and at everybody. Those not holding down a calf were busy trying to catch the next, chasing around the corral and yelling. Corral gates were being quickly banged open and closed. The pungent smell of fresh manure was mingled with the acrid smell of the burning hair and hide. Dilute Lysol poured into the castration wound as a disinfectant added its own scent.

Calves were contracted for sale to a Jewish buyer who would come around in the summer. Older cows were sold at the auction sale in Shelby or to local stores. Raleigh White would come out from his grocery store in Sunburst to shoot and dress an old dry cow on the range. Tough meat for tough customers.

This entire process would be repeated a few days later at Gilbert and Grandpa's place about ten miles away. That was always a longer day since they had over 100 head of cattle. Mom and I would have to cook both dinner and supper for everybody in addition to morning and afternoon work breaks.

My brother Henry remembers me as a young girl bringing morning break out to the corral for the men, probably cookies and an icy thermos of Kool-Aid, only to be scared and chased by the mama cows who were mad as hell at everybody for hurting their babies.

Post-operatively the castrated calves had to be checked every couple hours for the first two days to see if they were bleeding or developing an infection. The poor things could hardly stand and walk but we had to chase them and make them move in order to assess their health. We counted them carefully to be sure there wasn't a weak, sick one lying down behind a hill. We rarely saw a complication but vigilance was always necessary.

We maintain a sense of nostalgia for this ritual of branding because it was a day different from all the other routine days. And also because the brand represents the farm that we loved. My sister took the retired branding irons to display on the wall of her kitchen. My son Buzz had the "lazy T H bar" tattooed on his upper arm. Pop asked, "Why the hell did he get a tattoo; I could have done it with the real branding iron."

Violet Suta Moran

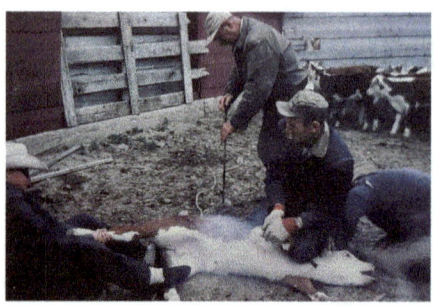

Manure by Mark Seeley

I hope there's manure in Heaven I know that sounds a bit strange But some folks might agree with me If I'm given the chance to explain

Now by outward appearance, manure Is a smelly goo, no doubt. But think about what went into that cow Before that manure came out

That cow might have grazed in a pasture Filled with clover and grass green and lush And that sweet smelling pasture on which that cow dined Was transformed to this foul smelling mush.

Or maybe she dined with a range herd On a wide open prairie somewhere Making meals of scattered bunchgrass And leaving a pile here and there

That cow might have grazed in the mountains Beneath pine trees that whisper and sigh And the grass and wild flowers from meadows Are contained in that cow's special pie.

So I hope there's manure in Heaven Cause that means there'll be cows when we die And pastures and prairies and meadows Beneath mountains that reach toward the sky.

Haying

When I was very young hay was cut by a sickle mower. Rakers gathered the hay straw into windrows (a row of cut hay) where air could dry the crop. Prior to using a machine to cut the hay, people cut the stalks by hand using a long curved knife named a scythe but we didn't do that.

Hay was left to dry for a while because wet grain could develop mildew and that could make the livestock sick. Dried hay was picked up by "pitchforks" and tossed onto the back of a truck. A pitchfork has four or five long forks that could stab into a bunch of hay. When the truck was full it was driven to the barn where the hay could be thrown by pitchfork into the hay loft. Another person or two would stand inside the hayloft to toss the hay back further into the loft, stacking the loft full of hay. Old barns have large open spaces cut into the front to allow hay to be tossed in for storage and out for the cattle to eat.

Soon there were machines that would cut the hay and gather a bunch of stalks together into a sheaf, tying the sheaf with binder twine. These machines were called reaper-binders. The bunch of individual hay stalks form a sheaf, or plurally were called sheaves of hay. As a child I participated in gathering about five to eight sheaves or bundles and standing them upright with the seed heads or fuzzy parts on the tips of hay standing at the top. Leaning these sheaves together allows air to circulate around the standing

Pop and his brothers shocking hay when they were young.

Putting hay bales into the hayloft of the barn.

sheaves and dries the grain. Doing this gathering of sheaves is called sheaving or shocking. Many people call this simply part of the process of "Haying."

The grain was ripe when it was cut for hay, but it still contained a lot of moisture which would be a problem if all the hay was put together in a haystack. If the hay contained moisture it might develop mold during the winter. Also chemical processes inside the haystack might cause combustion and the entire haystack would suddenly burst into flame.

When the sheaves of hay were dry, they had to be thrown up from the ground onto the back of a truck, and then they were unloaded by hand into the hayloft of the barn. You can see a large opening on one end of older barns which allowed the hay to be thrown from the truck into the hayloft. Someone had to be inside the hayloft to keep moving the new hay toward the back of the loft.

I don't know when it was changed to stack hay onto a free-standing haystack rather than into the barn. And now the hay is gathered into bales and tied.

When the cattle were unable to graze on grass in the winter, someone (usually Pop) would have to climb on top of the haystack and cut the binder-twine off a sheaf or bale before throwing the hay down for the cattle to eat. You wouldn't want to leave a piece of the twine on because the cows might eat that along with the hay. The twine would stay in their stomach and make them sick. Pop would also have to use an ax to chop holes in the ice on the reservoirs for the cattle to be able to drink.

The Old Testament and a hymn talk about "Bringing in the Sheaves." The imagery is to encourage believers to share the Gospel with others. The idea is that one day believers (sheaves) will come before the Lord, bringing others with them with whom they shared the Gospel, thus the metaphor of *bringing in the sheaves*.

In 1947 we got a J.I. Case baler that was a three-man operation. Pop drove the tractor, Ted punched wires to form the bales and Henry or Benny tied the knots. The puncher and the person tying knots sat on the back of the baler working in a blizzard of chaff. It took a while for the boys to convince Pop that he should replace the machine because they were so miserable. Then it took a while for Pop to replace this machine because it wasn't bothering him.

Years later we had a baling machine that cut the hay, gathered it into a hard rectangular bale and tied it. These bales could be forty to 100 pounds each and had to be tossed from the ground onto the bed of a truck. It is very hard work to lift a weight from the ground to above your head. Pop tended to make them large, but he didn't have the hardest job of lifting those bales. Young men all found it hard work to lift those bales, but Mom could still lift bales from the ground onto the back of the truck while in her sixties. Pop would stand on the truck bed to grab each bale and stack them. Pop knew a specific way to place the hay bales so they wouldn't fall off the end of the truck. Pop also knew how to stack the bales on the haystack so that the haystack would not collapse or have bales fall off. He probably also knew a method to allow circulation of air to prevent spoilage.

For many years after their sons moved away, this was a Mom and Pop operation with Mom tossing bales from the ground up onto the truck where Pop would grab and stack them.

The thought that Mom could do this amazes me because women do not have the upper-body strength that men have. And Mom was not a very large person. But she always did a lot of hard work. In later years Pop hired young Hutterite men from the Colony across the road to do this lifting.

Today in 2025 on other farms the hay is baled into very large round bales which can be left in the field because of good keeping qualities. Haying now doesn't require very much physical labor. Of course it would become easier after we no longer had cattle or sheep on the farm.

Ford Fairlaine

A true story written by my friend Sara Williams

In the summer of 1961, my sister Susie had just married and gone on to a new life with her husband. Mama had been home from a psychiatric hospitalization and shock treatments for about four months. Dad was farming as well as working for the Federal Land Bank as a farm loan officer. I was drifting the current between high school graduation and the start of college. I had a lot of freedom to take Mom's red and white Ford Fairlane into the town of Klamath Falls, Oregon, where I hung out with my girlfriends, dragging Main Street and stopping for burgers at our favorite drive-in, Rob's Big Boy.

On one such evening, I drove home to the farm in a thunderstorm, watching streaks of lightening split the sky. When I arrived at our large circular farm yard and pulled into the garage, I was greeted by Sherrie, our golden collie. Sherrie hated storms. She was trembling with fear but I knew Mom wouldn't allow her in the house so I petted her, trying to calm her down. Then I got the idea to leave the car door open so the dome light would comfort Sherrie. I was pleased with my idea as I went into the house to bed.

The next morning, Dad came into my room before he left for work. "Indian, you left the car door open and ran down the battery. I jumped the battery, started the car and left a stick under the brake and over the gas pedal. I want you to get up and take the car into town to get the battery charged." Well, okay.

I was still a little sleepy when I got in the car and backed out of the garage. I saw the stick under the brake and over the gas pedal. I left it there. When I stepped on the brake, I heard the sound of gravel flying and I realized I was going even faster in reverse. "Oh my god, I'm having brake failure!" I floor-boarded the brake. The next thing I knew, the car was perched precariously on top of a haystack beside the barn, a cloud of dust was rising from the big farm driveway and sheep were scattering in all directions through a downed section of corral fence. Stunned and shaky, I tried to open the car door, but it was stuck. I tried the passenger door. It opened so I got out and slid down the haystack. I had no idea how this happened.

Mother was washing dishes, looking out the kitchen window when she heard the sound of gravel and saw the dust cloud. She thought, "I told that girl not to peel out of the driveway like that!" Then the cloud began to disperse, and she saw the car just as I emerged climbing down the haystack. She hurried out to meet me. Halfway across the farmyard she started laughing.

When she laughed, I started laughing. We stood together staring at the car, watching the sheep wander off. Every time she tried to ask me what happened, laughter stopped her speech. Finally she gasped, "Oh my, I've wet my pants!" Just then the mailman came down the road by the house, nearly hitting the mailbox as he saw the car. The few cars or pickups on the road slowed down, drivers staring in astonishment.

Mother went into the house to call Dad but when he answered his office phone, all she could get out was his name before laughter took over. Mother was not known for her sense of humor and Dad just heard, "Bryant!" followed by

Sweetgrass

what must have sounded like hysteria. She tried several times to tell him what happened but couldn't get the words out.

Dad jumped into his pick-up and hurried the twelve miles from town to our farm. His mind was racing, imagining that Mother had totally snapped. When he got to the farm, all he could do was shake his head repeating, "Holy Moses, Holy Moses!" Finally he asked me, "Why didn't you take out that stick from under the brake and over the gas pedal." Sheepishly I replied, "I thought you put it there for a reason so I left it." At that point, I realized what had happened.

One of the neighbors helped Dad get the car off the haystack and into town for repair. I had to call the insurance agent to give a report. The clerk made me repeat many parts of the story because she couldn't stop laughing. Everyone who heard this found it hilarious—everyone but Dad. He never scolded me but he never laughed either. He just shook his head. We were all aware of the old pipes stacked on a stand beside the barn which would have impaled me had I been a foot closer to the barn.

Less than a month later, I went swimming with friends at a community pool about twenty miles away. Mother was out of town staying with friends in a cabin at Lake of the Woods. I was to pick her up the next day. Driving home from the pool, enjoying soft serve ice cream dipped in chocolate from the Dairy Queen, I noticed the red oil light was shining brightly. When I got home, I woke Dad to ask him what to do before I went to get Mother.

"Put oil in 'er before you leave. You've seen me put oil in the pick-up." So the next morning, I turned the crank on the oil barrel in Dad's shop to fill his old oilcan. Things got a little confusing when I popped the hood of the car. It didn't look like the pick-up. Finally I saw a cap labeled "oil," opened it and poured in the dark engine oil. Satisfied, I washed my hands and headed for town. The damned oil light was still on and I knew Dad was away visiting farms for the day. I stopped at the first service station on the edge of town and told my story to the mechanic. He opened the hood, looking at me dubiously while he pointed at various places and asked, "Lady, is this where you put the oil?" I felt my confidence slide away.

Turns out I'd put engine oil into the automatic transmission. The whole transmission had to be taken apart, cleaned and drained, and engine oil replaced with lighter automatic transmission oil. For a second time that summer, Dad shook his head. He kept saying, "I never even thought of that." Again he didn't scold but he must have breathed a sigh of relief at the summer's end when he and Mom drove me to college in that red and white Ford Fairlane.

Cooking with Mom

"Well, of course I planned my delivery route so I'd be at your farm for dinner," laughed the man who delivered gas to the tanks on our farm, when, as a teenager, I accused him of that. He continued, "I could always count on Pete to invite me in and your mother was the best cook on that route. Hell, she was the best cook on any of my routes."

Mom had started cooking at a young age. From age nine or ten she was sent out to live on other farms, where she worked as a Mother's Helper to earn money to help her father support the family. I was never sent out to another family to work as a Mother's Helper, but I sure was a helper to my own Mother from my earliest days.

Mom did a lot of cooking with my help while making three large meals every day for a family of six kids. Summer farm work then added as many as four hired men to the table. Family, neighbors and, of course, salesmen of various types, often dropped in unexpectedly during those days before we had a telephone. If we were cooking and noticed a clearly visible cloud of dust coming in our one-and one-half mile dirt driveway, Mom would tell me to peel more potatoes and maybe add another vegetable to the pot. Since we were already cooking a large quantity, we could always stretch a meal to include any number of surprise guests.

Most of the time we could identify the vehicle coming our way and then we would know how many people to expect and whether they were big eaters. Each brand of car in those days was distinctly different from others, unlike today when it is hard to tell one from another.

If the potatoes were boiled or cooking in with a roast I would add one medium potato for each person. Mashed potatoes required more potatoes per person. If the vegetable was carrots, I would add two large ones for each person. These additions might have to be started to cook at a high temperature to catch up with the food already cooking. Because we canned a lot of foods, we could open a jar of another vegetable or add fruit to dessert. We had time to get the meal ready because there would be time spent with people greeting each other. Greetings would take place in the porch and the first part of the kitchen, not interfering with the work area of the kitchen.

We served our meals family style with a bowl or platter of food being passed around and each person helping themselves. We children served ourselves and were expected to take only what we could eat. We weren't forced to clean everything off our plate, although we usually did. We weren't forced to eat any food we didn't like but we weren't given special substitutes.

Sometimes my brothers couldn't wait for the food to be passed and they might reach across the table or even stand to be able to reach the food they wanted. When we had company they behaved with better manners.

We ate the organ meats of kidney and heart with stuffing. Our Hungarian grandparents had a smokehouse to make ham and sausages. They cleaned the intestines to be stuffed with seasoned ground meat mixture and smoked for sausage. Grandma Suta also made a mixture called "head cheese" which was a seasoned mixture of meats stuffed into the cleaned cavity of the cow's head and was eaten as a cold meat after it was cured.

My mother was complimented frequently on her cooking, and she deserved accolades, but it was usually not acknowledged that I was cooking right alongside her. Most of the time it would have been impossible to identify which of us had cooked something because we shared responsibilities from my earliest childhood. Mom was smart enough to just gradually give me assignments that were increasingly difficult. I was little when I set the table, helped clear off the dirty dishes, and dried dishes.

Because I gradually took more responsibility I cannot say exactly when I learned to cook, but I know for sure that I cooked entire meals when I was eight years old. And that was using a coal stove. Mom had some sort of abdominal surgery and in those days patients were told to stay on bed rest for six weeks. Mom would think of menus and give instructions from her bed on how to cook things like roasts.

I know for sure that we were still using the coal stove because I let the fire go out one day while the mid-day meal was only about half cooked. It was a good thing that this happened in the middle of summer and not when it was the busiest time of the year, such as harvest time. I expected Pop's volatile temper to erupt but he just told me very sternly to never let this happen again.

I shared all chores with Mom except I knew I wasn't strong enough to chop the heads off chickens or to punch down a large batch of dough for bread.

I usually had to wash the dishes, but occasionally during the winter when the boys weren't doing much outdoor work, Mom tried to spread the assignment around. We had to laugh that one of us kids would invariably have to go to the outhouse with what we called "dishpan cramps" or "dishpan trots."

We always had a limited supply of water, and I realize now that our dishes were not very hygienic after being washed in a small basin of soapy water and rinsed in a small amount of water. If the person wiping dishes found some food still on a plate, Mom would say that you were doing a poor job if you couldn't wipe off a little food.

Doing dishes was enjoyable if we had a lot of company because all the women gathered in our large kitchen to share the work and a lot of laughs. The men went into the living room and napped on the sofas and chairs or else went outside and did something.

We had an advantage in cooking well because all of our food was grown on the farm.

Mom baked bread at least once or twice a week. She insisted on buying Canadian flour, only about eight miles away as the crow flies but a drive of fifteen miles on a winding, narrow graveled road, usually in poor condition. She felt strongly that Canadian flour made better bread and bought large sacks of flour. I think they were 100 pounds. I have learned that their flour has a higher amount of gluten.

On school days we arrived home while the loaves of bread were still warm, and each of us kids cut off a crust or two on which to put home-churned butter. Those loaves of bread were left a little squished after each of us four children had removed slices off the ends.

Fillings for sandwiches were leftover meats, never cold cuts. The closest thing we had to cold cuts was home-made head cheese or blood sausage. Cheese was rarely added because we had only Velveeta, a cheese product, and that was reserved for grilled cheese sandwiches or macaroni and cheese casserole.

The home-made quality of our sandwiches caused me a lot of embarrassment when in high school the girls had to bring sandwiches to sock-hop dances in the gym. I tried to quickly hide my sandwiches under others because I thought it was bad that I didn't have store-bought bread and cold meats. There were always a lot of the popular girls and boys hanging around nearby, and I didn't want them to see the sandwiches this country hick had brought. It wasn't until a class reunion ten years later that one of those boys told me that they stood by the table just waiting for me to arrive and then they fought over who could have the excellent sandwiches I had brought. I wish I had known that.

That Canadian flour also was essential in making large quantities of excellent egg noodles. Mom used a skinny rolling pin to roll portions of dough into very thin circles. Each circle was then rolled up and sliced into different widths. Mom's specialty was cutting the noodles as narrow as possible. She had a very thin knife dedicated only to this purpose. Every time Mom made noodles Pop sharpened the knife using a whetstone.

We fluffed up the noodles and spread them across our large yellow Formica kitchen table to dry. There always was sunshine coming in those windows and with our dry climate, the noodles dried quickly. After thorough drying, the noodles could be stored for months in three-pound coffee cans. When I became an adult Mom bought coffee in three-pound cans labled with the brand of MJB, which my children liked because those letters start the names of Morgan, Jeffrey, and Brent. We always took some of those noodles home with us. Any soup became heavenly when those super-thin noodles were added. We also had some wide noodles which we fried mixed with fried breadcrumbs. This simple dish was included in a Hungarian cookbook I had purchased. It was excellent due to the home-made ingredients.

My favorite "comfort food" that Mom made is chicken and dumplings. My three sons always loved this when they ate at Grandma's during summer vacation in Montana. I tried recipe after recipe until I thought I had finally perfected it. But at the end of every meal the boys one by one stood back from the table and announced, "That was good Mom but not as good as Grandma's." Well, it was difficult to make this as good as Mom did because she would go outside and freshly kill a couple of chickens. And she had that Canadian flour to make the dumplings. There was no way I could ever compete with that. I had successfully made that recipe when I was a child on the farm but I no longer had access to those same good ingredients.

I don't remember ever seeing fish for sale in the grocery store of our home town, Sweetgrass. It was just as well because we were happy eating freshly caught trout. I thought trout was almost the only kind of fish. But I know there were rainbow trout and brown trout.

When I was a little older fish peddlers would work their way east from the west coast traveling with an insulated box on the back of their truck keeping the fish on dry ice. Mom one time bought lutefisk which is cod, dried and soaked in lye water. The salesman didn't say anything about how to prepare this Norwegian delicacy, so she breaded and fried it in lard the same as she fried trout. This caused it to liquefy and exude a terrible odor. Lutefisk has a strong odor even when it is poached. She threw her favorite extra-large cast iron skillet outside into the trash can, opened all the windows and we went to Uncle Rudy and Margaret's while the house aired out.

We often had people, relatives and neighbors, dropping in un-announced to visit and eat before we had telephones and TVs. We never had phones or TVs when I lived on the Suta farm. Our kitchen was large, and everyone gathered there to talk instead of in the living room. We never ate in the dining room because that table was filled with Mom's many plants, especially a lot of Christmas cacti. In the kitchen our large Formica table could be expanded and seat twelve to sixteen people when we added to the back of the table the narrow bench Pop had made for the porch. If more room was needed, then we would set up the card table in the kitchen rather than isolating children in the dining room. Holiday gatherings and birthdays, or some ordinary days, might include as many as forty people eating in shifts, with the children eating first and the women eating last.

Without telephones we didn't know who might drop in at mealtime or how much more food we would need. It was easy to add another potato or open another jar of vegetables. We could always stretch a meal to include any number of surprise guests.

Dessert was likely to be pie made from fresh or home-canned fruit or cooked fillings made from scratch. Favorite home-made fillings were lemon meringue, chocolate pudding, banana cream, or custard. Mom made excellent pie crust using real lard while I cooked fillings from scratch without lumps.

The beverage at meals was always Kool-Aid. For Pop, the Kool-Aid could only be green, as was also his requirement for Jello. We usually made two pitchers of Kool-Aid, one red for a little variety from lime green.

If we were going to have a picnic, usually in Glacier Park, we always made fried chicken. We didn't deep fry the chicken. We simply dredged each piece in egg and seasoned flour and pan fried it in plenty of good lard.

Mom went about once a month to a Women's Home Demonstration Club meeting. They always had potluck and Mom was always expected to bring her cold macaroni salad that she and I had developed in a hurry one day and which was loved by everyone. Her fame depended on that Velveeta cheese which melted from the heat of the cooked macaroni, and we added a little heavy cream to lighten the cheese. I honestly didn't know until I moved to Wisconsin that there were more than a couple of cheeses that weren't Velveeta.

As an adult, my cooking was very basic, like Mom's, until an unusual introduction to gourmet recipes. When I bought a washing machine in 1965 to wash my oldest son Morgan's cloth diapers, I discovered a surprise bonus inside. There was a leather-bound edition of a cookbook authored by Vincent Price, a sophisticated movie star famous for roles in horror movies. Sears Roebuck Company had contracted with him to choose artistic items for them to sell. The padded leather cover and heavy paper of this cookbook felt so exquisite that I began reading it like a novel. Vincent Price and his wife collected recipes during their extensive travels abroad, and each recipe had an introductory story. Included in the book were beautiful full-page glossy colored photographs of food, menus and household collections from foreign countries. Their travels appealed to me as I had already started on my "trip around the world" by leaving Montana for Madison.

As I read the cookbook I soon began to identify recipes that did not look very hard to make even though they were pretty exotic for the time. That was the beginning of my interest in gourmet cooking.

I guess you could say that my skill in cooking is the result of dirty diapers, horror movies, and the Sears Roebuck Company.

These days I don't have any salesmen dropping by at mealtime. If that gas delivery man came here, he would probably join my boys in saying that my mother's cooking was better than mine. Mom was an excellent cook, but it made a big difference that she started with better ingredients.

Three Meals and More

When I was growing up on the farm, all of us worked hard and needed to eat a lot for energy, especially in the summer. My three teen-aged brothers always ate a lot because they were growing boys. They had to be fed more than three times a day and our meals were referred to by different names than I use now in the city.

Our three main meals a day were referred to as breakfast, dinner, and supper, all being substantial, full meals.

Because physical work makes you hungry, we also provided food between meals that was more substantial than what might be called a "coffee break" or snack. This between-meal food was more like a light meal and might include a sandwich as well as some sweet dessert. We usually referred to this between-meal food as lunch.

So we served Breakfast – Lunch – Dinner – Lunch – and Supper.

By the time Mom and I finished clearing the table and washing dishes by hand, it was time to give the men something to eat for a between-meal lunch.

We called our noon meal at home dinner but at school "lunch" because it was a light meal, consisting usually of a sandwich and dessert. We didn't have self-stick paper like Glad in those days. Our sandwiches were wrapped in wax paper which always came undone and let the bread dry out.

We didn't use aluminum foil because that was all saved for the war effort. We carried our lunch to school in re-usable metal lunch boxes. Plastic had not been developed and paper bags were never used because paper was conserved because of war effort.

We seldom had fresh fruit because we didn't go to the grocery store very often. Actually I doubt whether fresh fruit was even delivered to our small town store on a regular basis. It's possible that Mom thought it was too expensive when it was available. We had canned a lot of fruit during the summer but there were not any small containers like Tupperware to carry wet products in a lunch bucket.

On the farm both the noon meal called dinner and the evening meal called supper were equivalent, both being substantial meals featuring meat, potatoes, more than one vegetable, salad, and dessert.

We made fried chicken frequently during the summer. This saved us from having to go to our freezer box in Sweetgrass to get meat.

When we decided to fry chicken, Mom would go out and chop the heads off the number of chicken we needed. For our family alone we needed at least two fryers. Of course, in the summer we usually had more people than our family to feed at a meal.

We didn't make a thick batter for the chicken but rather just rolled it in seasoned flour.

If we had to feed a lot of people, we would put each batch of fried chicken into a roaster on low heat in the oven.

Ben and Pop ate the gizzards while Mom and I ate the heart and liver. Mom was so accustomed to being the last at the table that she had developed a taste for the neck and the rear-end of the chicken. She would pick on the neck until she had eaten every little morsel and the bones had separated.

We also made potato salad to go with fried chicken. I think the thing that makes potato salad good is to use lots of hard-boiled eggs. We used a little thick cream to lighten the mayonnaise. Actually we did that every time we used mayo as a salad dressing. For potato salad, we added a little dab of mustard and some finely chopped pickles. Then we sprinkled paprika on top for color and to add a little flavor.

The meal on our farm at noon was large because of energy needed for working, which is why it was referred to as dinner rather than lunch. Usually the work day for those farming ended when it became dark, so the workers ate a heavy evening meal called supper. They needed to work outside as long as it was light, and in northern Montana the sky stayed light until very late.

Breakfast was always more than a bowl of cold cereal. Most often it was eggs, bacon or ham, and toast. Sometimes Mom made pancakes for breakfast, and she would make fresh ones as each of us strayed out to the kitchen. Pancakes were made in winter or when there was more time, and not during seeding or harvest. A common meal for dinner and supper might be some type of roast: beef or pork. Our meats did not need much seasoning because they were from our own home-grown free-range animals. That meat always tasted better than anything I could buy in a store, no matter how much seasoning I use. Salt and pepper were necessary and maybe a small amount of garlic powder or paprika.

Surrounding a roast, cooking slowly in the juices, would be potatoes, carrots, and onions. The potatoes might be cut up and roasted. If the roasting pan was too full, we would boil or mash the potatoes. Another vegetable would also be served. If we served peas, we would have one bowl of fresh peas just picked from the garden and steamed or lightly boiled. Pop did not like fresh peas; he would only eat the large canned peas. Without question, gravy would be made of the roast drippings.

We sliced some of Mom's home-made bread for every meal because Pop couldn't eat a meal without a slice of bread in his left hand. Salad in the summer was usually fresh leaf lettuce and tomatoes. Our salad dressing almost always was mayonnaise thinned with some thick cream. Store-bought Thousand Island dressing was also popular. For the lettuce salad, I would have to make a run to the garden and pick the outer leaves of lettuce plants, leaving the smaller leaves to continue growing. I never pulled up an entire plant. We often also had Jello with a meal, either plain or with some type of fruit, but always green lime Jello as Pop preferred. Pop also liked his Kool-Aid to be green.

Rather than baking dessert three times a day, I also had to make something for between-meal lunches during the summer. So I may have been baking some dessert five times a day, or at least increasing the number of pies or cookie bars or whatever I had baked.

If I was making chocolate chip cookies I used two large bags of chocolate chips and doubled the batter recipe for each. That made eight normal-sized batches of cookies. The boys usually didn't like nuts in their cookies. An entire batch of these cookies, actually four batches of cookies, would be eaten at one lunch. If the men were in the house, they would be eating the cookies as quickly as they baked. Hands were already reaching for the hot cookies I had just removed from the oven. By the time I took the last cookie off the baking sheet, all the other cookies had already been eaten. I had to hurry if I wanted one cookie for myself.

My family was quite poor as I grew up. We didn't dress well but we had plenty to eat. Our poverty was not as devastating as it is for families in the cities because we were able to plant a large garden and raise animals for food. When the first of us children were young we also had a couple of milk cows to provide milk and butter.

Coal Stove

I was required to cook full meals independently when I was eight years old while Mom had to stay on bed rest following a surgery. This unfortunately occurred during summer when there were more than four men to cook for. Mom dictated a simple menu and directions from her bed.

We had only a coal stove for heating the house and for cooking. My worst experience was letting the fire go out while cooking dinner one day. When the men came in to eat, the food was only half cooked and my father had to re-light the coal stove and waste time waiting to eat. I was afraid my father's explosive temper would erupt but he surprised me by being patient. However he did sternly tell me to never let this happen again. I was lucky that the men were only picking rocks and plowing because Pop would have been very angry if this had been the high-pressure time of harvest when everything had to be done quickly before the erratic Montana weather began to snow.

We used a coal stove rather than wood because we had absolutely no trees on our land. It was more convenient and less expensive to have coal delivered rather than wood. Coal burns longer and hotter in the stove than wood does. My brothers told me that the coal was delivered in large chunks to one of the old homestead buildings on our land and they had to use a sledge hammer to break it into pieces of appropriate sizes to use in the stove. There always was a bucket of irregular-sized pieces of coal in a bucket on the left side of the stove.

I have read stories about people who are poor following a train to pick up pieces of coal. We couldn't do that because the nearest train was over fifty miles away. But we had something more accessible to use when necessary. Once in a while Mom sent us kids out on the pasture to gather dried cow pies which burned very quickly and didn't provide much heat but were better than nothing.

I discovered this old photo of Ted finding our discarded coal stove. Ted at 92 YO can't remember where he found it and I can't remember taking this picture. But it was our stove. You can imagine this standing upright as a stove. The stove was black and some of the front apparently was enameled. The model of the stove was Monarck which was a common brand. The circle on the front of the oven door might look like it was a temperature gauge, but I can tell you there was no such thing.

There were no knobs to control the heat for whatever food you were cooking. Whether the heat under a burner was high, medium, or low was learned by experience if I happened to burn something I was cooking. Of course, I quickly learned to judge the temperature of a burner on the stove by holding my hand over it. The entire top of the stove was flat so we could move pots around to the area with the desired level of heat.

Coal burns from the bottom up and I suppose that is what kept the oven hot. I still think it was an amazing skill to put my bare hand inside the oven to determine whether the oven was 450, 350, or 300 degrees Fahrenheit. I did that so often that I am still able to discern the oven temperature in this way. It was critical to judge the correct temperature of the oven when baking cakes and cookies, which were usually my responsibility. It was definitely essential to have the correct temperature when baking an angel-food cake which we did often because we had a lot of eggs. The cake would not rise unless the temperathure was correct.

Shelves could be inserted to cook foods such as cookies on more than one level. The oven was big enough to hold a large roasting pan.

There was a large venting pipe from the stove to the outdoors through a hole in the wall.

On the right end of the stove, where Ted is standing, was a water reservoir that could keep water warm for any use. It was another task of mine to keep it filled with water to be warm by the time the men came in to wash their face and hands.

A washbasin was kept in the porch on a chest that Pop had made. The men brought the basin into the kitchen to get warm water from the reservoir on the stove to wash their face and hands. Farming is dirty work. Dirty water was thrown out the front door and prevented grass from growing there. We did not try to grow a lawn anyway.

There wasn't time for the men to change clothes before eating so they were a dirty bunch. Needless to say, we did not use upholstered chairs.

The kitchen stove was the only heat inside our house until the living room was added and included two wall heaters.

Mom knew how to "bank" the fire in the coal stove so it would keep burning at a low temperature all night long. The banked fire didn't provide any heat but made it easier to start the fire in the morning. In the winter the house would get very cold overnight with no heater, as we commonly had temperatures way below zero. Twenty below was not uncommon but we once had a temperature of forty below zero.

The house would be very cold in the morning. Each of us kids would often bring our clothes out to the kitchen where we could undress and dress in front of the open door of the oven.

Violet Suta Moran

If you have to start a new fire from scratch in a coal stove, you begin with some paper and very small sticks and then slowly add small sticks of wood as the fire begins to burn. Continue adding pieces of wood until there is a small fire going. Then you can begin to put in a couple of small chunks of coal and wait five to ten minutes before slowly adding more pieces of coal. You have to have a base of burning coal with some coal above the base to maintain your fire. Once the coal ignites and you see blue flames, you can adjust the damper and damper control.

Nailed to the wall by the stove was a turquise colored tin box that held a box of Farmer matches and was open at the base to dispense matches, like some toothpick dispensers. Farmer matches are about two inches long and light with a big flame. You would singe your eyebrows if you used one of these to light your cigarette. It was popular for businesses to advertise by giving away paper matchbooks. A lot more people smoked cigarettes when I was young.

Ted found our coal stove in a junkyard. It was used until 1947.

Feeding the Men in the Fields

During the summer, those who were picking rocks were given their between-meal lunches in lunchboxes. We had only the large metal type with a rounded top because plastic had not been invented yet and paper bags were not used because of the war. Rock pickers usually came into the house to eat dinner and supper.

For the other men who were working in the fields, Mom and I either packed lunchboxes, or the men came into the house, or we delivered food out to where they were working.

Mom speeding food to men in the field.

Where these field workers ate lunches, dinner, or supper depended on several factors: whether they were working near or far from the house, whether they would have to return home anyway to refill gas or seed, and what type of work was being done. The different types of work being seeding, haying, harvesting, or simply working the field with a plow or disc.

During the busy time of harvest, we had to catch the men "on the run" out in the field to deliver food. Our growing season was so short that we were anxious to harvest the grain before the unpredictable weather might ruin the crop by raining, snowing, freezing, or hailing. Workers would not stop while harvesting grain unless there was no choice. We delivered food when they had to pause anyway to empty a hopper of grain from the combine into the truck. There often were two combines and two trucks working a field at the same time.

Mom and I had to watch the field where they were working and time everything just right so that we had the food prepared and loaded into the pickup or camper ready to meet the machinery when they were at the end of the field closest to the house and had made enough rounds that they would have to empty the combine hopper into the truck. Thinking back, that really took a lot of planning to coordinate everything, timing everything just right. Just cooking a meal requires a lot of planning and coordination to get everything done at the same time.

Mom serving food in the field.

Supper during harvest time would be delayed until dark, at least 9:00 or 10:00 pm when the grain began to get moist from the dew and was difficult to cut. We lived so far north that it didn't get dark until late. Combining could not start in the morning until the dew had evaporated a little.

If we were delivering dinner or supper to the fields, we prepared the same type of food as we would have if they

Sweetgrass

were eating the meal in our kitchen. My sister-in-law Sherry photographed one typical harvest dinner. For that noon-time dinner, Mom was serving the following food out of the back of the camper: homemade soup, homemade bread, iced tea, broiled T-bone steak, lettuce salad, baked potatoes with toppings, and their choice of apple or huckleberry pie. Supplies for washing face and hands also were included. This type of meal had to be made every day for lunch and supper during the hard-working days of harvest time.

Mom and I had to be alert to the time the harvest crew would be coming into the house for supper which would be late since they wouldn't want to take time to eat when they could still be combining. We had to be ready to put the meal on the table as soon as they had washed their face and hands and were ready to eat. They would be anxious to eat and fall into their beds after a long day of hard work and be ready to start again early in the morning.

Of course, that left Mom and I to clear off the plates, put leftover food into storage, and wash and dry the dishes. We could not go to bed yet after our hard day of work.

Oh, I almost forgot that we had to get everything ready so that we could give the harvest crew a good Breakfast early and quickly in the morning.

Oops, I wouldn't dare forget to pack lunch boxes for the next day.

Before we go to bed, Mom and I had better make a good plan of what we are going to cook tomorrow so we can check our supplies.

Miki and I took food to my nephew Mark and his hired man prior to seeding.

Garden

When I was very young our large garden was just outside the kitchen window facing east. This land slanted downhill and probably was not the best place for a garden. I think Mom might have wanted the garden close to the house so she could quickly get what she wanted while keeping an eye on her four very young children.

We liked to play in the garden when we were supposed to be hoeing. We chasesd each other around, trying to hide behind some of the plants, and we ate everything raw that could be eaten. Mom never said a word to stop us from being in the garden because she was probably happy to see us eating vegetables.

Mom had to do most of the hoeing when we four were very young, but we were taught as soon as possible. Every one of us had a hoe to use. Mom was able to get me a child-size hoe so that I could help along with everyone else even though I could barely walk.

We planted a lot of potatoes because we ate them at every large meal and we didn't eat rice or noodles as side dishes. I spent many days removing the string and shucking green peas for summer meals and for canning. Cucumbers and dill were grown so that we could can dill pickles, but we didn't make sweet pickles. We pickled a lot of beets. I don't remember head lettuce but we had a lot of leaf lettuce and tomatoes for salads every day during the summer. We planted and canned standard vegetables of green and yellow string beans, carrots, squash, and onions. We planted some vegetables that were commonly used by our ethnic groups, such as turnips, rutabaga, kohlrabi and parsnips. We never even knew that Brussels sprouts, broccoli and eggplant existed. Some vegetables we didn't even know about because Mom either didn't like them or had never been exposed to them. We planted a lot of cabbage and chopped it to make sauerkraut, but we didn't keep five gallon cans of it as my Suta grandparents did. We didn't grow corn, berries and fruit because our climate was cold and too dry. Instead we went up to the mountains to pick cherries, which the growers allowed us to climb stepladders and pick by ourselves. That would not be allowed today because of possible injuries and lawsuits.

We grew only a small amount of corn because it takes up a lot of space and needs more water than we could provide. We used fresh tomatoes in salads all summer, but we didn't make tomato sauces. My parents may not have been exposed to Italian foods and I don't remember an Italian restaurant in our town. Pizza was the closest we came to Italian. We bought fruits like peaches and pears by the crate from the grocery store and canned them ourselves.

Mom loved flowers and we always planted some in the garden but didn't take the time to bring bouquets into the house every day. Flowers I remember fondly are bachelor's buttons, snapdragons and black-eyed Susans. In later years Mom tried to grow roses in a raised garden but the chickens and dogs spent too much time scratching and sleeping on that soft soil. Our climate wasn't the best for roses but eventually Mom was overjoyed to have one red rose blossom on a plant.

When we kids were older we often drove to Lethbridge, Alberta, Canada to eat Chinese food. There were quite a few Chinese restaurants around because some Chinese people who had built the railroad tracks across the upper part of the United States stayed around in our area. We were never exposed to foods we considered exotic, other than Chinese.

We didn't plant any spices like basil, thyme, and oregano because we rarely used spices. We didn't plant strawberries because they would have needed water and would have been eaten by the chickens anyway.

The chickens liked our garden when it was close to the house because the dirt was loose, good for scratching and rolling around to clean their feathers.

When the new garden was plotted on flat land down below the hill, enough space was allowed between rows so that Pop could use a machine to destroy weeds. Then we only had to hoe to remove the weeds that grew closest to the plants.

Mom tried to keep the vegetables growing all summer by teaching us to only harvest a partial amount from each plant instead of destroying an entire plant. I had to dig around each potato plant and take away just one potato that was the largest. Doing this digging around every plant until I had enough potatoes for a meal took a lot longer than it would have taken to just dig up the entire plant. But the remaining potatoes left behind could continue to grow. This was Mom's method of conserving food and it worked. We did the same with other plants.

I had to pick the outer leaves off the leaf lettuce plant, leaving the smaller leaves to continue growing. I had to dig around the carrots and just take the largest ones, thinning them out so that those left behind would grow larger. I couldn't just pull a carrot out of the ground anyway because our gumbo soil was so hard that the carrot would break off.

The only time we removed small potatoes was to serve them with fresh peas in a cream sauce, one of my favorite dishes. Mom liked to leave a few potatoes to grow as large as possible so she could show off and brag to other women about the large potatoes she grew, implying that all of her potatoes were that large.

Part of our basement was simply packed dirt because the house had been built in stages. That part of the basement was used as a cool root-cellar for storage of potatoes, carrots and onions for as long as they would last into the winter. I hated to go down there to get a bucket of potatoes because in the darkness before electricity there were always mice darting across my feet and running up my legs.

Since we didn't have a freezer at home we also canned meats: beef, pork, chicken and fish. I still long for Mom's canned trout. We canned all vegetables, plain and pickled, fruits, jam and jellies.

Mar's Grocery Store in Sweetgrass used some type of generator to create a large walk-in freezer that served the entire community. None of us had electricity. It would have cost too much to freeze our vegetables and fruit and store them in Mars grocery store, so everything was canned.

After we butchered an animal, steer or pig, the carcass was taken to Mar's to have their butcher cut up the animal, wrap the pieces, label and store them in a separate section for each customer.

One memorable year their butcher cut every part of our beef animal into steaks. He didn't leave any piece large enough for roasting. Mom knew only two ways of preparing steak, either pan-fried or broiled. We became sick and tired of steak before we had eaten that entire beef animal. I know now that the steak meat could have been sliced or cut-up and made into various stir-fry or mixed dishes. But Mom was not a creative cook and Pop would not have tolerated casseroles or mixtures anyway. We reluctantly ate steak for several months. We even welcomed a change to organ meats of liver, kidneys or heart which was stuffed and roasted.

A Woodpecker Visited My Parents

Have you ever seen a woodpecker living on the prairie? I grew up in north central Montana where there was not a tree growing anyplace on the thousands of acres we farmed. There was also no lake or river. It is odd that there are a lot of seagulls flying around even though there is no longer a sea, but I never had seen a woodpecker. I wouldn't have believed that a woodpecker would be present and surviving on this land.

Of course I didn't believe Mom and Pop when they told me on the phone that they had a woodpecker coming to visit them every day. I kept asking doubtful questions but they both said that they were telling the truth. And they gave details. Neither of them had been known to make up stories or tell lies, but this was difficult to believe.

They said that almost every day a woodpecker would come and talk to them by pecking on the living room window. It would come about noon while they were watching their favorite soap operas on television and eating their lunch of soup and half a sandwich. The television was at an angle in a corner of the room against an outside wall and the bird perched on the wires that ran outside. Mom and Pop sat at the opposite corner of the room on their matching blue

Sweetgrass

La-Z-Boy chairs to watch television and eat their lunch on TV trays. I could not believe their story. They repeated this same information to me several times. It was even more unbelievable when they insisted that the same woodpecker had visited them last year.

I happened to make a trip to Montana by myself when I wanted to tell my parents about my decision to divorce my husband. This would have been in the fall of 1989. Harvesting was finished and my parents had time to visit with me and to watch television in the middle of the day as they were accustomed to doing.

I had completely forgotten their story about a woodpecker as we sat in the living room eating lunch. Mom and Pop were in their chairs and I was sitting on the sofa close to the television. I was startled and jumped about a foot when I heard pecking on the window just a few feet away from me. I was utterly amazed when I looked and saw a woodpecker—<u>their</u> woodpecker—pecking at the window. I couldn't believe my eyes and ears!!!

The bird was perched on wires outside at the level of the television and was looking into the living room. I am not a bird person, and I didn't notice details of its color and shape that would distinguish it from other woodpecker families. But it definitely was a bird, and it was purposefully pecking at the window.

Pop quickly jumped up and turned off the television. Both Mom and Pop started greeting and saying friendly things to the woodpecker. Both were excited and talking at the same time, as they often did. The bird stopped pecking while they talked and tilted its head as though it was listening to them. It started pecking again when my folks stopped talking for just a little bit. When they started talking again, the bird would stop pecking and turn its head again as though it was listening.

Violet Suta Moran

It felt surreal when Mom introduced me to the woodpecker, telling him, "This is our daughter Violet here for a visit from Madison," as though the bird might know where Madison was. While Mom said this, she moved her hand and pointed at me, and that of course caused the bird to look at me. That almost made me think that it understood who I was. I couldn't understand if it pecked a greeting to me but it seemed obvious that the bird and my parents were having a conversation.

The bird would stop pecking while my parents talked and then it would start pecking again when they stopped talking. This went back and forth between the woodpecker and my parents as though they were having a social visit. A polite conversation. I couldn't believe what was happening right in front of me. I was flabbergasted!!! This conversation must have gone on for more than five minutes.

Although I couldn't understand anything the bird was saying, Mom happily said, "I think it's speaking German to me." Pop responded in his irritable growl, "Don't be stupid, it isn't talking to you!"

I wish I could have recorded this amazing event but in 1989 I didn't have a telephone that took photos and videos. I had a camera but didn't have it ready to record this unusual event. I had not believed my parents when they told me about "their" woodpecker and neither did anyone else. I asked other members of my family who might have visited them and seen the bird but all thought that I must be crazy to think that it was possible. I am the only person other than Mom and Pop who ever witnessed this phenomenal event. I have no proof but I swear that I witnessed exactly what my parents had been telling me. And nobody believes me either.

I can't remember if Mom and Pop gave their visitor a name, but I think they just said "You" when addressing the bird, as in:

"We missed you."

Sweetgrass

"I'm glad to see you again."
"It's good to see you."
"How have you been?"

This woodpecker visited them for two or three years before it saddened my parents by not returning. And not even dropping in to say goodbye.

I wasn't surprised that it left. I thought if this bird was smart enough to visit my parents it ought to have been smart enough to notice that it would not find a woodpecker mate here. It was about time that it realized that there was no future for it to keep returning to the Suta Farm on the prairie.

Postscript: This is the last story I read to my son Jeff on 5 April 2024, just a short time before he died of brain cancer on 17 April 2024 after twenty-eight years of battling the disease while living a good life. He and his brothers had requested stories about the Montana farm. He enjoyed this story and believed that we really had talked with a woodpecker, unlike many people who doubted me and my parents. He grinned as he used his sense of humor telling me to add this plausible but fake scene about the bird speaking German to Mom and thereby upsetting Pop. I enjoy that Jeff maintained a sense of humor to the end of his life.

Raising Chickens

We raised many chickens on the Suta Rock Farm and it was a lot of work to get them ready to be fried and eaten or to be sold. Our chickens were completely free range, and that makes a difference in how they taste.

Springtime can trigger a hens instinct to incubate or brood, wanting to make a nest, lay a number of eggs and sit on them for several weeks until chicks hatch. A broody hen will stop laying during that time. If you prefer to get production of eggs rather than hatch your own chicks, you have to keep taking her eggs away and remove her from her nesting site until she loses that broody instinct. We watched closely for hens showing broody signs because we didn't want them to make a nest somewhere outside of the hen house where predators, even the family dog, could easily eat the eggs.

Violet playing with chickens and ducks.

Sweetgrass

Roosters can be useful. Hens will lay eggs with or without a rooster in the flock but a rooster is needed to fertilize the hen before she can lay eggs that will hatch. If raising chickens to reproduce you need about one rooster for ten hens. Having a rooster in your flock can be a good alarm system when a predator is disturbing the chickens. People expect roosters to routinely crow at sunrise, but they may start crowing a couple of hours before sunrise and may crow anytime and all the time. The crowing of the roosters all day didn't bother us because we weren't in a confined space.

Cities that permit raising chickens in backyards do not allow roosters because of their disruptive crowing.

Every spring Mom ordered 350 eggs that were in the process of hatching into baby chickens. When ordering, there are quite a few choices to make between breeds having different characteristics in color, speed of growth and size, tolerance of cold weather, production of eggs and so forth. We usually got mostly white Cornish hens because they grew quickly and would be ready to butcher as fryers in eight to ten weeks. Raising fryers to sell was a money-making venture for us.

Our order of eggs and hatchlings would be delivered by train from Minneapolis in 2 x 2 foot cardboard boxes. They were kept warm while enroute by train from Minneapolis to Shelby, Montana. A postal carrier then brought them from Shelby to Sweetgrass in his warm car. When we picked them up after their 1,100 mile trip most would have hatched while others would still be pecking their way out of their shells. Their feathers quickly dried and the chicks became fluffy, yellow and soft. Some real feathers can start to appear on the wings and tail in a week and then they aren't as cute and cuddly to hold.

Keeping Chicks Alive

Hatchlings usually do not know how to drink water and are in danger of dehydration within forty-eight hours. It was necessary to pick each one up and gently dip its beak into water, watching to see that it actually took a drink. After being watered they were moved from one box to another to be sure we didn't miss one. Usually this only needed to be done once.

We had some finely-ground special chick feed close by for them to eat, but they would start scratching and scattering the chick feed. Scratching comes from their instinct to take dust baths, perhaps to remove oil from their feathers. As they get older, gravel or dirt is best for them to be able to scratch enough to raise dust and be able to roll around in the dirt. Then they will fluff out their feathers and shake like a wet dog to get rid of some of the dirt.

After starting with special chick feed, they will gradually progress to a different kind of feed in larger sizes. Even if they are given grains to eat and are allowed to eat anything they find on the range, they may have to also be given various supplements.

Chicks Can Be Mean

Chicks had to be watched closely to keep them alive. Sometimes they cause suffocation by all crowding tightly together. Crowding could mean that the heat is too warm or too cool or it could just be a stampede like the mosh pit at a rock concert.

Chicks could be mean to each other and we had to watch frequently for that. After an aggressive one starts pecking on a specific chick, others will gang up and attack the same chick, especially if there is blood drawn. The sight of raw meat will excite the chicks to peck even more as they are omnivores, eating all kinds of food, both plant and meat. The weak and the bullies had to be separated.

In addition to suffocating or pecking to death another chick, they did other stupid things. They pooped in their food and water all the time. Despite having special feeders and water holders, they would get their food, drinking water, and straw bedding dirty. You will wonder how on earth they did that when you had bought special equipment. But they will find ways.

They will stand in water getting themselves cold, or even drown themselves. Fluffy yellow chicks are cute but they don't have any common sense at all. A mother hen could help raise baby chicks but they are not always good mothers and may actually kill rather than protect their young chicks.

Food and water containers had to be cleaned out once or twice a day. The straw bedding had to be kept clean and dry. Every week or two the chicks had to be moved into a temporary location so that we could do a thorough cleaning of their permanent living area.

The baby chicks had to be kept all day and night in the "brooder" house where they could be kept warm and safe from predators. A light bulb or heat lamp was mounted at just the right height to keep the area the right temperature, warm but not too warm.

Roosting

Mature chickens had to be cooped up at night in the "hen house" or "chicken coop" for protection from predators. Sometimes a predator would sneak in anyway. Snakes and weasels can get through even a very small hole. Weasels would kill all the chickens in the hen house and not eat any of the meat. That really made us mad.

In the hen house there were layers of wooden rods to roost on, layered like seats in an auditorium. Chickens are perching birds, and it is normal for them to want to be elevated. Roosting also gives them more space without crowding each other.

If you watch them going into the chicken house, you will notice that there is a "pecking order" among chickens and they will push each other or fight for a given space. They exhibit a pecking order just as people do in a human business.

Gathering Eggs

There were nests lined with straw in the hen house for those chickens that were laying eggs. To gather eggs, we had to steal the egg from underneath a chicken that is sitting on a nest. You quietly slide your hand under her body from the rear or she will become alarmed and peck at you, which hurts and may draw blood.

Free Range Chickens

Our chickens were always what is called "free range" being allowed to roam around in the yard eating bugs, worms or anything they could find. We scattered some grain in the area near the hen house and kept their food and water there so that they wouldn't roam too far away. They usually stayed close to home even though they were free to go anywhere. When it was feeding time or bedtime when you want them to go back into the hen house, you just had to holler in a high voice, "Here, chick, chick, chick. Here chick, chick, chick."

Butchering Chickens

Chickens were considered fryers at about four-to-six weeks of age, weighing about 2 ½–3 pounds. When you wanted a fresh fryer for lunch, you had to first catch one by chasing it into a corner and very quickly grabbing its legs or catching it in a butterfly type of net. It has to be killed by wringing its neck or chopping off the head. Chopping off the head and letting the torso jump around on the ground has the advantage of bleeding out the chicken. The torso really jumps around like crazy for a few minutes, thus the adage of someone " jumping around like a chicken with its head cut off."

Mom was strong and skilled at chopping off the head by laying the neck on a stump, putting one foot on the head and holding the legs with one hand while holding the axe in her other hand to quickly chop off the head. I was afraid I would chop my foot, and I wasn't strong enough to do this.

Plucking Feathers

Holding onto the legs, Mom would dunk the entire chicken into scalding water to make it possible to pluck the feathers. Water temperature was important because you couldn't pluck out the feathers if not hot enough, or the skin would peel off if the water was too hot. We were careful to not tear the skin since we were selling some of these fryers, and that would not look good.

Left behind were quarter-inch "pin feathers" that had to be pulled out one by one. Then they were held over a flame to singe off any tiny feathers. Then you were ready to clean out the insides of the bird.

Cleaning the Insides

A cut would be made between the thigh and body in order to pull out the intestines and other organs. Saving the liver, heart and gizzard to eat is up to you. You have to remove the crop at the base of the neck which is an expandable storage compartment where food can remain for twelve hours. Food trickles from the crop into the stomach where it is ground up and digested.

Finally you are ready to cut up the chicken into the desired pieces.

Repeat, Repeat, Repeat

If you had ordered hundreds of hatching eggs as we did and planned on selling fryers in town to the grocery store and individual people, or eating them yourself, you had to do this entire process of plucking millions of feathers and cleaning out the inside 350 times. My hand and fingers would be sore every summer from plucking millions of feathers.

Making Butter

I was having lunch with a friend who was slathering a thick layer of butter onto her bread when she turned to me and asked, "How is butter made?" I was surprised at her question since she has spent her entire life in the dairy state of Wisconsin but not on a farm. I don't know how they make butter in the large commercial processing plants, but I can tell you how we produced butter on our family farm.

Obviously, the first thing you need is milk and we had to milk our cows by hand twice a day. Certain breeds of cows produce a higher butterfat content in their milk than do others. Other animals such as goats and llamas could also be milked, but we didn't have those animals. On our farm we milked only a few cows for family consumption of milk and to be able to sell some butter. Ours was not a dairy farm.

The milkmaid, or man, sits on a three-legged stool which allows her to tilt inward, leaning her head against the side of the cow if needed to get a comfortable reach to the teats. You can expect to probably get slapped across your face by the dirty tail of the cow as she swings it side to side. She may swing often and forcefully to send a personal message to you if she doesn't know you or doesn't like your method of milking. Keep an eye out for a cow that is a little testy and might kick because they not only "kick the bucket" but may also kick you. These creatures are not as docile as they look.

Sweetgrass

There is a process for milking. You can't just grab a teat and squeeze with your whole hand. You have to use a procedure like squeezing the last drop of sauce out of a plastic bag. Start squeezing the teat at the top with your index finger and thumb and follow with each finger down to your pinky finger, at which time a stream of milk should come out. Like all skills, it takes practice to be able to milk a cow efficiently.

The commercial process of pasteurization not only takes care of pathogens, but it also mixes the cream and milk together so that they don't separate when left standing. That is why you can buy a half gallon of whole milk at the store and the cream will never rise to the top. If you leave a jar of unpasteurized milk in your refrigerator, the cream will gradually rise to the top and become thicker and thicker until it is clotted. I liked to put the clotted cream on my cereal. The rest of my family preferred the plain cream below that layer of heavy "clotted" cream.

To make whipped cream or butter you have to start with "heavy whipping cream," not half and half. You can make whipped cream by using an electric mixer to add air to heavy cream. Actually, if you keep whipping cream past the stage of "firm peaks" it will begin to turn into butter. Alternatively, you can churn or beat out the water to get butter. There are other methods to add air to cream such as shaking a jar containing cream. That's a fun activity for young children.

We had a "separator," a machine bigger than an electric washing machine, for the purpose of separating cream from the milk. The separator had about eight or nine discs that were installed one above another. The milk went through a center hole in the discs but exactly what physics process was involved to divide the cream from the milk, I don't know. All I know is that we poured the milk into the holding tank and then cranked a handle to run the milk through the separator—cream came out one spigot and milk out another. There was a weight in the crank handle that clicked and it only stopped clicking when you were turning the handle quickly enough for the separation process to occur.

There was a screw that could be tightened or loosened to control how much cream you wanted to have removed from the milk. We didn't have today's measurements, but I guess you could use that screw to obtain the equivalent of 2 percent, 1 percent, or skim milk. We wanted as much cream as possible because we sold cream and butter, so we adjusted the screw to produce skim milk.

Something I know very well about the separator is that it was a beast to clean and it had to be cleaned thoroughly immediately after being used twice a day every single day. There were many pieces of different shapes and sizes and each had to be washed with soap and water very carefully so that bacteria would not grow. At this point you are welcome to think about all the swear words that might have gone through my mind day after day. I never learned how to put all the pieces of the separator together again and my oldest brother says that he didn't either. It was a complicated machine. It must have been Mom who knew how to do that. We are amazed that someone invented a machine this complicated and that we didn't get sick because we hadn't been thorough enough in cleaning all those pieces.

Finally, getting back to the original question of how butter is made. You can now pour the "heavy" cream into a churn of some type. We had a large glass jar with a lid that had two flat paddles and a crank handle attached. We turned and turned the crank attached to the paddles and eventually were rewarded by little pieces of butter separating from the liquid. Cranking had to continue until the little pieces of butter came together to form a large chunk of butter. The liquid is buttermilk, but the taste of it is different than store-bought buttermilk which is richer.

I know of another type of churn that is a tall wooden holder that has a stick coming out the top. This method of churning requires you to keep raising and lowered that stick until you feel the firmness of the butter pieces that have come together.

The process was not complete when butter formed in the churn. The butter still had to be worked to remove all remaining liquid. This was done by hand using a single flat paddle. We kept turning the mound of butter and pressing it with the paddle until there was no more water coming out. Then we could put the butter into any type of container desired. We had a wooden form that would make precisely one pound of butter when filled. After the form was filled, we could push up the bottom of the mold to release the butter. This measurement was very useful since we were selling our butter by the pound to local stores or individuals. There also are molds to make the butter any size you wish and press into the butter any fancy design desired.

If you like "whipped butter" you have to practically reverse the process and whip air into the solid butter. You could also whip in a small amount of flavoring if desired.

Have I answered the question?

Mortimer Snerd

Like the nursery rhyme of "Mary Had a Little Lamb" I had Mortimer Snerd who followed me wherever I went. Mortimer and I met when I was seven years old as a result of my joining the new Rimrock 4-H Club being formed west of Sunburst, Montana. At that time the national rules of 4-H said members had to be ten years old, but an exception was made to let me participate along with my big brothers and some neighbors. I was always doing things for which I was supposedly too young.

The question then was what we would do for our 4-H project. Somehow the decision was made that my brothers and I would all raise sheep. Nobody asked me if I wanted to raise sheep or would rather do a project of sewing or decorating. But that was okay because I usually wanted to do what my brothers were doing anyway.

It was an odd choice to raise sheep since we only raised some cattle on our ranch and farmed. My older brother says the County Agent told Pop we should have a flock of sheep to keep the land cleanly grazed and to diversify options to make money when beef and grain prices were low. This is an example of bad advice sometimes given from inexperienced County Agents. Never having raised sheep, we were unaware that they would break through all the fences designed for cows, run amok eating and trampling the farm crops, and

Sweetgrass

eat the grass so low that we couldn't graze cows on the same land for at least two years. We didn't know that the sheep would require so much work.

The sheep seemed to appear suddenly without me knowing what was going on. The idea was that we could get Rambouillet sheep quickly and cheaply from Simmes' large sheep ranch below the rim. It was a surprise to me when Pop and my brother drove up to our barn one day with a truckload of old ewes and bum lambs. Bum lambs are newborns that are not being fed by their mother either because of rejection, lack of milk, or inability to feed twins or triplets. A rancher may try all kinds of tricks to fool another ewe into accepting the bum as their own, but that seldom happens. Usually these lambs have to be bottle fed; a time consuming and labor intensive project. Undoubtedly the Simmes family was happy to be relieved of the work of hand-feeding the bum lambs that we bought.

As the sheep were being unloaded, they were divided between the four of us kids. Since I was the youngest with three older brothers, I ended up with the oldest, broken-down ewe and the skinniest runt of the bum lambs. I simply accepted what was, but everyone knew and would admit that I got the short end of the stick. However, justice prevailed when my old swaybacked, toothless ewe consistently produced healthy twins for me, and her lambs often were prize winners at the county fair.

The minute I was handed the scrawniest runt of the bum lambs, I named him Mortimer Snerd after the ventriloquist's "dummy" on the popular weekly radio show of Edgar Bergen and Charlie McCarthy. Even though I had only heard this show on the radio I could tell that the Mortimer dummy was not good looking or smart but yet was sweet and lovable, clever and always happy. Just like my scrawny little lamb.

Mortimer, like the other bum lambs, had to be fed by hand using a nipple on a soda or beer bottle filled with cow's milk.

Like an underweight baby he had to be fed more often than the other lambs, every two or three hours around the clock. Knowing even then that I wanted to be a nurse, I enjoyed this opportunity for caregiving. I was also lonely for a friend. I really poured my affection onto Mortimer.

For months I spent all the time I could talking and playing with my lamb. He grew to be healthy and large with an ideal shape for a sheep. I was constantly carding his wool and trimming loose hairs with a scissor or shears. Carding is essentially combing the wool to fluff it up and remove foreign objects like straw and grass. The carder is a chunk of wood about 4x4 inches fitted with a handle and numerous bent metal projections, like nails resembling teeth on a comb. To card a sheep, you push the metal projections down into the wool and use a forward rocking motion to pull them up through the wool. Trimming the wool with a scissor is done to accent the appearance of a nice flat back and square shape.

Like a good parent, I taught him how to behave appropriately. I didn't know about the concept of "positive reinforcement" but that's all I used: my voice, hugs, and an occasional sugar cube. He liked to be hugged and scratched. I loved him so much! I talked to him about all my personal problems, as I would a best friend, while he looked at me with his soft brown eyes and listened attentively.

Mortimer Snerd wanted to hang around me rather than be out in the pasture with the herd of sheep. I was his Mom!! The sheep were in the pasture nearest the house and he would stand close against the fence watching for me to come out of the house. He paced back and forth to keep me in view as I walked in the yard. Finally my parents said he could stay in our yard instead of in the pasture, resting with the dog at the bottom of our front steps, waiting for me. When I came out the door, he would jump up and follow me wherever I went.

If it's true, as many say, that sheep aren't as smart as dogs, then Mortimer must have been an exception. Mortimer

Sweetgrass

could follow my commands like a well-trained dog to shake hands, kneel, lie down, roll over, and dance while I held his front hoofs. And of course he gave me kisses by licking my face, whether or not I asked for a kiss.

I trained Mortimer so well for showing at the county fair that I didn't even have to touch or push him to move into show position. I could just give a signal for what I wanted him to do. Usually when showing a sheep you have to firmly grasp a bunch of skin under the chin with one hand and place the other hand firmly over his anal area in order to control his movements. And you have to place the sheep's feet in the correct position straight under the body. Mortimer assumed "show pose" by lifting his head up high, looking straight ahead, and "squaring off" with his feet placed exactly right. If you pushed him out of position, as I knew the three male judges would do, he quickly resumed the correct pose. I taught him to not flinch when the judges poked and prodded to check his body over. All I had to do to keep him in show position or to lead him around the arena was to place one finger under his chin.

He and I surely should have won a blue ribbon on show, but my brother Henry did instead. Mom told me later that she overheard the three judges having a lengthy argument to resolve the dilemma of whether I was really "showing" the animal when I barely touched him, while the other kids were wrestling and pushing their animals into place. What a stupid decision!! Did they think this sheep had taught himself how to do those things? Like referees, judges can make wrong decisions and we didn't have television replay for challenges. Who knows if their decision was influenced by sexism (I was the only girl showing an animal), reverse ageism (I was younger than anybody else), jealousy or other factors. Mom was really angry but didn't feel that she could speak up and criticize the group of judges. It still bothers me as something unfair that I experienced.

Eventually Mortimer Snerd suffered the same fate as other male farm animals. Pop loaded him into the truck with all the other sheep that needed to be sold. While he and my brothers did this, Mom kept me busy in the house doing chores so I wouldn't know what was happening. My folks kept me away thinking it the best way to save my feelings. I didn't even know there was a plan to sell Mortimer and I didn't get to tell him goodbye. It seems strange now to recall that nobody talked to me about my feelings, my grief. I don't remember crying over my loss, although I do know that I was sad and missed him a lot. Farm kids just had to accept things like this as a fact of life.

Steers and pigs raised by 4-H kids bring ridiculously high prices at the auction sale after the fair. We actually didn't get much money for Mortimer because lamb was not a popular food in Montana at that time.

In my adult years I began collecting little stuffed sheep and then anything and everything with sheep on it—sweaters, bowls, towels, bigger sheep, necklaces and earrings, cups, buttons, anything. Friends would ask why I had these sheep things so I would tell about raising Mortimer when I was a child. They would then add gifts of sheep to my collection. It grew and grew.

One year my parents came to visit and Pop sat staring for a long time at the large flock of stuffed sheep I had arranged in a corner of the room. He said, out of the blue, "If I had it to do over again, I think we could have figured out something else for Mortimer Snerd instead of selling him to be butchered." Pop talked about how Mortimer "cried and cried," bleating more than the other sheep, while they were being loaded into the truck and also during the entire fifty-mile trip to Shelby. He said, "I know Mortimer was crying for you. It made me want to leave him behind, but we needed the sale money for your college fund, and we didn't need a male sheep in our herd." He admitted, "I felt like crying myself by the time we got to Shelby."

I was shocked to hear Pop express his sentiments about Mortimer. My father was never known to be a sensitive man, far the opposite. Yet with these statements he validated that he did care about my feelings as a child. And I had sometimes doubted that caring.

Pop's comments also jolted me into awareness that I was collecting sheep things not just because they were cute but because of unresolved grief over Mortimer Snerd. My grief had never been discussed, never expressed. Despite sadness over his loss, I don't recall crying. Becoming aware that I had unresolved grief, I was then able to emotionally say goodbye to him.

I have now given away almost all of my stuffed sheep, making children proud and happy because their friends only have Teddy Bears and such. They have told me that now their friends want to come and play with their sheep.

I kept a couple of stuffed sheep and a whole lot of Christmas ornaments that either were sheep or had paintings of sheep on them. I keep my grandchildren busy trying to count how many sheep I have on the Christmas tree.

Many years after his glorious life and sudden demise, memories of my precious Mortimer Snerd still bring me feelings of comfort and love. And because of him I was able to make some other little girls happy.

Henry and Violet holding Mortimer.

County Fair

When my brothers and I were in the 4-H Club and had sheep at the Toole County Fair in Shelby for judging, we had to be at the Fair every day, much to the delight of us four children. We were given some money to go on the carnival rides which the boys loved. I didn't like the rides that much because I was afraid of heights and didn't like getting dizzy. I spent most of my money by riding the little ponies on the merry-go-round. Once in a while my brothers persuaded me to go on a ride with them. They had figured out that taking care of me on a ride was a way for them to get an extra ride.

Eating trash like cotton candy at the Fair was fun because we ate such healthy food otherwise.

We always spent some time attending the rodeo and there were sometimes horse races. In the evening there was always some fairly good stage show with a singer performing. During the day we watched other animals being shown and judged. It was a lot of fun to watch the judging of kids showing their pigs because the owners usually didn't have much control over their pig. There also were contests for fun, such as trying to catch a greased piglet and being able to shear a sheep in the fastest time.

Most of the exhibits at the fair were made or developed by members of 4-H Clubs. When I was a child it seemed as though 4-H clubs were only for those who lived on farms or ranches even though you could choose almost anything for a project. Guidance was given to Clubs by the County Extension Agent, but volunteers were in charge. I've learned that today there are 4-H Clubs in cities as well as in the countryside and in every state and many countries.

The 4-H's stand for Head, Heart, Hands and Health. I was proud of myself for being able to remember these seventy-five years after I had learned them. I remembered that these were part of a pledge we said at the beginning of every meeting, but I had to look up that reference. It is:

I pledge my Head to clearer thinking,
my Heart to greater loyalty,
my Hands to larger service, and
my Health to better living;
for my club, my community, my country and my world.

These are the basis of the values worked on through the programs.

4-H Clubs help children develop friendships, commitments to work, and leadership skills. A volunteer parent was present at the Club meetings, but we members elected our own officers.

When we went to the Fair, there was no question that we would look at all the exhibits and go through all the animal buildings. Mom required that. Some of the exhibits were more interesting than others but we looked at all the projects as a way of paying respect to the 4-H kids who had worked hard on their project. It was interesting to see why some projects got higher ratings than others. The variety of chickens always amazed me. We also went through the exhibits of canning, sewing, baking and such. Mom thought we should pay respect to the girls as well as the boys for the work they had done. Sometimes my brothers even learned something.

When I became the mother of three boys who were not in 4-H clubs and we went to the State Fair, I took them through the animal barns and some of the exhibits showing "women's work." Projects that used to be considered women's work are now sometimes done by boys. I think the 4-H exhibits are the main purpose of county and state fairs; otherwise the event is just a carnival.

I was happy to realize that paying respect to the 4-H kids who do this work was being carried on by at least one of my sons when I heard a grandson complaining about having to go through all the animal barns. My city-raised grandson begrudgingly admitted that some of the things he saw in the exhibits were a surprise to him.

Dian and Rudy feeding their 4-H calf.

Boarding the Plane

My sons and their wives swear they will never board a plane with me. I don't understand because, really, all I had said to the Security Guard was, "It's just my vibrator" when he pulled me over to inspect my suitcase. This occurred several years before 9/11 when we weren't told and didn't think about things you shouldn't pack in your carry-on suitcase.

My oldest son and his wife, Morgan and Garmit, who live in Chicago, had invited me to join them on an inexpensive flight to see Jeff and Susan's new house and new baby in Lawrence, Kansas. I met them in Chicago, and we were in the Southwest Airlines boarding area when the incident occurred.

Having spent time recently with Jeff and Susan to help with Jeff's health issues, then the new baby and now the move, I knew that both of them had chronic backaches. Now they would be tired and aching from packing for this move to a new city with their new baby (Becca) and two-year old (Hannah). Those stressors plus that of starting new positions as a lawyer and a professor had them both in need of relaxation.

I thought that I had discovered just the thing to help them relax and feel less stress. I had bought this piece of electric equipment through my Chiropractor. It's called a "Thumper" and is a hand-held electric massager about two feet long. I packed it very carefully in my carry-on suitcase. My worries about it being damaged on the trip were overshadowed by my desire to share this wonderful invention with Jeff and Susan. I'd found muscular relief from using Thumper and I wanted them to have the same experience. I was certain that they would love it and then buy one for themselves.

So here we are in the Security Inspection line for boarding Southwest Airlines in Chicago; me in one line and Morgan and Garmit in a line just next to me. The Security Guard looking at the image of my suitcase got a puzzled frown on his face and said, "I'm going to have to open your suitcase, Ma'am." That's when I told him, "Oh, that's just my vibrator in there."

I heard Morgan speak loudly in a stern voice, "Don't say that, Ma," but in my rush to get on the plane, I didn't know what he was talking about. Morgan didn't know I had packed Thumper, and I thought he just didn't want me saying something incorrect.

Not realizing what was wrong, I thought I had to explain this new devise to the Security Guard. As he was taking me to the Second Security Level, where they open and inspect your bags. I told him, "This is a different kind of vibrator, it does more than vibrate. It has these two round balls that move around and it thumps up and down quickly which is why it's called Thumper." I added the fact that, "It has a long enough handle that you can do it yourself," and, I commented, "It's really a great vibrator and very relaxing."

By then I noticed that the Guard was giving me an odd look that I didn't understand. And out of the corner of my eye I could see a blur of Morgan and Garmit literally running down the hall with their suitcases and turning a corner out of my sight.

I thought it unusual that they didn't wait for me while the guard was examining my suitcase. But Southwest at that time was a first-come first-served, no-reserved-seats kind

Sweetgrass

of airline so I figured they wanted to hurry in order to get seats in the same row for all of us. Because of my delay at Security Check-in, I was one of the last to board the plane. I wasn't concerned because I was sure Morgan and Garmit would have saved a seat for me. But I didn't see them waving at me. I squinted and looked carefully but couldn't see them anywhere so I sat by myself.

I learned later that they were actually ducking down behind the seats to avoid me because they didn't want anybody to know they had anything to do with me.

They also didn't wait for me when exiting the plane after we landed.

It wasn't until they were describing the event to Jeff and Susan that I realized the implication of the word "vibrator."

To this day none of them will stand next to me when boarding a plane even if I tell them quietly that I don't have a vibrator with me.

When planning a trip to Montana last summer, years after this incident had happened, Morgan phoned to ask what seat I had reserved. Instead of him reserving seats near me as I expected, when I boarded the plane I found they were seated at a distance.

I don't think I can expect that my family will take me on interesting trips when I'm older and have physical impairments. They'll never trust my mind and mouth.

Although I didn't laugh at the time of this incident and neither did my poor mortified son, the story has been told over and over again with a lot of hilarious laughter at my expense.

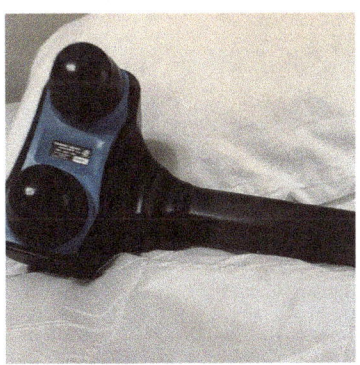

Thumper the vibrator

One-room country school.

Oilfield school was surrounded by oil pumps, but no oil was ever found on our land.

One-Room Country School

I felt so sad when each of my three older brothers started going to school. I wanted to go to school, too. I pestered my brothers a lot wanting them to play school with me, but Henry was the only one who agreed at least once. I was the teacher and made him be the student—maybe that's why they did not want to play school with me.

I finally was allowed to start school when I was less than five years old. Our country school did not have a kindergarten, so I started in the first grade when I was four years old. I knew how to read and print, and I had begged to go to school. I was so happy to be going to school that the building looked like a cathedral to me.

Our one-room school was painted white with windows along one wall. There was a small entry porch where we hung our coats on hooks along one wall. Our muddy overshoes were mixed together on the floor. Behind the school and to the left was an outhouse for boys and one on the right for girls. The school was located on a barren piece of land with no trees or shrubbery and very little prairie grass. The only piece of equipment on the school ground was an old metal swing set with a couple of seats low to the ground for younger children and a seat that was wider and higher for older children.

When my oldest brother Ted, five years older than me, started going to that school, there were eighteen students spread out over all eight grades. That must have been quite a challenge for the teacher. By the time I attended, the number of students had decreased to nine.

Our teacher lived in a small, one-room cottage, called the "teacherage," built adjacent to the school. The teacher was responsible for shoveling snow as necessary for access around the school. She was to start a fire in the morning so the room would be warm by the time students arrived. The school had a large potbellied stove with gas jets rather than burning wood or coal. Burning gas was an advantage as we were located in the midst of multiple oil wells, making gas convenient and easiest to use. Not a surprise, our school was named the Oilfield School. Even though the teacher had the stove going early in the morning, it was often cold in the room, and we all gathered as close as we could to the stove.

Our school was located only a few miles south of Canada and a couple miles west of Sweetgrass, the border crossing with Canada. Inside the school room was a blackboard/chalkboard large enough to cover almost all of one wall. Every day someone was assigned to take the erasers outside in all kinds of weather and clap them together to remove the chalk residue so they could be used again to wipe the board. At the top of the blackboard were all the letters of the alphabet diagrammed to show exactly how to print the lines forming each letter, upper and lower case. I believe this was the Palmer Penmanship Alphabet. To improve our handwriting we had exercises such as repeatedly making overlapping circles on lined paper. The circles were to be the same size with the tops and bottoms touching the lines on the paper.

Mounted on the wall above the blackboard was a pull-down map of the world. I was very impressed with the large number of countries and hoped to someday travel the world, but countries other than the United States were never pointed out or talked about. Sometimes the pupil who pulled down the map forgot to hook it over the little nail at the bottom of the blackboard and there would be a terrible racket startling everybody as the map quickly rolled itself back up into the rack.

In a corner of the room was a cupboard about the size of an armoire which held books and was called the school library. I loved to read and finished reading most of those books within the four years that I attended Oilfield school, even though many were intended for older students.

I had a head start in reading because Mom taught every one of us six kids to read before we started school. At the time I started school we had only two books in our house. One was a simple book with repetitive words, such as "See Jane run," "See Jack run," "Run, Jane, run." I very quickly became bored with that book. This type of reader years later was highly criticized and removed from all schools. The other book at home was the opposite in difficulty. I had no choice but to start reading Mom's eighth-grade book. Of course I had to frequently ask her what a word was as I spelled or sounded it out phonetically. Years later Mom told me that she had started to become impatient with my constant questions even though she had always wanted to be a teacher. She was happy to send me off to first grade. A few years later, Pop bought a set of Encyclopedias from a salesman brave enough to find his way across the countryside. I made good use of those.

Everybody carried a lunch which we left in the coat room of the country school because it was cooler in there. Our lunch boxes were made of metal. Plastic wasn't invented, and paper bags were a waste that no one could afford. When we had liquids, they were carried in bulky glass canning jars. Sometimes we had "soup day" when everyone was to bring a soup, homemade or canned, that would all be dumped into one big pan set on top of the stove. One time someone brought a cream soup which did not mix well with the others. Adults today remember how awful that made all the soup taste.

My brothers and I always had good sandwiches made with the bread baked by Mom and leftover roast beef, ham or chicken. Another favorite was a fried egg sandwich. We always had some sort of dessert such as cake or cookies but rarely did we have fresh fruit. Either our grocery store seldom had fresh fruit or Mom might have thought it was too expensive. At home we had fruit that we had canned but there was no portable container like Tupperware to take that to school.

Our nine-month school year started March 15 and ended before Christmas. Yes, we had school during the summer because snow made the road too dangerous in the winter. Believe me the snow was much deeper in past years than it is now. We had a spring break and a fall break so that we could all help our farm families with the busy times of seeding and harvest. When we got home from our day at school in the summer, we then had farm chores and rock picking to do before bedtime. Farm kids were expected to do adult work at an early age. Pop taught Ted, my oldest brother, to drive the tractor when he was nine years old.

The County Health Nurse came to our school once a year to give immunizations to all the children whose parents had approved—they all did. The nurse also gave basic vision and hearing exams. She always demonstrated how to wash our hands under running water from the spigot of the five-gallon jug of water we used for drinking water. At home and everywhere else we washed our hands in a basin of water, usually used by more than one person until the water became dirty enough to throw out. None of us had running water at home but nobody ever told the nurse. At school we drank water out of small, flat paper cups that you had to open up and run water into. The cups were flimsy and it was hard to not spill. At home, and at all the homes we visited, we drank water from a ladle dipped into a bucket of water, with everybody drinking out of the same ladle and the same bucket.

Older kids sometimes picked on the younger kids but not a lot. Ted remembers that Eldon Bye threw Mike Buckley's boot down the outhouse. Excrement in the toilet was piled not too far from the top and so Mike just reached way down and retrieved his boot. We were all poor kids, and he couldn't afford to go home without his boot.

My adopted cousin Louis joined us in the country school when he was in the third grade. Uncle Rudy Suta had married his first cousin Margaret who was Louis' mother, after Louis' father had died. Louis had grown up in Bethlehem, Pennsylvania with his grandmother and an uncle who was not a good role model. Louis was an overgrown, big-mouthed, nasty brat who I never liked very well. He was a swaggering bully who was a bad influence on the other boys, swearing and teaching them dirty rhymes and jokes. My brother Ben remembers that Louis was teaching the other boys to gamble by rolling dice when he was stopped by the teacher, Mrs. Scalese. She told him, "I heard about you and your big-city ways and I won't let you act like that around here." Another time Louis was in the outdoor toilet for a very long time. Mrs. Scalese opened the door and pulled him out while hollering at him: "There is no way that I will allow you to skip out of school."

I remember only one Christmas pageant at school, but we probably had something every year. I don't remember ever having had a role in a play. I do remember that all the parents attended, and we sang Christmas carols. We always were given multicolored curled ribbon candy, which we only got at Christmas and was considered a big treat. We sometimes had peanuts in the shell. The biggest treat, remembered by every adult, was to receive a large, fresh orange.

I never had a friend in the school because the other students were boys. It was too hard for me to play ball with the boys because they were so much bigger. Winter snow was always so deep that our school was scheduled in the summer instead of winter. We went to school from April to December. We were given vacation at the times when we could help our families with seeding and harvest. All the students in our school were country kids.

We country-school kids had to go to the county seat, Shelby, to take a standardized achievement test at the end of each year. That was a hundred mile round trip, and we never went to Shelby otherwise except for some years when we went for one day just before Christmas. The test covered all the content we should have learned during that school year. This was a way to check on the effectiveness of teachers who did not meet all state requirements for their education. I think my grade school teachers were wonderful, but some might have been only high school graduates, and some attended a "Normal School" which was a one-year college-level program to prepare teachers.

When people find out that I graduated high school at fifteen they automatically say, "Oh, you skipped some grades." But I never "skipped" any grades. Instead I took two grades a year for two consecutive years. One year I took the comprehensive final exams covering everything that had been taught during that year for both first and second grades. The following year I took the exams for both third and fourth grades. In this way, I caught up with my brother Ben and we attended grade school and high school in the same grade.

In those years, until about 1950, Montana State College mailed every student's grade report to their parents. One evening when we were home from college and Ben and I were doing our usual argument about who got the best grades, Mom came out to the kitchen waving the two report cards she had saved to compare us on one specific quarter. That quarter included swimming in which I got a D. (Ben didn't take swimming because he got a doctor to lie that he had a back problem.). There wasn't much favoritism in our family but Ben really was Mom's "baby." I still have my third-grade report card with a handwritten note stapled to it from my teacher, Mrs. Dell T. Scalese. Her note says, "I suggest that Violet is put into the same fourth-grade class with Benny Suta and Jerry Buckley since her achievement tests show she is equal to or better in her grades." This was done after I had already been advanced from first grade into third grade on the recommendation of Mrs. Taft. My advancement was not automatic on the recommendation of the teacher but also required that I pass the comprehensive exams for each grade.

I never realized or thought that I was too young for the grades into which I was advanced. I just knew I was capable of doing anything I wanted.

Beth Volbrecht

"Oh, how wonderful to see you," exclaimed Beth as she opened the door to her home. "I've been thinking of you and hoping you were safe in this snowstorm." "Come in out of the snow and cold," she invited while holding back several dogs trying to sneak outdoors. Beth acted as a volunteer Humane Society in the little town of Sunburst.

I quickly slid through the door while she tried to calm down the dogs. Beth selected one of the two large, upholstered chairs filling her living room and invited me to sit down after she had removed a cover sheet and brushed off some of the dog hair. The next routine was to have tea. She said, "I was just going to brew some tea for myself. Would you like a cup?"

Beth was one of the teachers I had in my one-room school, and she was now teaching in Sunburst. When the roads were too bad for the bus and I had to stay in town, I would walk to visit her in her little house. I felt so grown up visiting her and sipping tea when I was only ten years old, and she was about seventy. Beth conversed with me as though I was an adult and never spoke down to me.

After preliminary greetings she might say, "I have a book of poetry I've been eager to share with you." She would tell me only a little about why she liked this author and this book. I remember her saying, "I don't want to spoil your discovery with my opinions." The books she loaned me were written for adults, far above my age level. But she never revealed any doubt about my ability to understand what she loaned me.

If I was returning a book there followed a series of questions and discussion. Questions such as: "Did you have a favorite poem in this book?" "I was puzzled about the meaning of such-and-such poem. What do you think he meant?" "Tell me, did you like this book as well as the one written by so-and-so?" And I also had some questions for her.

Before I left she would hand me another book, saying, "This book is new to me, and I look forward to hearing what you think."

I often picture her as the gutsy, attractive nineteen year old woman who came to Montana to claim land that the government was giving away to anyone who would commit to working the land. Beth said that at her high school senior banquet she was required to tell the other students what she planned to do with her life, and without hesitation she told them, "I'll have my own land and be a farmer." Now she thought she had to prove that.

This prairie land was full of rocks, most of the soil was hard clay and it deserved the name of dry-land farming because it seldom rained. It was difficult to get anything to grow. This land was free but required a lot of work and wasn't really such a great gift. She hired itinerant men to do the physical work while she taught in one-room schools to get enough money to pay them. Four out of ten homesteaders failed and left as quickly as they could, but Beth was tough and stayed.

Beth had a steely mind and a commanding voice when needed, even though she was quick to smile. She resembled Katherine Hepburn in stature and, like Hepburn, wore slacks all the time while doing outdoor farm work.

Beth was a farmer, a sheepherder, an artist, and a teacher. Her oil paintings of Glacier Park sold for a fairly high price to tourists. She wrote poetry, was a singer and taught painting to quite a few of the local farm women.

Before her husband died, Beth said she herded their 4,000 sheep. She wrote about her memories of seven years in a row, 1923 to '30, when they had no crop at all to harvest because it had been so dry. When winter came there was so much snow that their animals couldn't graze and had no hay to eat. There were some temperatures of 20 below. They cut and stacked Russian thistles and she stomped on them to make them flat between every layer of adding salt and then another layer of thistles. They called this "thistle sour kraut" and the animals liked it and lived through the winters.

Our conversations were interrupted when Beth moved to Nevada because that state, unlike Montana, would allow her to continue teaching after the age of seventy-two. Little country schools didn't have any retirement plans and Social Security didn't start until after 1935. Before she retired in her late eighties she was actually teaching the grandchildren of people she had taught. It amazes me that Beth actually taught for a short time my father and five of us six children.

Beth told me how much she "admired my parents who, with not much formal education themselves, raised six exceptional children and sent them all to some form of higher education." She was amazed that my parents could "eke out a living" on that hard, dry land. She also told me that I was her favorite student of all the years she had been teaching. Because I had such admiration for her, that was one of the greatest compliments I ever received.

I treasure an oil painting of a scene in Glacier Park that she gave me as a wedding gift. I cried then and feel sentimental when I think of her. I have the painting on the wall of my office.

The last time I spoke to her on the phone she was a bright ninety-two year old who cared for herself. She had failing vision but a clear mind until she died at the age of ninety-six.

Beth Volbrecht was one of several strong pioneer women I knew and admired. She was an intelligent, liberated female who demonstrated that women could do anything they wanted to do. I couldn't have been luckier than I was to be influenced by her.

I don't remember what facts she taught but I do remember that she inspired her students, prompted us to think critically about what we were reading, and fostered a love of music, art, and literature.

School Bus

While enrolled in the one-room country school, we were usually bused to school in Pop's car or Uncle Rudy's. There weren't other people riding with us so the drive to or from the school was about eight miles. It helped a lot that the country school scheduled some vacation time in the winter when the roads were most likely to be bad. That road west of Sweetgrass was seldom plowed during the winter when the road was frequently in bad condition. We often got stuck, either in snow or mud, and everybody had to get out and push the car. School would be cancelled if the weather was too bad. We didn't have a telephone to notify the teacher, but she could assume we weren't coming if we were very late and the weather was bad.

When we began going to school in Sunburst we had to ride in a typical old bright yellow school bus with plank seats and no seatbelts. The bus made the same circular loop every morning and afternoon. Because the bus went the same direction every time, we were the last to be picked up in the morning and go directly twelve miles to the school. In the afternoon we would have to ride the bus forty miles until we were dumped off at the driveway to our home. The school bus was very slow so we usually did not get home until 5:30 pm after getting out of school about 3:00 pm.

The school bus picked us up and dropped us off at the "Suta corner," which was one-and-a-half miles from our house. That was a lengthy "driveway," which was really a trail on the prairie with a little gravel here and there. My three older brothers and I crammed ourselves into our old 1932 truck named Hildegard to make the trip to and from the corner on school days.

I don't remember any of us playing games in the school bus to make the ride seem shorter and less miserable. My brothers had each other to talk with but I was the only girl on the bus.

A boy about my age, George Baldwin, rode the bus until they opened a one-room school closer to his home. George always had big greenish boogers running out of his nose and down to his mouth. He never had tissues or a handkerchief, so usually wiped his nose on his sleeve. George was such a sad-looking sight that my brothers teased me about him being my boyfriend. They would sing, "Georgie, Porgy, Pudding and Pie. Kissed the girls and made them cry." It made me angry at my brothers and I didn't like George at all. The joke was on me many years later when George came home for a class reunion and I saw that he had grown up to be a very handsome man. He worked as a model and actor in Guam, where he lived. And he was accompanied by a beautiful woman.

All bus kids had to have an alternative place to stay in Sunburst when weather prevented the bus from taking us home. We stayed home if bad weather was forecast, but snowfall during the day may have been greater than expected. Our bus would be cancelled, and we had to stay overnight in town. Forecasts were inaccurate and emergencies happened. The two other school bus routes from Sunburst drove on paved roads and were plowed early. My route had the worst road, graveled rather than paved, and our bus was more likely to be cancelled.

An area of the road between us and Sunburst went through what was known as "Hendricks Coulee." This coulee, a small ravine, was part of the rimrock where Sunburst was below

Sweetgrass

the rim and our home was on the elevated area above the rim. The road through Hendricks Coulee had twisting curves on a narrow road with a deep drop on one side poised over a pond. I always feared we would go into that pond. The road became more dangerous in the fall when farmers were hauling truckloads of grain to the granary in Sunburst. The truck drivers were always in a hurry to unload and get back home for another load of grain. The road was almost too narrow for a truck and a car to pass by one another.

One of our memorable school bus drivers was the shop teacher, a grizzled, skinny old man who everyone called "Crowbait." When Crowbait was nearing the Coulee, he would holler for us to balance the weight on both sides of the bus to make it easier for him to drive. We were willing to oblige in this or anything that would help us be safe because he was not a very good driver.

The roads in all directions from the Suta corner were narrow, with two lanes and no shoulders, providing barely enough width for two cars to pass by each other. The gravel on the roads was large, rough stones, not finely ground. When the road had been newly graveled, you had to be careful because the loose, rocky gravel stones were like driving on ice. In fact newly laid gravel caused Mom to slide into the ditch near Baldwin's and frightened her from ever driving again.

It was important to have gravel for traction when driving in snow or mud. The soil of the road was gumbo, which when wet became extremely slippery and sticky. When the road was wet, you had to simply try to stay in the deep rut in the middle of the road made by a previous driver and hope that you would not meet anyone coming from the opposite direction. If you met someone coming toward you there would be a brief moment of decision making as to who could most easily stop or move over, almost like a game of chicken. When the gumbo soil dried out, it would be about as hard as cement and the road would be very rough with deep ruts. We would hope for the road grader to come and smooth it out a bit, but the road grader always came at the wrong time. Inevitably the grader came shortly after a layer of fresh gravel had been laid, and it would push a lot of the gravel off the road and into the ditch. Then there would not be enough gravel left to help you drive safely the next time the road was bad.

Snowfall was definitely heavier in those days before climate warming. Every winter we would be snowed in several times for a day or two at a time. There would be at least once a winter when we would be snowed in for a week. I remember a frustrating winter when we were stranded for two full weeks. Most of the time we were plowed out after a day or two.

When snowed in at home, we played cards and board games after chores were done. Monopoly was most common but sometimes we played card games of Canasta, Pinochle, Crazy Eight, Hearts or Poker. Also Checkers and Cribbage. I did a lot of reading.

When we arrived home from school on a day when it had been snowing, our old truck Hildegard would need some attention. There often was a half foot of snow on the seat, and there was no heater or defroster. She was often hard to start when it was really cold and there wasn't a hill to park her on at the Suta Corner. We would begin by seeing if Hildegard would start with Henry cranking her. We often had to start walking the one-and-a-half miles home in deep snow—up to my knees and over the top of my overshoes—and freezing temperature. This is the truth and not just one of those stories an old grandfather would tell by making everything worse than it was. I was stupid enough to carry all my books and clarinet home every day, and my brothers never offered to help. They said it was my problem. It was just a force of habit to carry everything every day.

Ben was in the same grade as me and he never brought a single book home to study. Ben was really smart and could get decent grades without even trying and he didn't see any reason why he should try to get higher grades.

People today complain about the heavy weight of the backpacks their children have to carry but they ought to try carrying that same weight in front of them, stacked on outstretched arms. It is much harder to carry the weight that way. When I was a kid nobody even thought about having backpacks. Our mothers could have sewn them.

We were snowed in for a day or two quite a few times during the winter. A few times every winter we would be snowed in at home for a week. Pop got really antsy when we were snowed in. He kept going out with the tractor to try to plow out the road. But the wind would blow the snow back as quickly as he plowed the road clear. Our driveway had to be plowed frequently because it was more of a trail on the prairie than a road. Pop tried to keep some gravel on it in the areas where we got stuck in mud or snow.

The school bus seldom got stuck because the school would simply cancel the bus when they thought driving would be a problem. Then we would have to stay home or stay overnight in town with the people who had agreed to keep us in case of emergencies. However, I remember a few bad times when the bus actually got stuck because the road had drifted over after the snow plow had gone through. We were just stuck inside the bus. We did not have phones in those days, but I think the bus had a walkie talkie that reached the school, so somebody knew where we were. But it didn't help very much when nobody could reach us.

We just had to just sit and wait until the fathers got worried about us being so late. I remember one time when Pop plowed through the snow about six miles first to get a neighbor, Bill Baldwin, to come and help him. They had to drive tractors to pull us out and our old tractors didn't go very fast on snowed-in roads. It sometimes was 9:00 or 10:00 pm before we got home from school.

We were cold while waiting. The heater on the bus was not adequate to keep it warm—at any time—and the drivers were reluctant to keep the motor running because they were afraid of running out of gas. They wisely thought it was best to conserve gas by only running the motor periodically for heat.

At those times I was really thankful that Mom made me wear those ugly long brown cotton stockings and pants under my skirt.

Hildegard took all four of us to the Suta corner and back.

Transition from Country to City School

When my one-room country school merged with the city school of Sunburst, Mom told me about an incident involving my grade placement. I was starting seventh grade at the age of nine and the school board wanted to put me back into fourth or fifth grade, appropriate for my age. I had not "skipped" any grades but had taken two grades a year for my first two years of school.

Advanced placement each year was recommended by my teachers, and I, like everyone in the Oilfield School, had to take a comprehensive state exam at the end of every year.

At the end of each school year I had to go to the County Courtroom and take two comprehensive exams, one for each grade. It should have been obvious to the Sunburst school board that I had the required knowledge verified by the state exams I had taken for every grade.

I was also gaining half a year because the two schools had been on different yearly schedules. Our country school year was March to December while the school year in town was September to June. The schools made some type of adjustment and we country students just didn't have any vacation that year.

Ben and I started school in Sunburst. Rudy wasn't born yet.

Ben and I all dressed up for our first prom. Mom made my dress.

All in all, that meant that I was two or three years younger than most of the kids in my class.

My father was put on the Sunburst school board to represent the country school. He was very proud of being on the school board because he had very little schooling as a child. The School Board thought I should be put into the lower grade that matched my age. My father was a forceful person and thought I had already proven that I knew everything taught in lower grades. I guess it was quite an argument. The school board accepted me into the seventh grade on a six-month probation. Neither Pop nor Mom told me that I was on probation because they didn't want me to worry. When Mom later told me about this she said, "We had no doubt that you could handle the school work."

I didn't notice any problems while speeding through grade school. However, when I transferred to school in the city I became painfully aware that my appearance was different from classmates. I was truly an "ugly duckling."

To this day I am amazed that I had a smooth transition from country to city school. This was mainly because of the extraordinary support of Theodora Simmes, who was a farm neighbor of ours but had always gone to school in the city.

Everything was new and a little overwhelming, from finding my locker to turning on the bubbler for a drink of water. I was full of fear when I cautiously entered the seventh grade classroom. But I was warmly welcomed by Theodora who sat in the desk next to the door so that she would be the first to see me arrive. She greeted me and invited me to sit on the top of her desk while the teacher, Mr. Haines, was making some remarks. She introduced me to a friend of hers named Betty Lee. I asked at least a couple of times, "Betty Lee what?" or "Betty Lee who?" She sounded irritated when she said, "My last name is Lee and I don't have a middle name." I felt stupid and was afraid I had made an enemy.

However, Betty Lee and I are friends even now that we are in our eighties and live in different states.

Theodora and Betty took me under their wings and let me hang out with them during lunch breaks. We usually walked downtown, about seven long, cold blocks, and had cherry phosphate cokes at the soda fountain in the corner drug store. I was so happy and could hardly believe that Betty and Theo chose to be friends with me.

Several years later, Betty Lee told me that Theo had prepared the class for my arrival. She had explained to the students that it would be a big change for me to be coming from a one-room country school. Betty said Theo told them, "Violet would be much <u>younger</u> than them because she was <u>smart</u>." Betty said Theo threatened the class, saying, "If I ever hear of somebody teasing or picking on Violet I will beat them up." And everyone, even the boys, knew that she was capable. Theodora was big for her age and definitely muscular from helping her father with farm work. Nobody ever teased me or treated me differently than the other students. This is amazing now that I think of it. I couldn't believe how lucky I was to be accepted as a friend by Betty and Theo.

Betty and I exchanged overnight visits at each other's house. We both had double beds to sleep in, but we each envied the other. I slept in flannel sheets which she loved, and I thought her smooth cotton sheets were more "the way things should be." It was a case of city-country contrast.

When my sister was born on my ninth birthday, Betty told Mom that she wanted a baby for her birthday, too. And it is hard to believe but my youngest brother, Rudy, was born exactly on Betty's birthday. I sure don't know how my mother managed to do that, but it made Betty happy.

Let me explain how I knew that I was an "ugly duckling" when I started school in the city. Not only was I several years younger than my classmates and small for my age, but

Sweetgrass

I was also a "late bloomer" developmentally. And I dressed like a dork.

Mom made me wear old-fashioned brown cotton stockings attached to a garter belt, and they sagged around my ankles immediately. Mom thought I should have home permanents to make my hair manageable, but they just made my hair frizzy. I wore round, wire-framed glasses at a time when everybody else had plastic frames. My parents thought I had to get wire frames because they would be sturdier, but I had never broken a frame. I wasn't an active rough-and-tumble girl; I was a book reader.

Mom sewed dresses for me out of colorful printed bags that held flour or chicken feed—"gunnysacks" in other words. I think it's humorous, now that I dress like a fashionista, that I used to select the color and print of my next dress by going to the grain elevator and looking at the stack of feed bags against the wall. The fabric was stiff and scratchy.

Mom did her best to make clothes for me, but she wasn't a seamstress. She had to use a treadle sewing machine that skipped stitches and she didn't use patterns because of the cost. She tried to add pretty touches of ruffles or lace but I have never looked good in ruffles and lace. My attire was a big contrast compared to the Lund sisters who always wore Jantzen twin-set sweaters. Not everybody wore Jantzen but all the girls dressed in nice casual clothes that were obviously not home-made.

Girls were not allowed to wear slacks or jeans in school, but Mom made me wear slacks underneath my dress in order to stay warm on the bus. That was appropriate but it was very embarrassing to take off and put on pants while standing in the school hallway.

When I was in high school, I pleaded for some store-bought clothes. I ordered from the Sears-Roebuck or "Monkey Ward" (Montgomery Ward) catalog a reversible skirt and weskit or vest. I spent that entire year mixing and matching those two pieces that were solid navy on one side and a navy-white plaid on the other side. I had a white short-sleeve sweater and a white blouse to complete that ensemble. I added some fashion when I was able to get saddle shoes like those that everybody wore. That's all that I remember wearing that school year.

I think it was my junior year that "poodle skirts" became the rage and I begged for one. They were made of felt material and were a full circle wide. Some even had a poodle applique. We were in Cut Bank one day when I saw a poodle skirt in red, my favorite color, and in my size. I begged and begged Mom for that skirt. Pop was pretty stingy with money unless it was to buy drinks or dinner for other people. Mom had plenty of money to buy groceries, but she wasn't given a salary or allowance to buy extras. The money from the sale of eggs, pullets, and butter should have been Mom's, but it was spent on groceries. When she began receiving a social security check she definitely claimed that as her own money to spend as she wished. By that time our farm was well established, and while we were still poor we were no longer as poor as when we began farming. She had to go find Pop who was in a bar drinking with a friend and beg him for money to buy this for me. Pop didn't mind buying drinks for friends at the bar but thought $6.00 for girl clothes was outrageous. Having to cajole and beg him must have been humiliating for Mom. But I was never so happy.

The only other item of clothing I ever begged for was "saddle pants." Girls could not wear pants of any kind to school until my senior year when we could wear pants on Fridays. Saddle pants had become a must-have fashion item for girls and young women. They were made of heavy twill material and were cut to be worn tight. There was no stretch in the material, the pants were just plain tight.

Despite my feelings of embarrassment and shyness in high school, I finished successfully and was accepted to begin college when I was fifteen years old. When I told the college at the last minute that I decided to stay out a year, they made it known that they were upset because they had held a special board meeting to discuss whether to admit me at the age of fifteen. Colleges were not as flexible then as they are now.

Instead of college, I spent that next year working as a carhop and waitress at the 49er Drive-In and living with my friend Betty Lee. That is another story, but it might never be written.

Postscript: When I wrote this in 2021, I thought it would be good to send a copy to Theodora with a thank you note. I didn't know her address. I knew she and her husband John Wiegand had a large farm near Shelby, Montana, a town of over 3,000 and the county seat. I decided to just address the envelope to her at Shelby with a notation to "please forward." It was a long shot but I thought that their farm was large enough and her husband might be involved enough in Shelby that someone in the post office might know their box number or address. I didn't hear anything for a long time and thought the post office just threw the letter away. But in April 2023, two years later, I received a wonderful letter from Theo's caregiver saying she was living in a facility in Missoula, a long way from Shelby. Somehow the letter had made it to her. Theo could dictate only a brief note but the caregiver said that Theo showed my letter to everyone and got a lot of joy from it. I can hear her loud laugh in my head right now. Her phone number was included so I called, and Theo was able to talk for a short time. Sometime during the next month, Theodora died. With my permission, a son read my story at her funeral and said that this story best described Theo. The entire situation reminds me that I should never put off something my gut says to do because I don't know what might happen. This story made her very happy, and I was happy because of that.

My Hillbilly Relatives

My mother had two sisters, Madeline and Hulda, who both married and lived hidden away in the extreme northwest corner of Montana. The forest surrounding them was so thick that you couldn't see anything but trees. They didn't even have a view of the other mountains surrounding them.

The place where Madeline and Hulda lived is named Trego, but you would not have found it on any ordinary map. They received mail addressed to Trego and there was a post office within a house that also served as a grocery store and gas station. There was a large freezer shared by the community because everybody hunted but they were too poor to have their own freezer or didn't have electrical wiring. That house and the elementary school made up the entire town of Trego.

In 2025, that house, which is the entire town of Trego, has been expanded and enhanced, and it can be found on the tourist map of Montana.

If you look at a map of Montana, you can locate the area where they lived as being far west and north of the town of Whitefish, which now has an airport and a wealthy ski area. When I was a child, the store in Trego was the only place that had a telephone. Even today you might not be able to get phone service on your fancy cellphone because there is no internet service in many places in the mountains.

Aunt Hulda lived near Trego because she married a lumberjack. Walter definitely did not have a large, muscular body as you might picture when you think of a lumberjack. He also must have been the unluckiest lumberjack there ever was since he had a lot of accidents at work. It seemed as though every time Walter went back to work we would soon hear that he had another accident. There was no liability or health insurance available for them.

Hulda and Walter had three children about my age and I loved spending a week with them in the summers when I was seven or eight years old. I rode with Grandpa Lozing and Uncle Gilbert when they went to get a truckload of fence-posts and then stayed with the Farleys before they came back to get another load. Gilbert was my mother's only brother and he was fun to be around. He sang old country songs and taught me the words to sing along with him.

Hulda and Walter were very poor and lived in a house that could best be described as a shack. The family existed by eating produce from the garden, fish from a nearby stream, and animals they could kill. The children raised rabbits and chickens for their family to eat and to sell to other people in the community. I enjoyed helping them take care of the animals and the garden. We spent a lot of time playing with the rabbits. Other than that, we just walked around looking at things and playing. We threw sticks and rocks and made up our own games. We played hide-and-go-seek but had to carefully mark off the parameters to stay within so that I would not get lost in the forest. I envied my cousins' ability to always go barefoot, but my feet were too tender.

Walter died fairly young but surprisingly not of an accident while lumber-jacking. A few years later Hulda married a man who was truly the spitting image of Walter. He looked the same and even had the same voice and mannerisms. All of our family have talked about this amazing miracle that

Hulda found Walter re-incarnated as a much better version of himself. The new Walter was a good provider and never had any accidents.

My cousins all grew up to be good people. Shirley worked her entire life as a secretary for the State of Montana and Billy became an evangelical preacher. Joann was very significant to us because she would go into the mountains and pick huckleberries that Mom purchased. It was tradition that Mom always made huckleberry pie when we visited Montana. She used to pick the berries herself which takes a long time because they are a whole lot smaller than blueberries. Mom had to quit picking after her brother-in-law became scared when he saw a bear eating on one side of a bush while Mom was picking berries on the other side. After that, nobody would go picking with Mom.

Mom's other sister who lived near Trego was her non-identical twin Madeline. Madeline had married a retired railroad man who was quite a few years older than her father. The match worked out well because neither of them wanted to go out for entertainment and there wasn't any at Trego anyway. I don't know why they chose to live where they did but scenery was pretty and the land they selected was probably inexpensive years ago because it was only good for grazing Bill's horse.

They were able to donate a chunk of land for Trego to build a grade school. In return, the school offered to pipe running water to their place. Bill chose to have the water pipe run into the horse trough, rather than into the house. That makes a lot of sense when you think about who drinks the most water, but they could easily have run a second branch of pipe to the house. Instead, they continued to carry buckets of water to the house for personal use.

Madeline and her husband had a son who they named William H. O'Pelt, Jr. He was always called Junior except Madeline pronounced some words funny and she said "Choonyer" instead of Junior. Junior seemed to have mild cognitive impairment. He may have been that way at birth,

Sweetgrass

or he may have suffered brain damage from his father hitting him hard on the side of his head as discipline for any little infraction. That really bothered Mom because she would intervene even when she saw a stranger hitting their child in a grocery store. Her sister wouldn't have permitted her to intervene in this situation.

One time much later while Mom and Pop lived alone on the farm, Choonyer came to visit for a couple of nights bringing along a girlfriend. My parents did not like the girlfriend very well. Pop described her as a "slop hound" because her fingernails, hair and clothing were extremely dirty. Pop was a farmer and understood getting dirty from work, so his standards were not very high. This was the only time we ever heard Pop or anyone else use that derogatory phrase. But Mom agreed that what Pop said was true. On rare occasions my family now uses that name when we want to really insult a person we are gossiping about in private.

I have wondered what Choonyer has been doing these recent years. I wouldn't be surprised if he joined a Montana militia just for friendship and belonging. Also, he was very good with guns. But he had a good heart and I don't think he would hurt anybody or invade the U.S. Capital. At least, I did not see him on television during the January 6th insurrection.

Madeline and her husband with assistance built a sturdy small one-room log cabin. I was surprised the first time I saw the cabin as a young child because Madeline was sweeping the floor, but the floor was only packed dirt. A few years later they had a wooden floor, a better wood stove, and better seating. Bill tied a rope between the house and outhouse and between the house and water pipe so that he would not get lost in a storm considering his poor eyesight.

I thought their log cabin was wonderful and have always wanted to live in a log house.

In 2008, a friend went to Montana with me and by body memory I was able to find Trego and the log cabin. We spent a while taking pictures and trying to peek into the windows. A couple drove over to find out what we were doing. They said they were "city-folks from back east" and had bought the log cabin and surrounding land where they built a big log house. They use Aunt Madeline's log cabin for their guests from the city who they said just absolutely love the experience. They were glad to learn more about the history of the people who had lived there. And I was happy that the log cabin I feel sentimental about was being well cared for and was making other people happy.

Pete Suta holding Dian and Hannah Suta
William H. O'Pelt and Madeline, with son "Junior
Walter and Hulda Farley with Shirley, Joann, and Billy
Ben, Violet, and Henry Suta

Back (l to r): Madeline Lozing O'Pelt, Hannah Lozing Suta, Anna Ehli Lozing, Hulda Lozing Farley; Middle (l to r): Ted Suta, Henry Suta, Ben Suta, Shirley Farley; Front: Violet Suta, Joann Farley

Sunburst, Montana

When I tell people I grew up in Montana, they always ask where. That's a difficult question to answer since I didn't really have a home town. I lived on a farm that was about twelve miles from either the tiny town named Sweetgrass, or another named Sunburst. Both towns had their heyday when I was a child but one resembles a ghost town and the other isn't even a ghost town. My oldest son sneaked a preview of this story and asked why I didn't include the towns of Shelby or Cut Bank, which he has visited. The answer is that they were too far away and I never went there as a child. I only went to Shelby when we had to take comprehensive exams at the end of each school year. When we were more affluent, we also spent one day in Shelby at Christmastime.

Sunburst was a small town with no distinguishing characteristics until oil development occurred in the 1920s. In the height of the oil activity, the Texas Company (later Texaco) built a refinery in the town and production was consistently good. Jobs were steady and paid well in comparison to local incomes from farming and ranching.

To house the employees who worked in the refinery and those who checked on the pumps in the oil fields, the company built quite a few identical small two-bedroom homes with one bathroom, a one-car garage and a basement.

Main street of Sunburst.

For many years there was enough production from the oil wells to keep the refinery running on two shifts daily. That was pretty impressive. The population of Sunburst grew and was maintained at about 1,000–1,500 from the 1920s to the 1970s. The Refinery operated steadily since the late 1920s and it was taken for granted that it would continue. It therefore was a stunning, unexpected shock when the Texaco Company announced in May 1977 that they were going to pipe oil to their new refinery in Anacortes, Washington and dismantle the one in Sunburst, though oil production had not decreased around Sunburst. Approximately 2,500 oil wells were producing about 100,000 barrels of crude oil a day. Employees were offered jobs in Anacortes and, with no option of jobs in Sunburst, more than half of Sunburst's population moved to Anacortes within a couple of months.

The oil refinery had been very important to the city in many ways. Almost half of the local taxes were paid by the oil refinery. In the mid to late 1950s the Texaco company even subsidized a physician to reside and practice in Sunburst.

Sweetgrass

He left town when a high school girl died suddenly and the rumor was that he had performed a botched abortion. The rumor was denied by the family and boyfriend but no alternative reason was given for her death.

A Northern Development Association was formed by a group of Sunburst residents to identify resources to help them get along without the oil company.

They found that Sunburst's trading area stretched twenty miles east, fifteen miles west, and nine miles to the north and south and was rich in cattle, sheep, wheat, mustard, barley, safflower, rape seed, and bird seed.

It took at least two or three years for the natural change in ages and time to decrease the hostility.

My brother Ben and I transferred to school in Sunburst from our one-room country school when we both were entering the seventh grade. We later had the honor of being the first class to graduate from the new building of North Toole County High School in 1952. Lilacs were used to totally cover the gymnasium for graduation. Lilacs apparently don't require much moisture to grow because in our dry land lilac bushes formed hedges around almost every house in town. You could smell the strong and beautiful aroma of lilacs everywhere.

On Main Street was a pharmacy that had no pharmacist but safely held prescriptive medications that came by bus from Shelby. At this drug store you could buy basic things such as Vaseline, but you had to ask the owner for feminine hygiene products and for men's Trojans. These products were not on display, so there often were people standing around looking embarrassed while waiting to tell the clerk what product they wanted. Menstruation and sex were never mentioned in public in the 1950s, as though they were terrible things that never happened.

At lunch time groups of high school girls, including myself, Betty Lee, and Theodora Simmes, walked several blocks to the pharmacy which had an old fashioned soda bar. We could sit on stools at the counter and watch our cherry phosphate cokes made fresh. My younger brother Rudy added to this story that the soda fountain ten years later had more varieties, and he had chocolate cokes while Sherry had cherry cokes. The flavorings all had pumps mounted on marble containers. My sister-in-law Maxine worked there for a while and said that each of those heavy marble containers had to be emptied and carefully washed out every night after closing.

On Main Street there were two grocery stores, Rollie White's and Meagher's. Mom was able to sell some eggs and chickens to both stores and directly to some people in town who received a discount and free delivery to their door. The chickens were young, weighed about 2 ½–3 pounds, and were called pullets or fryers. Of course we had to do all the cleaning of these chickens before they could be sold as "dressed" fryers. When I say "we" in relation to cooking it means Mom and I. Plucking feathers of about 350 chickens every summer along with needlework projects caused the problem I have of "trigger thumb" which makes it too painful for me to bend my thumb and forefinger together.

The town had Catholic and Lutheran churches and a small Assembly of God church, attended primarily by one family. The community called this the Holy Roller church alluding to the movements of people being "healed" or "speaking in tongues."

There was a barber shop and for a few years in the 1950s there was The Tip Top Cafe which was good while it lasted. The husband cooked, and the wife waited tables while always wearing shoes with at least a two- inch heel. It was a point of conversation for women to wonder whether she could put her feet flat on the floor when she went home and removed her shoes.

Sweetgrass

For a few years, a pool hall operated on Main Street and was able to survive with patronage from high school kids. A movie theater was being built east of Sunburst but was never completed.

In the late 1950s a lumberyard was opened by Vern Mauritson, the band director. He may have been too optimistic about growth of the town, but the Texaco company had not left yet. Around 2000 a combined Senior Center and Library was built by the community with assistance from the federal government.

Of all the businesses Sunburst had, only three taverns and a reduced drug store remain in operation. A tavern at the top left of main street is Dutch's Bar and at the bottom of the block is the VFW Club. In the middle is the former Lutheran Church which had been moved and became the Mint Bar. The facade of former businesses on Main Street looks almost the same as it did but the buildings are vacant. I have heard there is a service station that sells a few food items such as milk and bread.

People talk about wanting to raise their children in a small town, away from the drugs and violence of bigger cities, not realizing that there is very little for teenagers to do in a small town and they still can get into trouble. There was quite a bit of beer drinking by the high school boys. Some of the teenagers must have spent time having sex because it wasn't unusual for sixteen year old girls in high school to have weddings. The contraceptive pill was not yet available. In those days sex was never openly talked about, even in the Health Classes.

It was a popular activity for high school students to cruise Main Street, traveling the long single-block before making a U-turn or "UUee." The drivers gunned their motors and drove as fast as they could for a block before making a U-turn, causing the elderly town policeman to go crazy hollering at them as they cruised past him without punishment.

The most significant occurrence of my high school years was selection of our band as the Honor Band to lead the Portland, Oregon Rose Festival. *See the story about the band.*

Despite becoming almost a ghost town after the refinery left, Sunburst built up a reputation of having an excellent school. Groups of high school kids in the last twenty years have received top awards in national math and science contests. I was surprised when I saw one of the math groups being interviewed on a national morning broadcast.

Other than the terrible loss of the oil refinery, Sunburst is a typical small town in America being destroyed by the progress of better roads and automobiles that allow people to travel to a larger town for a better selection of items.

In recent years I have heard that Amazon trucks are making quite a few deliveries driving on graveled roads to the homes of farmers.

Band from Sunburst

Vernon Mauritson, nicknamed Mort, wasted no time in recruiting me when I transferred from a one-room country school and entered seventh grade in town. He made band sound like a great opportunity. He had decided that it would be perfect for me to play the clarinet. I didn't even know what a clarinet was. He handed me an old metal clarinet, a book of beginner's lessons, and gave private and group lessons. My family suffered while I practiced a couple hours every night, but they never told me to quit. Pop called the clarinet my "squawk box."

Even though I was only nine years old, I was designated "first chair" of the band the very next year, which is a little like the concertmaster in an orchestra. Mort got sheet music for me to play solos in state competitions and during band concerts. He knew he could count on me to practice hard and play well.

I think Mr. Mauritson knew how important these achievements were to my emotional state. I was almost three years younger than my classmates and he gave me a way to rise above just being a country hick or ugly duckling. Soon Mort spoke privately to Pop and amazingly persuaded him to loosen his stingy wallet and buy one of the very best clarinets for me which made a difference because it had a better tone.

Basketball games and band concerts were a big deal in our rural community because there were few other entertainments. Our band received many awards in competitions, but we really shined as a marching band. We marched and performed fancy formations at half time of every basketball game. That was big entertainment for small towns. All the towns in our area were small and the high schools didn't have enough students to be able to produce football teams, but basketball was very competitive, and the bleachers were full for all games. I think they came as much for the band performances as for the game.

Because of the excellence of our band as judged at statewide contests, we were invited to be the honor band at the Portland, Oregon Rose Festival in June 1952. This festival is not as large as the one in Pasadena, but there were marching bands and floats made of flowers and the five-mile parade was watched by millions.

It was amazing that my Sunburst, Montana high school with a total enrollment of 150 students had 120 of them participating in the Portland Rose Festival. The entire town of Sunburst had a population of only one thousand.

We had a lot of extra band practices before and after school, causing me to miss the school bus. Mom arranged for me to board in town when necessary with a family who were devout members of the small Assembly of God church. This led to a serendipitous mind-opening experience. The family went to church on some week nights and it would have been inappropriate for me to refuse to go with them. The services were interactive with people waving their hands and continually calling out phrases such as "Amen," "Tell it Brother," and "Praise the Lord." There were times when someone would "swoon" or begin to speak in tongues. That excited everybody as a sign that Jesus was truly present with us. At my Lutheran church nobody even said Amen unless it was written as part of a prayer. I hadn't known there were different ways for people to worship.

Sweetgrass

To get the band ready for the Portland Rose Festival our town worked hard to raise money to purchase uniforms and pay expenses for the trip. In addition to standard band uniforms, they also acquired Western uniforms of custom-made ten-gallon cowboy hats and plaid Western-style shirts that we wore with new dark blue jeans. Portland may be further west on a map but Montana was always considered a more western place. The people in Portland liked it best when we wore our Western attire.

Mort recruited as drum major a tall and handsome former student, Raymond Gallup, who had recently returned from serving two years with the Marine Corp in Korea where he was wounded twice. He and Mort really put us through boot camp. At the five-mile parade in Portland on a hot day, there were first-aid stations to treat those participants who dropped out because of foot injuries, fatigue, heatstroke or other reasons. We were very proud that not a single one of us dropped out of the parade for any reason.

The Drum Major and Mort developed a series of whistles and baton movements to communicate what we were to do—which songs to play and which formations to perform. We could be marching down a street in standard parade formation and suddenly startle the onlookers by splitting apart with each row going in a different direction, some marching toward the spectators on the sidewalk before doing about-face and returning to formation. We could do these fancy formations even while playing a march. That was quite an achievement considering that some of our band members couldn't tell their right and left feet apart when we started practicing.

In addition to leading the parade, we gave several other performances in Portland. Most unusual was the day we went downtown in our Western-style uniforms and marched single file in heavy afternoon traffic, weaving between cars and never missing a note or a step. There were a lot of cars honking their horns and I'm not sure whether that was like applause or telling us to get the H_ out of their way. I'm pretty sure it was positive because I never heard anybody holler a negative remark.

Mr. Mauritson was not required or expected to work so hard in making the band excellent, but his hard work resulted in proud memories for the entire community. Being part of a group, such as an athletic team, debate club, or performing group has been proven to have a positive effect on intellectual and emotional development of young people. Plato said that he would teach children physics and philosophy but that the arts, such as music, are the key to learning. Our band members all had good attendance at school and to the best of my knowledge had passing grades in their classes.

I am not exaggerating when I say that I think my experience with the band saved me from suicidal thoughts that probably occur, even briefly, to most teenagers. Members of the band made a commitment to be the best they could be. Achievement does wonders for self-confidence. Those solos I played were great preparation for my leadership roles.

I have special appreciation for my favorite teacher, Mr. Vernon Mauritson, because of all that he did to help me develop self-confidence. The entire band and community developed a sense of pride. Mort was an exceptional teacher and person.

The Sunburst band wore Western uniforms.

Sweetgrass: My Hometown

We were very poor and didn't go to any town unless it was necessary. We couldn't afford to buy anything and didn't need to buy anything. Sweetgrass had all that we needed. We ordered essential clothing out of the Sears & Roebuck or the Montgomery Ward catalogs—called Sears and Monkey Ward. Shoes were ordered by drawing an outline around our feet. These large catalogs were recycled for use in our outhouse.

Mom made Violet's clothes, and the boys wore clothes handed down so only one item had to be purchased. Mom always bought clothes too large saying, "You will grow into it."

Sweetgrass was the only town we went to. It was about twelve miles away on a bad road that was partly graveled. During the recession Pop helped improve that road but it has never been paved. When we butchered an animal we stored the meat in a freezer at Mars's Grocery Store. Their butcher cut up the meat, wrapped it and labeled it. We went to town to get as much as we could use without a freezer or refrigerator. Mom canned chicken, meat and fish as well as vegetables and fruit.

Sweetgrass now exists as a major border crossing with Canada on Interstate Hwy 15 known as the Alaska Highway. Border security is a more serious business now than it was

Sweetgrass in the 1930s.

fifty years ago. When I was young the border guards knew our family and just waved us through.

All traces of businesses have been removed from Main Street. In the town there are presently a few small houses built by the government for the border agents and a few small houses of retirees who never went anywhere else.

This had never been a border crossing of concern regarding illegal immigration. After all, Canadians are happy where they are. But now there is no place to hide if someone did want to cross over illegally.

Sweetgrass isn't even a ghost town.

But Sweetgrass was our address, and we considered it our home town when I was a child. Let me tell you about the way Sweetgrass used to be.

After 1900 Sweetgrass became a major trade center for ranchers, homesteaders and border traffic. By 1912 it had two general stores, two hotels, two restaurants, four saloons, a bank, two lumberyards, a land office, a newspaper, livery barns, a bulk oil station, a school going through the eighth grade, and an implement dealer. A few years later it added a four-bed hospital, drug store, blacksmith shop, clothing store, grain elevator, more saloons, and a high school.

The population of Sweetgrass has never been over 150 but it was a lively town when I was a child, with seven bars kept busy by bored ranchers and Canadians. There was a Canadian law that prohibited men and women from drinking together in the same barroom. That was no way to have fun, so they poured across the border. Also, gambling was fun in Sweetgrass even though it was illegal in Montana for many years before it stopped in Sweetgrass. Sweetgrass came to life on weekends when Canadians came streaming across the border to drink and dance and gamble and fraternize in the seven bars.

My Aunt Margaret and Uncle Rudy loved playing the slot machines. They would lift me up to pull the handle of the slot machine, hoping I would bring them luck. Uncle Rudy loved those slot machines so much that he bought several to play in his own basement when Montana began to enforce the law against gambling.

Main Street was wide and dusty with almost no gravel. There was boardwalk in front of only one store, otherwise you walked on dirt or mud, maybe a little gravel. Storefronts looked like those depicted in old Western movies. Vehicles were parked at creative angles because there were no markings. I could see remnants of where horses used to be hitched up when owners used them for transportation.

I never saw the Livery Stable because it was taken apart, board by board, by Pop and Alex Toth, and used to make our barn. We could still see some marks on boards from the stable.

Curly Bob's bar on the top left of Main Street was the largest and nicest bar.

Of all the bars, Billy Kimble's was the worst; dirty and full of alcoholics. You had to go through the bar to get to the most gross outdoor toilets you have ever seen. Yet that was the place to go to when you really had to go because there wasn't much of a waiting line – everyone hurried out. Yes, I did go in there when I was a child.

My brother Rudy was told that Jimmy Prosser had a car repair and sales shop that was built to allow cars filled with bootlegged booze to hide by driving beneath the regular floor of the building. I can't confirm that but I can believe it because there was a lot of bootlegging from Canada to the United States during Prohibition from January 1920 until December 1933. Across our farm were tracks of a bootlegger's trail worn so deeply that the track was still visible in 1988 when we sold the land, more than fifty years after prohibition ended.

Sweetgrass

There was also some legal commerce in Sweetgrass. A Women's Clothing Store run by Jenny Kirkobough was next door to the Post Office in the home of Phyllis Crockford.

Marr's Grocery Store was a very busy place. They had a walk-in cooler where they could hang carcasses of animals to age for a while and a freezer that ran on some sort of generator. The REA had not reached our area, so nobody had home refrigeration. People slaughtered their own animal and the butcher at Marr's cut it into pieces, wrapped and labeled them. We rented a freezer locker there for storage. We drove in to town once a month or two to get meat out of the freezer and buy other groceries. In the summer we ate a lot of the chickens we raised, freshly killed as needed. During the winter we were able to keep some food cool using ice from our reservoir. Mom always stored roast beef on a plate in the kitchen cupboard at room temperature. I guess we ate it before it could spoil and make us sick.

We canned a lot of beef, pork, fish and chicken at home. I still wish I could have some of the freshly caught trout that Mom canned in her special way. We didn't buy fresh vegetables because we had our garden in the summer and canned our own for winter.

Our rare trips to Sweetgrass were exciting. The cover was torn off comic books and paperbacks when outdated and the price was reduced to a nickel. Mom usually had enough money to buy each of us a nickel box of cracker-jack. We could hardly wait to get home where we could empty the box into a bowl and claim the prize that was always included in every box. My bad luck at games or gambling was predicted by the fact that I am probably the only person who once didn't get a prize in the cracker-jack box.

I sometimes bought a small song book which had the lyrics of popular songs. I didn't know the tunes because our single radio station in Shelby played the same old records over and over. Not knowing the songs and being aware of my poor singing, I would walk out on the prairie where no one could hear me. Several years later when I started playing the clarinet I bought a book of Eddie Arnold songs that I could play on my clarinet while Uncle Gilbert sang and played his guitar.

There was a movie theater in Sweetgrass that we rarely attended. Uncle Gilbert took us four kids a couple of times and he would sing old songs while he drove. A couple of his favorites were "Corrina, Corina, Where you been so long?" and "Good Night Irene." I remember only two movies that I saw as a child. One was Black Velvet with Mickey Rooney and Judy Garland, and the other was Heidi with Shirley Temple as the lead actress.

Ted remembers that there was a four-bed hospital in Sweetgrass. When I was about four years old I was taken to see Grandma Suta as she was dying from stomach or some form of abdominal cancer. I don't remember being told how sick she was and how different she would look. She was a warm, caring woman who had special love for me because she had had two girls who died as babies. I was the first Suta girl to survive. I remember that I cried and was afraid to lie down next to Grandma, but I don't know why I cried. I think she just must have looked very sick.

There was a school in Sweetgrass for all 12 grades. The high school had only a few students, but they refused to merge with Sunburst when the new school was built there. Sunburst had been a competitor in basketball and the parents would rather drive their children about 26 miles twice a day to attend school in Oilmont than to have them picked up by the Sunburst school bus.

There is a cemetery located next to the Canadian border. It used to be just plain prairie, and I thought I would like to be buried there near many relatives and friends. But then they planted lawn seed and began watering and mowing the grass. That makes me angry because of the waste of water in a place where water is very scarce. So now I don't want to be planted there.

I wasn't sure if my memory was right when I thought I had seen a rodeo in that tiny town. How could that small town sponsor a rodeo? But my brother Ted confirms that they held a rodeo there every year. Ted remembers that they once called on him to compete with a monkey over which one could peel a banana the fastest. Ted laughed and said he won the race. I asked what his prize was. He laughed louder and said, "It was another banana, but I was happy to get it."

Now in 2025 there is nothing at all in my home town of Sweetgrass but the border crossing and a combination duty-free store and gas station.

However, the Glocca Morra bar still exists nearby, and it is family tradition that we must stop there for a beer any time we are passing through Sweetgrass.

The demise of small towns has occurred everywhere in the United States. With the economic boom after World War II people began to be able to buy cars. The roads have been improved and maintained better. Now the locals are able to drive to a larger store in a larger town where they can get a better selection of items they want to buy.

Country Gatherings

Country Dances

When I was a child there would be dances once a year or more somewhere in the countryside. The most common location was a one-room schoolhouse. The Boundary School about seven miles from where I lived was used most often. That school was north of Cut Bank, near Grandpa Lozing, and is where Mom went to school. The Fitzpatrick school which was halfway between the Suta House and Cut Bank was often used for dances. Also the Mud Lake Community Center, Red River School, Oilfield School, and the Bunyak's hay loft.

The dances usually were held at harvest time to celebrate harvest being finished whether the crop was good or bad. Fall was a good time because farmers were not so busy.

It was common for a family to have a dance when they completed a new building on their farm, no matter what the purpose of the building would be. We had a dance when construction was completed on our chicken coop. These were commonly called "Barn Dances" because the barn would have been the first building and the largest to be built on a homestead. A dance in the country thereafter would be called a Barn Dance even if it was held in a granary.

Sweetgrass

Mom and Pop met at a country dance when she had a fight with her boyfriend and Pop gave her a ride home. Sometimes years later when Pop had been drinking he would use a nasty voice to tell Mom if she was going to argue with him she could just go live with her boyfriend or her Father. This was mean when she had four young children, couldn't drive, had no money and there were no telephones to call a friend. At least he never hit her or anybody else even when he had been drinking.

Grandpa Lozing's birthday celebration.

We have a tiny black and white snapshot of "The Suta Band" consisting of Pop, Rudy and Kalman. They had one more brother, Willy or William, but I don't know why he wasn't part of the band. Rudy and Kalman were posing with guitars and Pop said he used to play the banjo and harmonica. They must have played before we children were born. Remembering that story, I gave him a harmonica for Christmas one year when I was a young adult. His face lit up when he saw it, but I knew he would not be able to play because his hands had become swollen from arthritis and work, and he had forgotten how to play. I just gave it to him for memories of younger days. My son Brent (Buzz) Moran claimed Pop's banjo, which was sixty years old or more and spent quite a bit of money to have it cleaned, repaired and tuned. He hung it on the wall in his house but never tried to play.

The usual band at the country dances I remember consisted of Mom's brother Gilbert Lozing playing the guitar and singing, Mom's uncle Stanley Bunyak playing the fiddle, and Pop's youngest brother Kalman playing the banjo and harmonica. Gilbert could yodel, and he said that skill made him a star in the barracks while he served in World War II. All of them were self-taught.

One of my favorite memories is dancing with Pop when I was very young by placing my feet on top of his shoes. When I was older I always had a dance with Pop. I'm thinking that these country dances may have been precursors of my love for music and dancing. They were notable because we didn't have many gatherings of people, and many other gatherings were not fun.

Women made sandwiches and dishes to pass for a late-night supper. The men brought whiskey and took frequent breaks to go outside for a drink or two straight from a bottle. They all smoked and had to go outside for a cigarette.

There usually was someone who had a little too much to drink, but I don't remember there ever being any trouble such as fights or car accidents. Everyone would have a good time relieving the loneliness of rural living.

Children always came to the dance with their parents unless there was an older child in their family to be the babysitter. Dances ran pretty late, and I remember us younger children falling asleep on the floor under a couple of chairs or school desks so we wouldn't be stepped on.

Nobody had to wait for an invitation to attend one of these dances. Everybody was welcome. Having no telephones, people were invited by word of mouth.

In the days when I was a child everybody knew how to dance. I think they mainly did the two-step, polka, a waltz, and the schottische. Sometimes there were square dances but those usually required more space and, of course, someone who knew how to "call" the dance. I find it strange that most young men today don't know how to dance. They may be picking the skill up again because I notice that there are lessons near the University for different types of dancing.

When my brothers and I were in high school we crossed the Canadian border a couple of times to attend a "Grape Dance" held in a country school. Hungarian friends of my folks sponsored these dances. Instead of planting wheat as we did they planted grapes as they had done in Hungary. There were grapes hanging from the entire ceiling of the room.

Years later when I visited the village in Hungary where my Suta relatives came from, I learned that grapes were the main crop grown in that region. The parents of my Grandma Suta left behind a vineyard in Veresedgehaz being persuaded by other relatives, especially the Vargos, to join them in America. People living there in Hungary about eighty years later had passed down the story as "this man Charley Boyza, who was so foolish that he gave up land, a good vineyard in order to go to America." People there thought it was a poor decision because Hungarians were always searching for their own land and this man just up and left land that he owned in order to go to America.

Mom and Pop once went to a Hungarian wedding in Alberta, Canada where there was dancing for three days. I think Uncle Bill and Ella Newmiller stayed with us kids. Mom told me that this apparently was common for old Hungarian weddings. One custom at the Hungarian weddings was for all guests, including the women, to take turns dancing with the bride. In order to dance with the bride you had to pin a piece of paper money onto her wedding dress. By the end of each evening the bride was a dancing bank, totally covered in money.

These days I go to bars that have good music and dancing. There is a problem in that very few of the men know how to dance so there are mostly groups of women moving their bodies on the dance floor.

Pop was able to dance as long as he was able to walk. In his eighties he had a very happy time dancing with women who were friends of Garmit at her marriage to my son Morgan. Garmit's friends were very impressed, surprised and happy to dance with my father. A group of them surrounded Pop in a circle for several dances. They were surprised because he was even able to dance a couples dance, usually the two-step and a polka.

The camaraderie of local dances has been lost with the closing of country schools.

Farm Auction Sales

A favorite activity of Pop's was to go to farm auction sales where he could visit with many neighbors, eat at the buffet, and bid on various items whether or not he needed them. Some of the items that he bought were still in their original boxes, unused, when we had an auction sale on the Suta farm. He and his brother Rudy enjoyed competing with each other and once had a legendary bidding war over a sealed box of unknown stuff. Pop won and the box turned out to be filled with rusty bolts and other unusable junk, but he was happy to have outbid Rudy. Auctioneers were always happy when they saw both Pop and Rudy at an auction because they knew the sale would then be successful.

The epitome of Pop's auction sale purchases was a toaster with a fifty-foot electrical cord. It was an old-fashioned type of toaster that requires you to physically open one side at a time to turn each slice of bread. We didn't need a toaster, we couldn't guess why it had such a long cord, and nobody ever used it. But the idea of that toaster with a fifty-foot electrical cord still brings laughter to our family.

Sweetgrass

There is camaraderie at these sales, but they are often based on sadness of the people selling out rather than the happiness of a new building or a good harvest.

Funerals

We always went to funerals as children. It didn't matter if the deceased was a close relative or someone who our folks hardly knew. This continues in the community even now. Funerals were a very popular social event with the opportunity to visit over the meal with people you seldom saw otherwise. You were expected to be there. The coffins were always open giving people a chance to talk about how well the corpse was looking.

The one funeral I was not taken to was that of Pop's mother. I was left at home to play mudpies with Charley Taft, a neighbor about four years old. This bothered me because I loved Grandma Suta. Nobody talked to me about this, and, in fact, I don't think I was specifically told that Grandma had died. I guess Pop may not have wanted us kids there because he was so distraught that he fainted at the funeral.

Many years later as an adult nurse I attended one of the first conferences given by Dr. Kubler-Ross who initiated openly talking in the United States about death and dying. I recall her commenting that she was certain most of us in the audience would have unfinished grief of some type. She paused for us to process our personal memories. I started crying for Grandma Suta and for my little self who never had a chance to say "Goodbye" to her.

At least we children never missed any other funerals.

Memorial Day

My parents considered Memorial Day as sacred as any other holiday. We always visited the graves of people significant to our family and put flowers on their graves. We put live flowers on some graves even though we knew they would wilt and have to be thrown away in a couple of days. It was the special feeling we had for that person that made us give live or plastic flowers. We spent the entire day visiting the cemetaries in Sweetgrass and Cut Bank. It was strange that we didn't have any family buried in Sunburst or Shelby.

The cemetary in Sweetgrass was completely natural when I was a child. It was hard to find some grave markers because of the grass that grew tall from snow or rain. I have to admit that it did look messy and not as beautiful as the one in Cut Bank, but I always had a good feeling about that place. I had known most of the people who were buried in Sweetgrass. Maybe it also felt like home because the grass was not watered and manicured. The one in Cut Bank was too manicured, green, and orderly, there were flags along the road, and you could see all the flowers people had brought. It was lovely but not natural.

I used to think that I wanted to be buried in Sweetgrass because I would be near relatives and also because it felt like my special place on the prairie of our farm. But now they have planted lawn seed and regularly give it water and then mow it. I think my main objection is the total waste of water which is very scarce there.

Memorial day is becoming less significant as families are scattered. My remaining two sons would probably not visit my gravesite on memorial day because of distance.

I plan to make an appointment to learn more about green burial sites near Madison where everything is treated more naturally. Dust to dust.

Another option, since I plan on cremation anyway, is to have somebody, preferably one of my children, scatter my cremains somewhere in Glacier National Park. Anyplace would be fine, but I think my favorite place is Many Glacier.

Needlework

Learning to knit, embroider, and crochet may not sound like an exciting activity in a young person's life, but these skills have been enjoyable and useful throughout my life. Needlework has not only helped me to pass time but has helped me relax and relieve any anxiety I might be feeling. I can let all negative thoughts go when I am creating needlework. I also gain a sense of accomplishment as I complete or partially complete an item.

When I was young I had no playmates. I lived in the country and had older brothers who didn't want me hanging around. I watched my mother, Aunt Margaret and a few other women their age sit around our large kitchen table visiting with each other while they each did some sort of needlework. Most of their lives were spent working hard to maintain their families and they all seemed to enjoy this break time when they could express themselves artistically while socializing.

I got tired of playing with dolls or reading and wanted to do what the adults were doing. Mom shooed me away at first, telling me I was too young to do these things. But she finally relented and started a crochet chain with large thread and crochet hook and taught me to keep making the same chain stitch, trying to make every stitch the same size by the tension I held on the thread. I pretty quickly became bored with that. Aunt Margaret volunteered to teach me to knit and I liked that because yarn is thicker and you can see progress of what you are making. Crochet thread is thinner and it takes much longer to make an item, such as a doily that I didn't want anyway. You can, of course, buy crochet thread that is thicker and make a variety of items, but generally not clothing such as you can make by knitting.

Aunt Margaret made me start by knitting a sampler, a square, in order to check my "gauge" keeping the same tension in all stitches. I don't like to do this, but you should always check your gauge at the beginning of any project. Your gauge will change with the size of your knitting needles, the type of yarn used and the tension you keep as you hold the yarn You want your little sample to have the same measurement as that of your pattern or else the item you make will be totally out of size and off-kilter when you finish.

To start knitting I bought a Beginner's Knitting Instruction Book but I didn't like any of the easy-to-make items. There were a lot of patterns for "soakers" which would be put over a baby's diaper to protect your lap from getting really wet while holding that baby. In those days there were only cotton diapers, not disposables—and there were no plastic pants to put over cotton diapers. In my pattern book there were also instructions for some baby clothes, such as booties and bonnets, but we didn't have a baby at that time. I had no motivation to make any of those easy patterns. I thought I had mastered the basic art of knitting and quickly wanted a challenge.

I chose to make the last pattern in that Beginner's book which, of course, was the most difficult. It was a pattern for a Norwegian-style sweater that had a star pattern knitted in around the top of the sweater. This is done by "carrying" the second color of yarn on the reverse side of the sweater. This was a very slow and difficult way for a beginner to make a sweater. Grown women were amazed that I was even attempting that pattern when I was about five years old. I was very happy and proud to see the progress that could be made with yarn, unlike crocheting with thread. But I was slow and became tired of that pattern.

I had finished all but one sleeve of that sweater when I moved on to other projects. Eventually my sister was born, nine years younger than me, and she found my unfinished sweater while she was still young. Dian asked Aunt Margaret to finish knitting and joining the pieces so that she was able to wear that sweater. I was happy to have made something that was useful and beautiful but I didn't continue knitting.

While I was in college I dealt with stress by crocheting a full skirt, using a thin yarn. It was a huge project and beautiful but I never wore it. I have realized that it was the process of needlework that I enjoyed more than making something useful. My most common and useful projects were embroidering scenes on pillowcases and crocheting trim around the pillowcase opening. I decorated many pillowcases and still use some of them about sixty years later.

Crewel embroidery is different from the basic stitches of embroidery I learned when beginning. Crewel is usually done with a slightly thicker embroidery thread. Usually the stitches are made to cover up or fill in an item, such as an apple, rather than just outlining it. These are generally done as pictures to be hung on a wall, rather than to decorate pillowcases. I made a lot of crewel pictures and kept only one for myself. The one I kept is a still-life arrangement of fruit that took a long time to make. I have framed it, and it is displayed on the top of my kitchen cupboards.

Mom's Hummel embroidery.

When my three sons were little I made small crewel embroidery pictures that hung on the wall just above the doors of the kitchen cabinets. These were useful because they had the words of blessings for food and the boys could look up for a reminder when they were asked to say a blessing for a meal.

When I was a working mother, I usually spent a little time doing "handiwork" after my husband and the children were in bed. I enjoyed some personal quiet time for relaxation.

One year I decided I wanted to learn knitting. I love the colors and feel of different yarn. I went to a local yarn shop for information on a beginner's knitting group. I told them that I wanted only a couple of lessons to learn the basics but didn't have time to attend their weekly group gatherings.

This particular knitting group turned out to be a wonderful mental health group for each other. There was some hilarious laughter at every meeting. Instead of attending only a couple of weeks, I participated with that group of women for several years. The leader was an exceptional knitter, and several other knitters were knowledgeable enough to give me help anytime needed. We all advocated the motto that "She who dies with the most yarn wins."

I wore only one or two of the sweaters I made for myself, but I enjoyed the process and the accomplishment. Making an item allowed me to express my creative ability.

This group was enjoyable, liked each other, and swore confidentiality. During the time that I was in the group we discussed the everyday issues we all encountered. But there also were some major events. The husband of one committed suicide. One member of the group entered legal proceedings of divorce and custody. One was married to an orthopedic surgeon and their differences could have filled a book. One woman became pregnant with triplets and there were many laughs in the process of trying to keep her physically and mentally comfortable. I had decided that I would get a divorce someday soon but hadn't started the process yet. The leader of our group was an unusually funny person. She

Sweetgrass

didn't understand why her husband objected to her knitting while she was driving.

Eventually there were changes in the group and we all decided at the same time to disband.

A lifetime of overusing the motion of "thumb-to-forefinger" in activities such as needlework and that of plucking millions of chicken feathers has resulted in my developing "trigger thumb" on my right hand. Trigger thumb is a condition that results when a ligament becomes so swollen that it cannot pass through a small opening of bone when you extend your fingers. The pain is brief but excruciating. Cortisone shots didn't work so I have changed my practices.

Now I knit plain shawls and lap blankets for my church to give to elderly people being visited at home or in a nursing facility. It is funny that the pattern for the knitted items I make now are similar to the "soakers" I should have started making when I was a beginning knitter.

Fun on the Farm

A topic suggested for me to write about was what we did for fun on the prairie. I admit that I was stumped by the topic. I asked my older brothers and they, too, couldn't remember us doing things for fun. Fun was not something we Suta children thought about when growing up on the farm. I don't think we knew the concept of fun.

Our childhood was spent in doing chores to help Mom and Pop and doing our homework, if any. But none of us feel as though we had an unhappy childhood. We liked each other and could laugh about everything. Even if Pop got angry with one of us that person had the rest of us to tell and we would all laugh and make it funny.

My brothers picked on me, but I always knew that they were doing it with humor and were not intentionally being mean. Frankly, I think I was just happy to have their attention. Sometimes they made me mad, and I would ask Mom to make them stop. It's hard for them to give compliments. They will bury a compliment within teasing or a funny statement. I knew it was a compliment if they were paying attention to me.

Winter Fun in the Snow

We got a lot more snow seventy or eighty years ago than we do now, but we never had equipment to go skiing or skating or even snowshoeing. Our family was very poor when the first four of us children were young—definitely too poor to buy useless equipment for fun. We didn't even ask for that type of equipment.

I remember finding an old pair of ice skates that were worn and rusty. They were probably from one of Pop's auction boxes. I remember stuffing the toes of the skates and going to our large reservoir to try them out. The experiment was doomed to fail. Old skates that didn't fit and nothing to hold onto while learning were problems, but the main problem was even worse. The wind that blows constantly had caused the ice to form in very rough ridges. Even a Zamboni machine would not be able to make it smooth.

To stay warm in those days we had to add layers and layers of clothing which was uncomfortable. Snowmobile suits filled with down feathers had not been invented. It wasn't comfortable to be outside in the cold. We spent all the time we wanted to have outside while doing essential outdoor chores, and we weren't anxious to spend more time outside trying to have fun.

My brothers did think it was fun to put snow down the back of my neck.

We owned one small snow sled and used that to sled down the tallest side of the hill where our house was located. Four kids with one small sled got tiresome pretty fast.

The best thing we did with all of our winter snow was to make home-made ice cream. We did this when the Baldwin kids and their mother were visiting.—Faye, Sharon, George, and Billy. They lived about six miles to the south of us and the children were about my age. But they went to a different one-room school than we did. We had to gather lots of hard snow to pack around the ice cream churn. We had plenty of cream from our cows to make into ice cream. The churn had to be turned for a long time with paddles connected to a handle. When the ice cream was ready, it was hard to stop everybody from taking spoonfuls before we had the paddles all the way out.

Violet Suta Moran

Visitors

We could count on our Uncle Gilbert to always make fudge when he visited. Mom kept a jar of marshmallow fluff on hand because that's the recipe he used. All four of us kids liked to be in the kitchen just watching him make the fudge. And he talked to us or sang. I think we always ate the entire batch of fudge before it ever had time to cool. Gilbert was the youngest in Mom's family, so he wasn't a lot older than us and always seemed like a really nice big brother.

We visited Grandma and Grandpa Suta fairly often since they lived only about three miles away. We didn't do any activities but just liked to talk with each other about what we had been doing, how school was, etc.

The Charles Taft family lived only a few miles away but soon moved away. They had only one child and Charley and I enjoyed playing together. As an adult Charley said that he didn't have any choice when I said we were going to play with mud pies.

I can say that Charles was my first love.

The Simmes family lived about five miles toward Sunburst. They had four daughters, but I didn't see them very often. They went to school in Sunburst. Mom would take me there evey six weeks when she wanted Mildred, the mother, to give us each a home permanent—which always made my hair frizzy, not curly. The youngest daughter was Theodora, who smoothed my transition from country school to her grade in the city of Sunburst.

After World War II when Pop's brothers were home from the Army we exchanged frequent visits with Uncle Rudy and Aunt Margaret. When they brought Margaret's son Louis from Pennsylvania the dynamics changed, and we didn't visit so much. Louis had been cared for by Margaret's mother, and he was a mean foul-talking city brat. To my dismay he was in the same grade in school as Ben and me.

Sweetgrass

Aunt Margaret and Cornelia Negu, who was married to another of Pop's brothers, Willy, had both been "Rosie the Riveters" during the war, working to build ships.

Gilbert and Grandpa came to our place for almost every Sunday dinner. We were very happy to have their company. Gilbert had interesting stories because he was unmarried, went out socially, and talked with a lot of people. Later when I learned to play clarinet in Sunburst school, I got a book of Eddie Arnold songs and Uncle Gilbert would play his guitar and sing while I played clarinet.

The boys were always on the lookout for baby kittens, and we all played with them.

We all liked to read and used the school library, but none of our small towns had a public library. Pop supported our education, but he couldn't help but holler at us , "get your damn nose out of that book and go learn something or do something." I read all the series written for children such as Nancy Drew and the Bobbsy Twins. I treasure the *Alice in Wonderland* book given to me by my favorite teacher, Beth Volbrecht. I also read the racy magazines Pop subscribed to such as *True Love, True Confessions* and the like. Those probably should not have been available to young children, but they were not hidden. Reading was probably my favorite leisure activity. My brothers read a lot too.

Glacier Park

I enjoyed going to Glacier Park and we went there often. We could easily go to Glacier Park and back in a day.

Pop liked to fish even though he rarely caught anything. No fishing license was required in the Park. We went there frequently, but we didn't explore very much because Pop didn't like to go hiking, and he didn't like to just wait in the car if the rest of us went hiking.

Sometimes without planning Pop would decide we could stay overnight near Glacier Park. Usually that was at

Ben holding Dian.

Me riding Bill Newmiller's horse.

Us four kids with Uncle Gilbert.

Sweetgrass

Glacier Park . . .

. . . for picnics . . .

. . . and overnights.

Swiftcurrent cabins which were very primitive at that time. But I loved it.

We always stopped to have a picnic at Glacier Park even if Pop didn't catch a fish. Mom was always prepared for a picnic. We often stopped at Lake Five. It was a small, calm lake and Pop wasn't too scared of the water there to go out in a row-boat and fish. Once we spent a week in a cabin at Lake Five with Pop's brother Willie, wife Nellie (Cornelia Negu), and two young sons who were not well disciplined. One, Dubby (Jon) would throw temper tantrums, kicking his feet and screaming before holding his breath and turning blue in his face. He wasn't much fun to play with.

Listening to the Radio

Primary evening entertainment was listening to the radio. Ted remembers that he had to take the battery out of Hildegard and hook it up to the radio. Ben said Pop traded chickens with somebody to get a Kolster radio and then put a propeller on an old car generator to keep the radio battery charged. And still the reception was poor. We all pulled chairs up close to the kitchen counter so that we could hear the sound. Favorite radio programs remembered these many years later are Fibber McGee and Molly, Gang Busters, The Lone Ranger, Amos and Andy, The Shadow Knows, Kate Smith Hour, The Great Gildersleeve, Lux presents Hollywood, and Jack Benny (from whom Mom decided that she was forever thirty-nine years old just like him).

We had a stereoscope that showed pictures in 3D and loved to look at that often. It was a wooden frame that you held up to your eyes. The photo you had put at the end of this devise was seen through the prism of a couple of different glasses, making everything 3D.

Board Games

We played board games often, primarily Monopoly. Mom would join us sometimes. We also played checkers and marbles. Mom taught us Solitaire. When we were in High

Sweetgrass

School we graduated to card games of Canasta, Euchre and others but not Bridge.

Traveling Salesmen

We didn't really have fun with Traveling Salesmen (honestly) but I think it was unusual for them to visit our farm since we weren't on any map at that time. They just drove around on the prairie roads, stopping when they saw a house. My brothers made fun of Pop for buying the encyclopedia set that they "never used." But I used it frequently and they did sometimes. I think that expenditure was a big effort of Pop to support our education.

Another purchase was an Electrolux vacuum which was relatively expensive, but we women liked it, and it lasted forever. I think that man made a lot of sales in our area, even to people who had nothing but linoleum.

You can see that we really did not know anything about the concept of fun when a visit by a travelling salesman makes the top of our list.

A Couple of Things My Brothers Did

There are a couple of things my brothers did that ought to be recorded whether or not they were fun. My oldest brother Ted was young when he heard Pop talking to Mom about needing to drain the radiator since winter was coming soon. Ted was a good boy and wanted to help Pop. He took a screwdriver out of the tool box and used it to punch a lot of holes in the radiator. He then proudly went into the kitchen to tell Pop that he had already drained the radiator for him.

My brother Henry was a little older when he saw horses in one of our wheat fields about half a mile away and wanted to scare them away by shooting a 22-caliber rifle above their heads. Amazingly, he hit and killed one of the horses which was Ted Simmes' favorite horse. It was rare to kill an animal that far away. Ted and Ben say that was the only big game that Henry ever killed, and we should have helped him mount the head.

Ben led me to steal something for the only time in my life. Mom had given each of us a nickel and we went into the Ben Franklin store where there were balloons laying out on the counter. Three clerks were talking to each other, and when they weren't looking Ben took two small balloons and told me to do the same. I did and we walked out of the store. I never went back into that store for years and years because I felt guilty and thought someone might recognize me. Well, at least I learned that stealing was not fun!!

For fun, we mostly spent time playing with young Dian and Rudy after they were born. Dian would cry whenever Ben came around unless he picked her up and walked around with her. She really had Ben trained. Dian's feet never touched the ground. Rudy wasn't the same novelty when he was born. But he did get a lot of attention because he had an esophageal constriction and couldn't get any nourishment. He was near death at one month of age and there wasn't a pediatric surgeon within hundreds of miles. A general surgeon operated on that tiny body, and Rudy hasn't stopped eating or smiling since then.

Easter When I Was a Child

My mother, Hannah Lozing Suta, loved Easter. She was a confirmed Lutheran, and the religious meaning was important to her. But I think she really liked Easter because there was no need to spend time and money buying toys or decorating as we did for Christmas.

When I was a young child there were four of us children making a mess of coloring hard boiled eggs. It was apparent that Mom enjoyed coloring eggs as much as we did. I'm sure her family didn't have egg dying kits when she was a child because Grandpa Lozing would never have spent money on such foolishness. Mom could indulge now in childhood fun.

My three older brothers liked to experiment when coloring the eggs: mixing the colors, dying eggs in two or three different stripes, and using a wax pencil to draw funny things on the egg which would be left visible after the egg was colored. Every year they had to discover anew that if you mix enough colors together you would end up with black. They always made a big mess on the table by pouring colors from one coffee cup to another.

It was fortunate that we had that huge yellow Formica table that could not be stained by anything. And it was big enough that we all had our own space

We raised our own chickens, and they laid enough eggs that we could color to our heart's content. There were two younger children in our family, and they say that Mom boiled as many eggs for them as she did for the first four children. Mom wanted a lot of colors and the fun of coloring. A large glass bowl of colored Easter eggs as a centerpiece on the table helped satisfy Mom's love of colors. She also liked color in the garden and painted bright colors on the walls of our house.

We always found an Easter basket alongside our bed on Easter morning which Mom would have put together after we children had gone to sleep. She always included a variety of candies that she had hidden from us. At the top of each basket would be the egg on which we had printed our name with wax pencil. She didn't hide eggs for an Easter egg hunt as I did years later for my own children. We learned that you have to count the number of eggs you hide so that none are left behind to spoil and start smelling.

Becoming baptized in the Evangelical Lutheran Church.

Sweetgrass

I was surprised and happy when I became older and still received a basket from Mom at Easter, long after I had stopped believing in the Easter bunny.

Most surprising was receiving an Easter basket in the mail after I had moved to Wisconsin. I remember the feelings of love and joy I had when receiving that basket. I knew how difficult it was for Mom to send that basket because she didn't drive, and Pop wasn't always willing to take her to town at her request. There was no UPS service in town to wrap and mail an Easter basket. Our small town in fact did not have any type of gift shop.

When Mom did get to town, there was seldom an appropriate selection of greeting cards. One year she apparently had bought a box of "all occasion" cards and used all the birthday cards. My sister Dian and I share the same birthday date and one year I received a Get Well card and she received a Sympathy card. We laughed a lot about that. But we had to give Mom credit for trying as hard as she could to send birthday greetings to us.

Easter was the one day of the year that Mom really wanted to go to church. However, spring weather in northern Montana was never good and it was not easy to drive the 1 ½ miles out of our driveway and twelve miles to Sunburst for church. The road to Sunburst was narrow, curvy and gumbo with a sprinkling of gravel. It wasn't improved until sometime in the 1960s. The road might be bad because it was snowing heavily, or a previous snow might be melting, or we could get an unusual rain. Our road of gumbo soil became very slippery when wet, worse than driving on ice. Gumbo also sticks like glue and can build up on your tires making it hard to drive. When gumbo dries, it becomes hard as cement and the deep ruts dried in the road make the road very rough. If a rut was deeper than your tires, you could damage the bottom of your car. The county occasionally put gravel on our road but there was never enough at the right time.

A few disasters that happened to us on the way to church were sliding off the road into the ditch because of the slippery gumbo, getting a flat tire, or getting stuck in the mud. We tried to leave home early enough to allow for emergencies and still get to church on time, but we always arrived late. The service would have already started. Our large family made quite a commotion taking off our muddy boots in the small entryway of the church and then trying to find seating for six people. None of the city people had mud on their boots; most had not even worn boots.

A happy memory of Easter was seeing Mom wear her only hat. It was maroon, a color that was very flattering to her. It was made of felt and had a two or three inch brim all the way around, and she wore it at a jaunty angle. A few colorful feathers were secured by a wide ribbon wrapped around the hat. I thought she looked beautiful in that hat which she rarely wore. At all other times she had to wear a head scarf to protect her ears. Her auditory canals were open to the air because most of the covering ear-drums were destroyed by repeated ear infections when she was a child.

When we got home from church Grandpa and Gilbert would be in the house waiting for the dinner Mom had started cooking in the oven before we left home. They had an easier drive than we did because the county they lived in, Glacier, took better care of their roads than did our Toole county.

New clothes are traditionally the focus at Easter time when the weather supposedly changes from winter to spring. Spring never came to the area where we lived by the time of Easter. A new sleeveless summer dress would look inappropriate when it was snowing outside, even if it was Easter.

One year I sewed myself a new outfit for Easter. I had just learned to sew in seventh grade and was only about nine years old. Not only was I a novice at sewing but I also had to use our old treadle sewing machine that skipped stitches. Nevertheless, the pink straight skirt and matching jacket with a large collar looked pretty good. However, when we tried to take pictures outside, the prevalent wind kept blowing that large collar over my face.

We had to take pictures outside because we never owned a camera with a flash attachment. For most of my childhood we didn't have any camera at all. I am sorry that many of my childhood pictures are of poor quality.

Easter was an interesting and enjoyable time for the Suta family but we never would have looked like we belonged in the Easter parade.

Wearing the Easter dress I made when I was 9 years old.

Christmas When I Was a Child

I recall Christmas being a happy time when I was a child. The adults were more relaxed than during seeding in the spring or harvesting in the fall when a lot of farm work had to be done quickly.

Buying presents for others was simplified by the fact that we didn't have very many choices. The nearby small towns of Sunburst and Sweetgrass did not have any shops at all where we could purchase gifts. We had to go to Shelby or Cut Bank, each about fifty miles away. We could count on only one shopping trip, usually to Shelby, or we could order items out of the Sears Roebuck or Montgomery Ward catalogs.

Our wish lists were not very long because we didn't have television advertisements bombarding us with all the possible toy choices. We didn't have much money and didn't get many presents. There was only one modest present for each of us from Mom and Pop. I think I usually got a doll. I didn't play with dolls a lot, but I had quite a few of them. One year I was very happy to receive an Easy-Bake Oven. I had been baking cookies and cakes in our real oven for several years, but this was fun and not a chore.

We always had a live evergreen tree, a fir with short needles. Our whole family never went to select a tree in a forest or tree farm because there wasn't a tree farm for about a hundred miles. Our tree had to be selected from a bunch of trees being sold in Sunburst. Pop was the only one who could drive to town to get a tree and he would never go as early as Mom suggested. He had a tendency to resist suggestions. By the time he went to get a tree the good ones had been taken. Our Christmas tree always had serious defects but it wasn't as bad as the Charlie Brown tree. We turned the worst side toward the wall and tried to decorate to hide the gaps.

Before we got electricity we didn't put any lights on the tree. I know there were countries that put burning candles on their tree, but that would be dangerous and there was no Fire Department for 50 miles and then no water for them to use when they did arrive.

Do you know about tinsel? I'll never forget that darn silver tinsel that Mom insisted be put on the tree. The threads of thin silver tinsel, about eighteen inches long and 1/16 inch wide, had to be put on the tree one by one, not bunched up. Tinsel was shiny and it did help to hide the bare spots on our tree. But I hated putting tinsel on the tree and hated it even worse when taking it off after Christmas. After Christmas we had to remove the tinsel very carefully to be re-used the following year. Mom had always been poor so she was frugal and saved everything she could.

If you weren't careful and neat, keeping each strand of tinsel separate when you draped it around a card, you would be very sorry next year when trying to separate the jumbled strings. The job of putting on and taking off tinsel was always done by me and my brother Ben. That took a lot of time and was very boring.

Our tree lights were large and of various colors. These old lights overheated and caused fires when people left them on too long. We never left any Christmas tree lights on when we were not home. Pop wouldn't have allowed that much waste of electricity.

We had a couple strings of "bubble lights" that I loved even though it was hard to make them stay upright so that they would make bubbles. They were made of glass and were so heavy that they kept tipping over.

I don't remember Mom ever buying new ornaments for the tree. There were old boxes that originally held sixteen small ornaments, but many had been broken. Each ornament was indented and inside the indent was a painted scene or just a different color, maybe silver or gold. Once in a while we children presented Mom with an ornament as her Christmas gift. Our tree didn't have many ornaments but we thought our tree looked better than Aunt Margaret's tree that she decorated with as many ornaments as possible. We criticized her tree, privately to each other, saying that you couldn't even see the green of the tree. We preferred our tree with fewer ornaments even though it was almost a Charlie Brown tree.

At our one-room school, we usually had some kind of gathering of families before Christmas. I don't remember performing any plays but we did sing Christmas carols and gave to our parents some things we had drawn or made out of construction paper. I remember gluing strips of colored construction paper to inter-twine circles making a long rope to decorate the tree. At school we received peanuts in the shell and other kinds of nuts, along with different kinds of cookies brought by the families. There wasn't anyone in my country school who had an allergy to nuts or anything else. We also made a lot of cookies at home, especially sugar cookies.

My brother Ted, at the age of ninety-two, has a favorite memory of how happy we kids were to each get a fresh orange at Christmas. We never had them during the year. I think the store in Sweetgrass probably didn't get them year round because shipping wasn't very good then. Or they may have been too expensive for Mom to buy. That fresh orange was a great treat!

Christmas was the only time we got ribbon candy which was an unusual, sweet treat All of the school kids were really happy about the ribbon candy. At home we always had some

Sweetgrass

Brazil nuts, walnuts, and peanuts in the shell, and that was unusual.

It was a tradition that we went to Shelby on the day of Christmas Eve or the day before to buy gifts. We were allowed only one day in town. Sunburst and Sweetgrass didn't have any gifts available. Pop didn't like to do any shopping but he was willing to take us to Shelby at Christmas because Buddy Dolan at the Hannah & Holmes auto and implement dealership always served Tom and Jerrys to his customers. Tom and Jerrys are usually made in large mugs but Buddy Dolan served them in coffee cups. The drinks were very strong because there was not much space to add hot water after a shot of whiskey and a shot of rum. Pop would get rather drunk, and it was always hard to get him to leave and go home.

When we were in Shelby we angle parked our car on Main Street. I remember turning around in the back seat of the car so I could look out the rear window, marveling at the magical lights and decorations in store windows. Everything was lovely and so exciting to me. I lived on the prairie with no close neighbors, no street lights and no holiday excitement.

Christmas music was piped onto Main Street and one of my happiest memories is hearing the song, Silver Bells. I still love that song with the original of Kate Smith's version sung in 1950 for the movie "The Lemondrop Kid." I get goosebumps and almost cry when I hear that beautiful rendition.

We opened presents on Christmas morning or may have opened one small present on Christmas Eve. We opened our presents carefully so that the ribbon and paper could be saved for re-use. We did not go to church at Christmas time as we did every Easter.

Aunt Margaret and Uncle Rudy, Pop's brother, always came to our place on Christmas Eve or the day before for Tom & Jerrys. The adults usually ran out of Tom & Jerry mix and turned to me to make more. I was only about seven years old when I concocted a mixture that could pass for Tom & Jerry Mix. Mostly it was whipped egg whites with lots and lots of powdered sugar added. The yolks were also whipped stiff with powdered sugar and then folded in. Whatever way I made it, they seemed to like it and continued to drink more than they should.

Margaret and Rudy always came to our place for Christmas dinner as did Gilbert and Grandpa Lozing—and sometimes others as well.

There were a couple of years when we experimented with rotating the place that hosted Christmas between Mom, Aunt Margaret and Aunt Mabel who was married to Pop's youngest brother Kalman. That experiment didn't last more than a couple of years. Mable wasn't a very good cook and there was friction among the grown-ups.

Mom made cabbage rolls as she did for every special occasion even though we also had turkey or ham. But Rudy always requested goose meat for Christmas. Mom always wanted to please Rudy and so she would buy a single live goose from the Hutterite Colony* a couple of weeks before Christmas.

One year the goose started running after Ben every time he went out of the house. It never bothered anyone else. I never knew a goose could run so fast. The goose would attack Ben by jumping up on his head and pecking at his face. A goose is a large bird and we thought it was going to peck out Ben's eyes. Mom killed that goose quickly—it didn't last until Christmas. But Ben hated that goose so much that he wouldn't even eat one bite of the meat.

*The Hutterites are a self-contained group of people who are much more communal than their spiritual cousins, the Amish or the Mennonites. They distance themselves from any interaction with the modern world. Their Colonies are totally self-contained with their own school. An elder monitors the classes so that only the required content and no current social content is taught. There

Sweetgrass

are many Hutterite Colonies along the western United States. They are agrarian. Their members provide free labor so they are easily able to purchase farmland because they can pay cash above the asking rate. There is a Hutterite Colony directly across the road from our farm and the manager seemed to enjoy tormenting Pop by telling him that he would soon be walking on Pop's land. None of us six Suta children wanted to sell to the Hutterites. They work every inch of the land as a business and we felt very sentimental and caring about our farmland.

Christmas stockings I made for family and others.

Sermon at the Funeral of G. Peter Suta

Pastor Patricia Callahan
Evangelical Lutheran Church
Sunburst, Montana
16 December 1999

**Grace and peace from God our Father
and our Lord and Savior, Jesus Christ**

The grace of God is a mystery to us, Paul says.
And he's right.
We, who are prone to sin,
who have trouble forgiving,
who cling to life because it's what we know,
how can we understand a God
who died in order that we might live?

It's a mystery.

But families can reflect a shadow of that grace.

In listening to Pete's family tell stories about him,
about their family,
about themselves,
we are reminded that families,

Sweetgrass

in their clear-eyed honesty about each other,
have a bond of love
that transcends the sins
they commit against each other,
a love that can accept each other's weaknesses
as well as their strengths.

No family is perfect,
no family can love and forgive
in the unconditional way God does,
but it's through families
that God gives us some hint of grace,
families that teach us whatever we know
of love and understanding,
of sin and forgiveness.
If we were perfect,
we wouldn't need each other.
If our families were perfect,
we wouldn't know how to cope
with an imperfect world.

Our strengths help us survive,
just as Pete's strength and energy
helped him break a living
out of Montana's hard earth.
helped him support a family—

but it's through our flaws and weaknesses
that we learn to love and forgive.
And it's through our flaws and weaknesses,
through our need for forgiveness
and our need to forgive,
that God enters our lives.

Paul says God's Power is made perfect in our weakness—
that's because it's our weakness
that teaches us that we need God.

Violet Suta Moran

I didn't know Pete when he was in his full vigor
and strength,
hard-working, with strong opinions,
friendly and outgoing,
maybe not always so easy to live with.

I knew him after illness gentled him,
making him patient and gracious.
In fact, the main thing I knew about Pete
was that he was always happy to be given
Holy Communion,
and I can still hear his voice,
confessing his faith
praying the Lord's Prayer,
even when he grew weaker
and couldn't say all the words.

Like all of us
Pete's weakness made him more aware
of his need for God.

There is another mystery here,

Even given God's unconditional love for us
—even given his ability to see our sin clearly,
and yet accept us
as though we are without sin,
how is it that we can be transformed
from earth-bound sinners
into heaven-bound members of God's kingdom?

How can we be changed in the twinkling of an eye,
at the blast of a trumpet?
How do our perishable bodies become imperishable?
How does our mortality become immortality?
We know the answer, of course—

Sweetgrass

We are changed by God's love,
compassionate enough to send his Son to die for us,
powerful enough to raise him from the dead,
forgiving enough to forgive us
even before we ask for forgiveness.

Paul says it is sin that kills,
sin that puts the sting of defeat in death.
But our sin is forgiven,
forgiven even when we cling to sin like it's our only friend.
Forgiven even when we can't forgive ourselves.

If all we had was the reality of life and death on earth,
we would indeed be perishable and mortal,
bound only for the grave.
But Christ, who with his Father, forgives us before we ask,
has changed all that.

Jesus says "I am the resurrection and the life.
Those who believe in me,
even though they die,
will live,
and everyone who lives and believes in me
will never die."

Christ has exchanged Pete's perishable body
for imperishability,
exchanged his mortality
for everlasting life with his Lord and Savior.

Amen

Jerry the Auctioneer

I have known a number of unusual people but one who popped into my mind had been a classmate of mine from first grade in a one-room country school until we graduated from high school in Sunburst, Montana.

As the son of an Irishman, Jerry had red hair and freckles and twinkling eyes. He wasn't the sharpest pencil in a box, but he was always cheerful and never caused any trouble. Jerry had inherited from his Irish father the ability to tell long interesting stories that may or may not have been factual.

My brother Ben was in the same grade as Jerry and noticed sometime in elementary school that Jerry had started talking differently. I agreed that he sounded different. He would say his name as (drawl: Jerr-yBuuk—ley)

Some native Montanans have a slight western accent, but Jerry perfected that, slowly drawling it out more than usual. Mixed with the Irish accent he had already developed from his father, his accent was unique.

I saw Jerry several years after we had completed high school. He told us that while he and his mother had spent the last two winters in Arizona, he had worked with a movie company. They were delighted to find someone who truly sounded like he was from the west. He said that his job was to "(slow drawl) tee—ch tha ac-trs how ta talk with a Wesstrn acc—cent."

Sweetgrass

Ben and I laughed and laughed about this because Jerry's accent was not like any other we had heard while living in the west.

Nobody has duplicated Jerry's style of speaking. And I'm not good at imitations but I'll try to tell you a story.

Several years later when I was in Montana Jerry came into the Sports Club in Shelby and sat next to me in a booth. After greetings, Jerry drawled to me:

(slow drawl) "I ws in yer neck a tha woods ths last year."

Oh, really. What were you doing in the midwest, Jerry?

(slow drawl) "Ya coudn guess. I was goin ta scoo-ul."

To school? What school did you go to?

(slow drawl) "Well. It was a spe-shel scoo-ul. In eye-o-wa." (Iowa)

Why did you go there? What did you study?

(slow drawl) "Well, ya might find this hard ta believe, but I went ta auk-shun-eeer-ing school."

I had heard about an auctioneering school in Iowa, but I never would have guessed that you would go there.

This was quite unbelievable until Jerry demonstrated a short sales pitch to me. He had amazingly developed the typical rapid fire speaking method of an auctioneer.

The success of an auctioneer depends on the audience that comes and then how he relates to them. In my area, a standard audience will attend almost any farm auction because of the farm implements and junk to be sold. Even if there isn't something advertised that a person wants to buy, there is always plenty of food and alcohol to share. The population in that area is low so many of the people know each other and have fun visiting. My father loved auctions.

Violet Suta Moran

Jerry auctioning our farm.

Sweetgrass

Mom told me that Jerry was being amazingly successful. There was a new phenomenon of women in the area insisting their husbands take them to auctions held by Jerry Buckley or even going with a group of women friends. Women never used to want to go to sales with their husbands, but now they want to go to auctions if Jerry is the auctioneer. Jerry was likeable, friendly, sort of good looking, and the women loved to hear him talk fast.

My siblings and I hired Jerry to do the auction of our farm (The Suta Rock Farm). I was impressed with the long hours of work he and his assistant did over several weeks to list and inspect everything and organize things in special groupings for the auction. Jerry thoroughly acquainted himself with the many pieces of farm equipment and household items to be auctioned. He may not have been very smart in school but when he began this auction it was apparent that he was an expert on the characteristics and value of all the items he was auctioning.

He did a great job, speaking in his slow accent when he was describing the item he was auctioning. He might pause if bidding wasn't going fast enough or high enough and give the audience a little lecture about what a good farmer Pete Suta was and how he took excellent care of all his machinery and tools. He reminded the group that Pete had loaned his tools to neighbors when asked, etc.

Then he began the typical auction spiel, something like

(speaking very, very quickly)
"We're starting at 50, 50, I've got a bid of 50 who'll make it 75, 75 ,75,

let's hear 75— I've got 75 over here let's hear.100, 100, <u>100,</u> give me 150, 150...

Jerry provided a good lesson for me that we should never underestimate somebody because we may be surprised at their skills and success when they finally find their niche.

Selling the Peter and Hannah Suta Farm

The day our parents made out their will they came home and told us that they were leaving the farm equally to us six children, but they realized that none of us could take it over. Mom said, "We know you will have to do something with the farm after we are gone but we aren't going to tell you what to do. We don't want to talk about it or to know your thoughts. Just know that you have our permission to do anything you decide."

After both parents were dead we siblings unanimously agreed that we wanted to keep the farm as long as we possibly could. None of us were anxious for the money and we weren't ready to let the farm go to someone else. The land was already in the CRP (Conservation Reserve Program) which covered the property tax so it wouldn't cost us to wait a few more years before selling.

We were reluctant to give up the land. We shared a special affinity with the Suta Rock Farm and with each other. There exists a spiritual connection when you give so much of yourself to something that it becomes a part of you. We hadn't enjoyed all the work required to develop and maintain this as a productive farm. But it may be that our hard work was the equity that supported our claim of the land as a very personal possession. We probably cared more about the farm than if we had not had to work as hard. We perhaps also cared more about each other after having to work together for a common cause.

It was fortunate when the CRP contract was nearing its end that Ted received a call from a woman who had been keeping her eye on our property. She gave an offer saying she didn't want any negotiation at all, take it or leave it. Her offer was acceptable to us. The buyer was a daughter of Rudy Judeman whose family had spent a few years farming in our area. She had learned from her father how to become a land owner by purchasing farms and leasing them to be worked by someone who lived contiguously. I realized that the farming would be done by a neighbor who cared about the land and wouldn't treat it as a piece of an assembly line which I believed would be done by the large Hutterite Colony right across the road from us. The manager had often taunted Pop in the years before his death by saying that he would soon enjoy walking on Pop's land.

The Peter and Hannah Suta family has left the premises.

We decided to accept the purchase offer and to hold an auction sale. We chose our friend Jerry Buckley to conduct the auction. The nice warm spring weather we had been having turned cold and windy with snow on the day of the auction. We laughed over the thought that Pop may have created that weather to convey his feelings about giving up the farm.

When we reached the end of the auction day the only thing not yet sold and carted away was the very simple narrow bench that Pop had made for the porch. It was on the ground, surrounded by people I assumed were potential buyers. I suddenly felt that we could not relinquish that bench.

I shouted loudly and tearfully that the bench could not be sold. My brothers recognized my distress and returned it to the porch. I just could not give up one more item. The auction day had been stressful, and I suddenly could not surrender that bench, even though I knew that neither I nor my siblings were able to put it to use. I was reacting in accordance with my feelings that I had given up enough, suffered enough losses, and could not let go of this item that represented far more than a bench. It represented the camaraderie of our family and sharing thousands of meals with people we cared about. At this point it was representing the entire farm –the millions of rocks we had picked to clear the land, sowing and reaping crops of grain, Indigenous People who had crossed or lived on the land before us, the gumbo soil, our unique Crocus Hill, wild mushrooms and flowers growing on the prairie, the animals that were returning to live on this land now that we had eliminated poisonous weed killers. It strongly represented memories of siblings and parents who had, against all odds, created a productive farm out of this hard, rocky, dry land.

It's hard to see everything go away when you have good memories of a place where you enjoyed your entire lifetime. Besides the connection to my family home we had also developed a spiritual bond with the land itself.

Sweetgrass

Now, twenty-seven years after the auction sale, we four remaining siblings decided to get permission to go onto the farm to briefly look around. We had no idea what to expect. We were not surprised that the house had been torn down; probably required by insurance. It was a little surprising that all the other buildings remained there even though they continued to collapse and be reclaimed by nature. The wind had rotated the outhouse off its foundation, but the building itself and the toilet seat were still intact, as a testimonial to Pop's skills.

The farmland, the driveway, the hills, the rocks on the reservoir dam, and the trails to the fields were still there. We all had strong feelings of nostalgia. We all had teary eyes. We shared memories and took a lot of pictures with the familiar backdrop of the Sweetgrass Hills. We didn't have time to look for Shooting Stars but that was okay after Crocus Hill had satisfied us by being completely covered in blooms. The Crocus had blossomed just at the right time for us to pick bouquets to place at the altar for Ted's Memorial Service.

This last trip seems to have satisfied my soul and that of my siblings. We know that the land has and will continue to be there even without our presence. I feel like I can now let it go without the pain I had been feeling.

Leaving this view breaks my heart.

Acknowledgments

I give special recognition to my late parents, Pete and Hannah Suta, who worked extremely hard to make a living on this hard-scrabble farm wanting to give their children a better life than they had. Their values will be carried on through their descendants. I have been honest in all portrayals of my family, but I lack the ability to convey the emotional connection we all had to the farmland, the physical location surrounding us, and the connections we had with each other.

I thank my oldest brother Ted for answering many little questions to complete or verify my memories about life on the farm and I thank Henry for verification of Ted's memories. The descriptions about machinery used on our farm were partially taken from an unpublished memoir written by my late brother Ben. My son Jeff Moran drew on his Harvard education to critique some of these stories before his early death of malignant brain cancer.

Sarah White, First Person Productions of Madison, has taught me a lot about creative writing and is an inspiration to many fledgling writers. I'm thankful for support from the Nova Scotia writing group of Sarah, Barb, Marg and Erin and the Storytellers Group including Pam, Judy, Cindy, Susan, Mary, Ellen and Enid.

My good friends Sally Lovchin, Karen O'Neil, and Blake Berton prevented this book from being completed earlier by distracting me to go out and dance to blues music. Other friendly dancers and lovers of the blues include Deb, Debra and Mike, Terry, Pam and Tom, Linda, Marcia, Sandra, Sue and Bob, Myrna and Al, Dave, Jack, Reid, and Vicki.

I couldn't get along without long-time friends Jacki, Patricia and her daughter Kathy, Miriam, Kaye, Ann, Jean Kollasch, Eleanor, Dorothy, and Donna Nelson. I have loved travels with Jane Zynda, Judy, Kathryn, and Connie and Robbie.

Thanks to Carol and Byron Beley, Mark and Miki Suta, Henry and Carolyn, Rudy and Sherry, and Dian and Jess and to my "bonus sons" Eric, Peter, Ken, and Brian. I can't list all of my relatives, but it has been a happy surprise to become acquainted with Los/zing second-cousins through sales of my book about our shared ancestor Anna Lozing. Your positive feedback has meant a lot to me and has spurred me on to write more.

I apologize to those important people I have not mentioned. I also appreciate the friendship of many more people whose names are not listed.

Violet Suta Moran grew up on a farm twelve miles from Sweetgrass, Montana, which in the 1930s and 1940s was a thriving little town with everything a farm family needed. In the 1950s, Sweetgrass went into decline and now is not even a ghost town. Every board has been removed from businesses that were on Main Street—being a border town is more serious than in the past, even if the Canadians on the other side are friendly people.

This book was written because Violet's three sons and five grandchildren wanted to know what it was like to grow up on the Suta Rock Farm without any modern conveniences. These stories tell that the families on a developing farm worked hard and did not have much time to play. But the siblings worked together with camaraderie, respect, and geniality.

Before retirement Violet developed a notable reputation in her nursing career. Among her accomplishments was creation of the first Intensive Care Unit in Madison, Wisconsin, in May 1963, one of the first in the nation. Her activities in the nursing profession included publications, holding elective offices, and providing continuing education. She also was a leader in the specialty of teaching staff to care for children who have profound developmental disabilities.

Although her heart remains in Montana, she enjoys living in the beautiful city of Madison, Wisconsin.

www.ingramcontent.com/pod-product-compliance
Lightning Source LLC
Chambersburg PA
CBHW050332230426
43663CB00010B/1829